Words Alone

Also by Denis Donoghue

The Practice of Reading
The Third Voice: Modern British and American Verse Drama
An Honoured Guest: New Essays on W. B. Yeats
   (editor, with J. R. Mulryne)
The Ordinary Universe: Soundings in Modern Literature
Swift Revisited (editor)
Emily Dickinson
Jonathan Swift: A Critical Introduction
Yeats
Jonathan Swift: A Critical Anthology (editor)
Thieves of Fire
Memories, by W. B. Yeats (editor)
The Sovereign Ghost
Ferocious Alphabets
Connoisseurs of Chaos: Ideas of Order in Modern American Poetry
The Arts Without Mystery
Selected Essays of R. P. Blackmur (editor)
England, Their England
We Irish
Reading America
Warrenpoint
The Pure Good of Theory
The Old Moderns
Walter Pater: Lover of Strange Souls

[Words Alone
The Poet T. S. Eliot]

Denis Donoghue

Yale University Press / New Haven & London

Published with assistance from the Kingsley Trust Association
Publication Fund established by the Scroll and Key Society of
Yale College.

Designed by Nancy Ovedovitz and set in Monotype Perpetua type
by Keystone Typesetting, Inc. Printed in the United States of America
by R.R. Donnelley & Sons.

Library of Congress Cataloging-in-Publication Data
Donoghue, Denis.
Words alone : the poet T. S. Eliot / Denis Donoghue.
p.   cm.
Includes bibliographical references and index.
ISBN 0-300-08329-7 (alk. paper)
1. Eliot, T. S. (Thomas Stearns), 1888–1965—Criticism and
interpretation.   I. Title.
PS3509.L43   Z668   2000
821'.912—dc21   00-035901

A catalogue record for this book is available from the British Library.

The paper in this book meets the guidelines for permanence and
durability of the Committee on Production Guidelines for Book
Longevity of the Council on Library Resources.

10   9   8   7   6   5   4   3   2   1

For Frances, and for David, Helen, Hugh, Celia, Mark, Barbara, Stella, and Emma

Contents

Preface

In 1990, I published *Warrenpoint,* a memoir of my growing up
in a small town in Northern Ireland. The book turned out to
be a tribute to my father; so much so that my mother without
my intending appeared only as a frail figure in the background.
My sisters Kathleen and May are noticed, and my brother Tim.
John, a brother who died in infancy, is recalled from time to time.
My life during those years was nearly bare of incident; it was
mostly a routine of ordinary lower-middle-class activities, with a
concentration on schooling, learning to read, transcribing momentous sentences from books. The ending of the book coin-
cided with the year I left Warrenpoint for Dublin, to become a
university student.

In idle moments over the past few years I have thought of
writing something about my first years in Dublin, when I was
developing an interest, necessarily secondary and discursive, in
music and literature. But the ambition has receded. I can't make
bricks without straw. I took some part in the musical life of
Dublin, but none in its literary life. Patrick Kavanagh, Austin
Clarke, J. P. Donleavy, Brendan Behan, and Flann O'Brien were
names to me, and they were occasionally to be seen in Grafton

Street or St. Stephen's Green, but I didn't meet any of them. Anthony Cronin's *Dead as Doornails* gives a far more vivid impression of Dublin literary life in those years than anything I could write. Besides, the literature that meant most to me at that time was the work of dead masters—Yeats, Joyce, Swift—and of living writers I had no prospect of meeting—Eliot, Stevens, Allen Tate, William Carlos Williams, Kenneth Burke, R. P. Blackmur, John Crowe Ransom, Cleanth Brooks, Robert Penn Warren.

Over a period of several years, I found myself reading Eliot more intensely than any other contemporary writer. His influence on poets was immense, even though few poets since the early Auden dared to imitate him. His influence on literary critics was such that none of them could write without a sense of his proximity: Leavis, Brooks, Bateson, Tate, Empson, Blackmur. If I were to write an intellectual memoir of my early years in Dublin, it would be a book about Eliot; or rather about my experience in trying to read him. If it had a more general interest, such a book would describe the process by which a young student tries to gain access, however limited, to a book of poems. What is entailed in submitting oneself to a writer?

The present book is partly a memoir, partly a study of Eliot's poetry. I see now that my early experience of reading him was complicated by Yeats and Stevens, two poets in their different ways as formidable as he was. But Eliot is strange in ways peculiar to himself. Yeats and Stevens are difficult writers, but each of them allows me to feel that I could, given time, understand the codes of his language, short of cracking them. Eliot makes me feel that his ways with the English language will continue to be opaque, no matter how much time and concern I spend on them. That is why, like other readers, I read his poems as if they were music become speech. If he were a composer, I think he would have gone to school with Schoenberg, Webern, or Berg. It is not a question of difficulty. Most of the cruxes in Eliot's poems have been elucidated, the allusions explained. But his ways with the language remain as bizarre as Mallarmé's:

Eyes I dare not meet in dreams
In death's dream kingdom
These do not appear:
There, the eyes are
Sunlight on a broken column
There, is a tree swinging
And voices are
In the wind's singing
More distant and more solemn
Than a fading star.[1]

The authority of these lines is so unquestionable, yet so irregular, that commentary seems defeated. The "I" has textual but no ontological presence, unless we settle for saying that the speaker is any hollow man. Exegetes say that "death's dream kingdom" is that of the lost souls in Dante's Hell. The eyes that do not appear may be Beatrice's, inadequately prefigured by the sunlight on a broken column. If that is true, the passage may enact a movement of will, only incipiently achieved but corresponding in gesture to the movement from *Inferno* through *Purgatorio* to *Paradiso*. But the authority I've referred to is musical rather than referential; it is internal to the syllables, and embodied in the full rhymes and slant rhymes that connect "dare," "appear," "are," "are" again, and "star;" the repetition of "There" and "Eyes"; the rhymes of "column" and "solemn," "swinging" and "singing"; the alliterations of "dare," "death's dream kingdom," "These" and "There." That the eyes "are" sunlight on a broken column can be true only according to a logic of imagination or association as distinct from a logic of reason: it is a distraught logic enabled by the rhetorical emphasis on "are" at the end of its metrical line, a gesture repeated for similar reason three lines later, "And voices are / In the wind's singing." This second rhetorical emphasis makes it a question whether the "are" is fulfilled in "More distant and more solemn / Than a fading star," leaving "In the wind's singing" a parenthesis; or whether it goes with "In the wind's singing" and lets the two last lines qualify the singing. Either way, in "And voices are / In the wind's singing," the meter is declaring itself independent of the official ways of English. The whole effect is of figures seen in a dream; or of a tone poem in which one state moves into another without syntactical intervention. It is as if the reasons of syntax were disabled, to allow our sense of reasons beneath or above reason to prevail. So Blackmur said, "To reveal the hidden analogies of things; Shelley's insight was Eliot's task as a poet; he has in his images to remind reason of its material, to remind order of its disorder, in order to create a sane art almost insane in its predicament."[2] So in "The Hollow Men":

Here we go round the prickly pear
Prickly pear prickly pear
Here we go round the prickly pear
At five o'clock in the morning.

Between the idea
And the reality
Between the motion
And the act
Falls the Shadow
  For Thine is the Kingdom[3]

I have called this book *Words Alone* to indicate both the authority of words and the perturbation of words that can't rely on an authentic syntax. The predicament to which Blackmur refers is that of diction with only unofficial relations to grammar; poetic rhythms enforcing themselves by fiat; phrases cut adrift from sentences.

The phrase comes from one of Yeats's earliest poems, "The Song of the Happy Shepherd":

The woods of Arcady are dead,
And over is their antique joy;
Of old the world on dreaming fed;
Grey Truth is now her painted toy;
Yet still she turns her restless head:
But O, sick children of the world,
Of all the many changing things
In dreary dancing past us whirled,
To the cracked tune that Chronos sings,
Words alone are certain good.[4]

If the shepherd is happy, despite the lapse of the pastoral tradition, the omnivorous success of realism and positivism, and the burden of one-thing-after-another, the reason is the claim he insists on making for words. Presumably he will discover that words alone are at best uncertain good, but that they are the only instruments we have. To read Eliot is to ponder the uncertainty of words and their certain force of presence in relation to other values: silence, form, pattern, speech, "the dialect of the tribe," "old stones that cannot be deciphered," prayer, "music heard so deeply / That it is not heard at all, but you are the music / While the music lasts," "the stillness / Between two waves of the sea," and "the communication of the dead."

I wrote most of this book while I was a fellow of the National Humanities Center. I am grateful to the center for providing, in Yeats's terms, "a scene well set and excellent company."

Words Alone

Beginning

"The Love Song of J. Alfred Prufrock"

I was born in Tullow, a small town in County Carlow about fifty miles southwest of Dublin, but I grew up in Warrenpoint, a town not much larger, in County Down, just across the border into Northern Ireland. For secondary education I attended the Christian Brothers' School in Newry, five miles away. The brothers were not priests; they were a lay order dedicated to giving lower-middle-class Irish Catholic boys a working education, nothing fancy, elaborate, or expensive. For English literature we had anthologies of stories, plays, poems, and essays. I recall with satisfaction *The Poet's Company,* an anthology predicated on the lighter Yeats—"Aedh Wishes for the Cloths of Heaven"—as an introduction to music might have been predicated on the lighter Elgar. I don't think we were ever told what literature was or how we might know a literary work when we saw one. A poem could be recognized at a glance: the words stopped short of the margin and every line began with a capital letter. I grew up thinking that poetry must be intimate with "the blue and the dim and the dark cloths / Of night and light and the half-light." The only alternative to early Yeatsian pathos was rollicking verse, preferably in anapestic tetrameters, easy to memorize. I can still recite the first two stanzas of Byron's "The Destruction of Sennacherib," a featured poem in *The Poet's Company:*

> The Assyrian came down like the wolf on the fold,
> And his cohorts were gleaming in purple and gold;
> And the sheen of their spears was like stars on the sea,
> When the blue wave rolls nightly on deep Galilee.
>
> Like the leaves of the forest when Summer is green,
> That host with their banners at sunset were seen:
> Like the leaves of the forest when Autumn hath blown,
> That host on the morrow lay withered and strown.

"Strown" was hard to deal with. Our English teacher, Brother Cotter, allowed us to turn it toward "strewn." Reciting the poem in class, I introduced for effect a pause, which I did not know enough to think of as rhetorical, between "deep" and "Galilee."

The Poet's Company did not include any of Eliot's poems. I suppose he was still regarded as foreign, difficult, and vaguely unpleasant. He didn't come into my life till I went to university in Dublin. It is my impression that I first read "The Love Song of J. Alfred Prufrock" in the National Library, Kildare Street, my home-away-from-home. I knew that it was a different kind of poetry from Yeats's or Byron's and that I would never forget it. My criterion for poetry at that time was simple: a poem should be memorable. Music during those years was my second avocation. At the Royal Irish Academy of Music, Dorothy Stokes taught me harmony and counterpoint, and Brian Boydell tried to make a singer of me, preferably a *lieder* singer. In one year I worked with pleasure if not success through songs by Dowland, Bach's "Es ist vollbracht," Schumann's *Dichterliebe,* and Peter Warlock's *The Curlew.*

Eloquence for me was Brahms's "Wie bist du meine Königen" as sung by Alexander Kipnis. In default of knowing what poetry was, I settled for having poems take possession of my mind as Schumann's "Ich hab' in Traum geweinet" did. I wanted every poem I read to be my singing school. "The Destruction of Sennacherib" was easy to remember, but I had to decide to commit it to memory, it didn't hold my imagination. There was some satisfaction in reciting it with Assyrian speed, but nothing much remained, the poem didn't take. The choice poems seized me without any decision on my part in their favor. "Prufrock" was one of those. At first reading, it took up residence in my mind. From that day to this I've never wavered from my conviction that it is a fully achieved poem or doubted that Eliot is one of the irrefutable poets.

I wonder about some poets I enjoy reading and much admire: why do their poems not lodge in my mind? Between readings, they sink into the vagueness of their reputation. I have read most of John Ashbery's poetry and reviewed three or four of his books, but I couldn't recite two consecutive lines of his work. When I go back to "Self-Portrait in a Convex Mirror," I assent to a cultivated voice as it leads me through the lines, but when I've finished reading it, nothing of the voice stays with me but a fading echo. If it is a superb poem—as I think it is—its quality is consistent with a culture that reads with the eye and keeps the ear idle.

"Prufrock" seemed to me a poem about a man's dread of being no good. Later readings have made me think that it is about spiritual panic, the mind whirling in a void, or the penury of one's being in the world. No one instructed me to think of the poem in relation to Allen Tate's assertion that "in Mr. Eliot, puritan obligation withdraws into private conscience."[1] Now that "Prufrock" seems to be the only poem of Eliot's that young people in America read, I find that my students at New York University take it as an uncanny description of themselves, their distress, their fear of having already failed. Prufrock is brooding on his insufficiency in mock-epic terms, but the terms don't remove his conviction of being inadequate. Growing up in Ireland, where there were no choices and one was lucky to get a job of any kind, I was likely to internalize the theme and to find Prufrock already defeated.

Knowing no Italian, I could make nothing of the epigraph to *Prufrock and Other Observations* or the further one to "Prufrock." The poem began for me with "Let us go then, you and I . . . " I'm still puzzled by the epigraph to the poem, but for different reasons. In *Inferno* xxvii Dante meets Guido da Montefeltro, confined in a single flame of punishment for having given false counsel to Pope Boniface. Guido answers Dante: "If I believed that my reply would be to someone who would return to earth, this flame would remain without further movement; but since no one has ever returned alive from this abyss, if what I hear is true, I answer you without fear of infamy." It's not clear what bearing this has on "Prufrock." In the "No! I am not Prince Hamlet" passage, Prufrock speaks of himself as if he were Polonius, but he doesn't confess to having given the king fraudulent advice. Perhaps the epigraph has him saying: I'll tell the truth about my life, however humiliating it turns out to be. Or it may be Eliot's device to clear a space for himself, ridding the reader's mind of extraneous matter, all the more effectively because the epigraph is in a foreign language. Or his way of insisting that what follows is a made poem, not what it might seem, a transcript of someone's confession. Eliot tended to choose an epigraph related to the poem it preceded by congruity or contradiction: either way, he enjoyed the latitude of keeping readers on their toes. I note, incidentally, that in his recording of the poem, he hasn't included the epigraph; he goes straight into "Let us go then . . . "

Like most of Eliot's early poems, "Prufrock" seems to have started as a bundle of unrelated fragments, bits of verse he wrote under the force of impulses amounting to inspiration and put aside till one day a certain loose affiliation among them might suggest a possible poem. Many years ago, when I was transcribing one of Yeats's notebooks for inclusion in his *Memoirs,* I was shocked to find that he started a poem by sketching the argument in a sentence or two. He then picked a word here or there, jotted down its nearest rhymes, and set about turning the sentences into verse. A rudimentary argument plus "colt," "dolt," "jolt," and "bolt" turned into "The Fascination of What's Difficult." It seemed a blunt method, though I recognized that in the process of revision his genius asserted itself, as it did in giving him the decisive word "indignant" in "The Second Coming." But Eliot's method was more bizarre than Yeats's. In the early poems he didn't start with a theme or something he wanted to say. By his own account, what came first was a fragment of rhythm, a motif he felt impelled to stabilize in a few words. Those words might suggest a few more—or might not—and the fragments would be set aside. Sometimes he failed to find a destiny for them. But on a happier day he would put one fragment beside another and stir some energy or reverberation between them. "Prufrock," even at a much later stage than that of its fragments, was called "Prufrock among the Women" and included a different epigraph, from *Purgatorio* xxvi, and a section of thirty-three lines called "Prufrock's Pervigilium."[2] In its definitive form it includes three rows of dots, dividing one sequence from the next, as if to acknowledge their origin as fragments.

The first line is odd, though I had to read it many times to see how odd it is. Who is speaking? J. Alfred Prufrock, presumably. But who is he? Hugh Kenner calls him a name plus a voice: "He isn't a 'character' cut out of the rest of the universe and equipped with a little history and a little necessary context. . . . He is the name of a possible zone of consciousness where the materials with which he is credited with being aware can co-exist."[3] He's more than that. But Kenner is right in maintaining that Prufrock isn't the man next door or a character set loose from a novel. We are not encouraged to think of him as someone who exists, as we fancy that Leopold Bloom and Stephen Dedalus exist, before and after the novel in which they appear. Prufrock begins and ends with what he says: if he seems to live beyond the pages of the poem, it is because his words do, moving out from their context in Eliot's *Collected Poems*. But the words don't repose upon an implied character or a personage. Who on earth would say to his friend: "Let us go then, you and I?" But Prufrock isn't quite on earth, nor is he quite "he." Eliot's language here and in the early poems generally refers to things and simultaneously works free from the reference. He seems always to be saying: "That is not what I meant at all. / That is not it, at all." When he gives a voice a name—Prufrock, Gerontion—he makes no commitment beyond the naming.

Let us suppose that Prufrock and his friend set out on a foggy October evening to visit an important lady-friend. Prufrock may make a proposal or he may postpone it:

> The yellow fog that rubs its back upon the window-panes,
> The yellow smoke that rubs its muzzle on the window-panes,
> Licked its tongue into the corners of the evening,
> Lingered upon the pools that stand in drains,
> Let fall upon its back the soot that falls from chimneys,
> Slipped by the terrace, made a sudden leap,
> And seeing that it was a soft October night,
> Curled once about the house, and fell asleep.[4]

Two verbs in the present tense—the same word, "rubs"—yield to a sequence of verbs in the past tense—"Licked . . . Lingered . . . Let fall . . . Slipped . . . made . . . and fell asleep." But the relation of the language to its ostensible referents is equivocal. The lines don't say that the fog and the smoke were like a cat. Nor do they quite describe a city under fog. The scene is internal to Prufrock's state of mind, or to a hypothetical state of mind we have to call Prufrock in default of another designation. The apparently objective references enable us to imagine a scene, but they don't establish it as independent of Prufrock. The plural nouns—"corners . . . pools . . . drains"—generalize the impression and release the language from the mundane duty of referring to something: no particular corner, pool, or drain is intended. Cat and fog do not hold their places, as they would if a definite relation between them were in view. The verbs— "made a sudden leap" and "curled"—point to a cat, but "Licked its tongue into the corners of the evening" is more fog than cat. The effect is to keep the reader among the words and their internal relations, as if the apparent local meanings were an unfortunate but necessary distraction, a gesture toward an external world that has to be placated, short of being granted its independence. We are not allowed to escape from the words into another place.

There is a minor difficulty with "you." Eliot told Kristian Smidt that the "you" is "merely some friend or companion, presumably of the male sex, whom the speaker is at that moment addressing, and that it has no emotional content whatever."[5] But in an interview in 1962 he said that Prufrock was a man of about forty and in part himself and that he was using the theory of the split personality.[6] This is a better hint, especially as it allows us to take "you" as a second self removed from the first—as in Conrad's "The Secret Sharer"—and fulfilling another mode of being, admonitory though silent. It is typical of Eliot to exert critical pressure on the matter in hand by establishing another scale of reference, another perspective. But some of the invocations to "you" in "Prufrock" are perfunctory, they hardly mean more than "one." It is hard to believe that the "We" at the end, "We have lingered . . . ," includes more than Prufrock's sole if notional self. I take it as a last flourish of the plural of majesty before the drowning.

When I first read the poem, I winced at "etherised." No one was etherized in a poem by Yeats. I didn't know Laforgue's "Jeux"— "Morte? Se peut-il pas qu'elle dorme / Grise de cosmiques chloroformes?" I had only the vaguest notion of Eliot's being an American Baudelaire, determined to make poetry out of distinctively modern experience, good, bad, indifferent; willing to live on his nerves. I didn't appreciate that the modern literature Eliot and Baudelaire exemplify is an affair of cities—London, Paris, Dublin, Prague—and that the friction, the crowds, and the desolate charm of urban life are its chief provocations. I knew nothing of Eliot's debts to Dante, Shakespeare, George Herbert, Beddoes, Baudelaire, Tennyson, Dostoevsky, Laforgue, Apollinaire, André Salmon, Gautier, Corbière, and apparently a hundred other writers. Nor did I see that Eliot's procedure in "Prufrock" is to refute Wordsworth. If Romanticism was—as F. W. Bateson called it—the shortest way out of Manchester, Eliot's early poems send the poor pilgrim back there. Instead of celebrating a spousal relation between man and nature, Eliot sets figures adrift in a modern city and makes them inhabit the confused exchange of energy between inanimate and animate states. Instead of taking human feeling for granted, he shows it dispersed among people and the streets through which they move. In "Prufrock" we read of the "muttering" retreats of restless nights, of streets that "follow" like a tedious argument, of a fog that "rubs its back," smoke that "rubs its muzzle," eyes that "fix" you in a formulated phrase, arms that "wrap" about a shawl, mermaids "combing the white hair" of the waves blown back. The transfer of feeling from scene to agent is most complete in

And the afternoon, the evening, sleeps so peacefully!
Smoothed by long fingers,
Asleep . . . tired . . . or it malingers,
Stretched on the floor, here beside you and me.

The effect is to remove the sentient privilege from human beings, or to show the desperate intensity with which we project our little grammars and dictions upon an objective life that is, so far as we know, indifferent to our yearnings. Isn't it pathetic to see Prufrock's mind lavished on such puny epiphanies?

The pervasive cadence of the poem is a tentative afflatus followed by inevitable collapse: these strivings rise, shine, evaporate, and fall. "All" is their leitmotif, as prevalent here as in *Paradise Lost*—"For I have known them all already, known them all." The rhythm of rise-and-fall begins with the rhyme of "streets" and "retreats" and the repetition of "Streets"—

Streets that follow like a tedious argument
Of insidious intent
To lead you to an overwhelming question . . .
Oh, do not ask, "What is it?"
Let us go and make our visit.[7]

The most complete fall comes when Prufrock's talk breaks down— "It is impossible to say just what I mean!"—and the next sentence barely gets to its feet with the helpless "But as if a magic lantern . . . " Again, this:

Should I, after tea and cakes and ices,
Have the strength to force the moment to its crisis?
But though I have wept and fasted, wept and prayed,
Though I have seen my head (grown slightly bald) brought in
    upon a platter,

I am no prophet—and here's no great matter;
I have seen the moment of my greatness flicker,
And I have seen the eternal Footman hold my coat, and snicker,
And in short, I was afraid.

"Should I?" joins other vain questionings: "Do I dare?" and, "Do I dare"; "Do I dare / Disturb the universe?" "And should I then presume? / And how should I begin?" "Shall I part my hair behind?" The most heartbreaking of these is "Shall I say?" as if saying or not saying made any difference. The verbal wondering collapses nearly as soon as it begins:

Shall I say, I have gone at dusk through narrow streets
And watched the smoke that rises from the pipes
Of lonely men in shirt-sleeves, leaning out of windows? . . .

—and the feeling declines upon lowly, primordial certitude:

I should have been a pair of ragged claws
Scuttling across the floors of silent seas.

That at least would have entailed an appropriate relation. But for the time being the afflatus is permitted: associations with John the Baptist, Salome, and King Herod allow Prufrock to indulge himself in "the moment of my greatness" before it flickers and dies in the unloving arms of Death, the eternal Footman. "And in short, I was afraid." "In short" retains a touch of dignity, like Buster Keaton before he sinks, his body standing to attention, beneath the waves. What is compelling in this passage is the force of rhythm, the inevitably controlling cadence; not just the rise and fall but the getting up again, such that the dying fall in "I am no prophet—and here's no great matter" is followed at once by another heroically blustering lift of feeling—"I have seen the moment of my greatness flicker, / And I

have seen the eternal Footman hold my coat." That second "And I
have seen" mimes the futile but not ignoble gesture of pulling oneself
up, starting over. It is the hero cheering himself down, as R. P. Blackmur said.[8]

The most elaborate afflatus comes at the end in the passage about
the mermaids, which begins as an astonishing change of reference:

> Shall I part my hair behind? Do I dare to eat a peach?
> I shall wear white flannel trousers, and walk upon the beach.
> I have heard the mermaids singing, each to each.
>
> I do not think that they will sing to me . . .
>
> We have lingered in the chambers of the sea
> By sea-girls wreathed with seaweed red and brown
> Till human voices wake us, and we drown.

In "Song," Donne gives a list of impossible achievements of knowledge and power:

> Go, and catch a falling star,
> Get with child a mandrake root,
> Tell me, where all past years are,
> Or who cleft the Devil's foot,
> Teach me to hear mermaids singing . . .

But Donne doesn't ask that the mermaids sing to him, as Prufrock
does. Claiming to have achieved one impossibility, Prufrock rises to
another and asks that the singing be in his sole favor. No wonder the
courage of his fancy fails him. His description of the mermaids is
a further claim to distinction, but it exhausts itself in the telling.
This little Ulysses can't get back to Ithaca, and besides, no Penelope
awaits him. In the first version of the poem, "sea-girls" was "sea-
maids." The change was an inspiration, making pathetically erotic the

relation between the siren-singers and the love-singer of the poem in our hands.

There has been much discussion of the "overwhelming question," though many critics end up claiming that there's no point in asking what it is. I don't see any reason to assume that Prufrock doesn't know. His gesture of impatience need not be a device to conceal ignorance. Empson once remarked that Hamlet keeps his secret by telling everyone that he has one. A comparison with Hamlet is worth pursuing, given that Prufrock glances at it. J. Peter Dyson has argued that since everything that Prufrock aspires to appears in the poem as an echo of something else, the overwhelming question is an echo of Hamlet's: "To be or not to be, that is the question." He reads the relevant line as if Prufrock were saying: "No! I am not Prince Hamlet, nor was meant to be. To be or not to be, *that* is the question."[9] It's an attractive suggestion, but I wish Dyson had gone further with it. He thinks that "Prufrock" is "a poem about the difficulties of realizing one's nebulous potentialities." It seems to me more than that.

If Prufrock is a dying fall from Hamlet, we might ask what Eliot thought Hamlet's problem is. His essay is a confused account of the play, but it reveals a lot about himself: "Hamlet (the man) is dominated by an emotion which is inexpressible, because it is in *excess* of the facts as they appear. And the supposed identity of Hamlet with his author is genuine to this point: that Hamlet's bafflement at the absence of objective equivalent to his feelings is a prolongation of the bafflement of his creator in the face of his artistic problem. Hamlet is up against the difficulty that his disgust is occasioned by his mother, but that his mother is not an adequate equivalent for it; his disgust envelops and exceeds her. It is thus a feeling which he cannot understand; he cannot objectify it, and it therefore remains to poison life and obstruct action."[10] Hamlet's buffoonery—his levity, repetitions of phrase, and puns—is "the buffoonery of an emotion which can find no outlet in action." In more general terms: "The intense feeling, ecstatic or terrible, without an object or exceeding its object, is something which every person of sensibility has known; it is doubtless a subject of study for pathologists. It often occurs in adolescence: the ordinary person puts these feelings to sleep, or trims down his feelings to fit the business world; the artist keeps them alive by his ability to intensify the world to his emotions. The Hamlet of Laforgue is an adolescent; the Hamlet of Shakespeare is not, he has not that explanation and excuse. We must simply admit that here Shakespeare tackled a problem which proved too much for him. Why he attempted it at all is an insoluble puzzle; under compulsion of what experience he attempted to express the inexpressibly horrible, we cannot ever know."[11] I don't understand what Eliot means by intensifying the world "to his emotions." I suppose him to mean that artists work up their sense of the external world to the pitch of intensity at which it seems to justify their emotions, however violent. I don't know under what compulsion Eliot attempted to express, in "Prufrock," an emotion that could not otherwise find an outlet in action. I can only suggest that Prufrock is Hamlet still further removed than in Shakespeare or Laforgue from having found an "objective correlative" for his emotions. What corresponds to Hamlet's buffoonery is Prufrock's rhythm of rise-and-fall: it takes the form of self-regarding irony, dandyish repetitions of phrase, amplitudes of interrogation—"And would it have been worth it, after all?"

But Prufrock's problem is not merely the lack of a sustaining context, the fact that he comes into the world—to the extent to which I can say this without being fanciful—bereft of parents, wife, or children, without a station in life, indeed with only a few minor possessions and an oppressive desire that he can't express. If we take Eliot's essay on Baudelaire seriously, we will not think that Prufrock's predicament might be relieved by a few sessions with a psychiatrist. In

Baudelaire's "Le Balcon" we find "all the romantic idea, but something more: the reaching out towards something which cannot be had
in, but which may be had partly *through,* personal relations." Again
resorting to general terms, Eliot says: "Indeed, in much romantic
poetry the sadness is due to the exploitation of the fact that no human
relations are adequate to human desires, but also to the disbelief in
any further object for human desires than that which, being human,
fails to satisfy them."[12] In the years between the essay on Hamlet
(1919) and the essay on Baudelaire (1930), Eliot had come to believe
that the finding of an objective correlative for one's feelings is not
enough, if that correlative is merely a human relation. After his conversion to Christianity, he could not have believed otherwise.

The practice of committing poems to memory is rare, I gather, but
while it lasted it had consequences good and bad. Among the good
ones for me: it allowed me to take pleasure in the sway of syllables
and rhythms, variations of tone, changes of inflection. I was willingly
kept among the words. Only with difficult poems like "Prufrock"
was it necessary to ask what the poem was about or what was going
on. Even though I wondered who spoke the words, I didn't fret over
the answer. The words seemed to have an acoustic presence that did
not need to be distinguished from their presence of mind. The merit
of memorizing was that I didn't reduce the poem to the implied crux
of the speaker and lose it there, replacing the poem by a quandary. But
I see that I've come close to replacing "Prufrock" by a predicament,
as Eliot replaced *Hamlet* by its hero's problem. In earlier years, the
risk I took was that I might find it easy to detach the words not only
from an implied speaker but from their referents. "In the mountains,
there you feel free": those words became a tune in my head, evocative but evocative of nothing in particular; they could be released
from "The Waste Land" and turned upon whatever mood in me
elicited them. Murmuring

(Come in under the shadow of this red rock),
And I will show you something different from either
Your shadow at morning striding behind you
Or your shadow at evening rising to meet you;
I will show you fear in a handful of dust . . .

the last thing I felt inclined to tease out was what precisely was going on, who was offering that appalling experience to whom, and why: the lines sounded as unquestionable as if they issued from a burning bush.

Long before I read Walter Pater's *The Renaissance,* I thought that poetry must be in an intimate relation to music, and I was dismayed if I found that a particular poem was in a more immediate relation to journalism. In later years I was happy to believe in a theory of inspiration, however unfashionable the theory was. Especially when Eliot's poems were in question, I thought of the words as preceding or provoking the feelings that somehow emerged from their conjunctions. I felt that he had recourse to writings in French, Italian, Sanskrit, Latin, and Greek not to learn how to write better but to force himself to engage with strange combinations of words and then to admit the corresponding feelings, all the better for being alien. He seemed to have found the words first and the feelings a split second later. Words were not for him the servants or vicars of his feelings, or instruments for their delivery according to a theory of literature as communication. They were feelings already inscribed, it seemed, in pencil or invisible ink, and they might be changed later to satisfy some formal requirement, but they appeared to have come first, or at some opportune moment after the inaugurally compelling rhythm or motif. It was pointless to assume that certain feelings, silently established, preceded them and awaited their verbal destiny with patience. In this respect Eliot's sense of language differed from Yeats's. It was an enabling period of his life when Yeats read Donne—it gave him another range of tones—but I don't think he discovered new feelings in himself by finding the words for them in Donne's poems. He read widely, but mainly to extend his field of reference and to find further adepts of the feelings he valued, mainly those in the neo-Platonic and other occult traditions. Eliot was a more learned poet than Yeats, but he didn't read to get ideas or enlarge his intellectual fellowship; he read to make himself so familiar with ideas that he could hold himself aloof from their claims.

He had another reason for studying the poets: to gain access to feelings other than his own. For many years it was common to say that Eliot was a cold, bloodless person. Bertrand Russell seems to have started this piece of lore, and Virginia Woolf sent it abroad through Bloomsbury. Michael Hastings's *Tom and Viv* is an extreme version of it. I can't speak to the issue with any authority. I met Eliot only once, by appointment, in his room at Faber and Faber, 24 Russell Square, London. The year was 1960 or 1961. We began with desultory conversation about my domestic life: was I married, had I children, and if so how many?—"Ah yes, a Roman Catholic." Eliot then recalled with pleasure his first visit to Dublin—January 1936—to give a lecture at University College, to address the inaugural meeting of the college's English Literature Society, and to see the UCD Dramatic Society perform *Murder in the Cathedral*: they did the Chorus, he said, better than the professional actors in London had done it.[13] Then we turned to talk about George Herbert, on whom Eliot was writing an essay for the British Council. The meeting ended in his asking me to send him the essays on Herbert that I had alluded to—one by L. C. Knights in the *Sewanee Review*, one by Kenneth Burke in *Accent*. Eliot said nothing worth making a note of, except for the minor reflection on my personal life. He was not cold, but he evidently saw no reason for being warm in my favor. Still, I'm convinced that in his early years he had been a man of exceptionally intense and dangerous feelings.

He feared for his sanity, and had cause to fear for it. The demeanor he turned toward people was palpably a mask to conceal the feelings he lived in dread of. I see him as a character in a novel by Dostoevsky.

If this is true, it follows that Eliot's theory of Impersonality, elucidated in "Tradition and the Individual Talent" and other essays, comes from acute personal need: "Poetry is not a turning loose of emotion, but an escape from emotion; it is not the expression of personality, but an escape from personality. But, of course, only those who have personality and emotions know what it means to want to escape from these things."[14] I take those sentences literally, and wonder what part the reading and writing of poems played in Eliot's desired escape.

In this context I have been puzzling over an early essay, the second of his "Reflections on Contemporary Poetry" (1917). One of his most detaining pieces, it begins innocently enough with a comparison between the poetry of Harold Monro and that of Jean de Bosschère (sometimes called de Boschère.) "Both poets are concerned with this thesis: the intimacy of the relationship between a man and his personal property." But in Monro's poems the man's utensils "are provided with adjectives which connect them with human emotions— 'the gentle Bed,' 'the old impetuous Gas,' 'the independent Pencil,' 'you my well-trampled Boots.' " Eliot didn't advert to the fact that in his own poems—and notably in "Prufrock," as I have remarked— not the man's utensils but the constituents of his "zone of consciousness" (evening, streets, fog) are provided with adjectives that connect them with human emotions. Not in the same way as Monro's poems, I concede. Eliot isn't much concerned with utensils or with the *petits faits vrais* that Stendhal recommended to the attention of novelists. In the "Reflections" he draws a contrast between Monro's poems and de Bosschère's, quoting "Homère Mare" to show that de Bosschère makes no pretense "of a quasi-human relationship," and "never employs his thoughts and images in decorating ordinary human sentiments." I'll quote the first lines of the poem:

> Homère Mare habite sa maison de planches.
> La maison est attachée à la montagne comme le nez à la face
>   abrupte.
> Sur la roche il plante des herbes alpines;
> Sur la terrasse, une vigne et des pavots.
> Il n'est pas un prophète ni un critique.
> Chaque matin il met lui-même le feu dans l'âtre.
> Tour le jour
> Il est l'époux du feu,
> L'aimé des flammes.[15]

Eliot makes the point that neither "époux" nor "aimé" has "any sentimental associations":

> M. de Bosschère is in fact almost a pure intellectual; leaving, as if disdainfully, our emotions to form as they will around the situation which his brain has selected. The important thing is not how we are to feel about it, but how it is. De Bosschère's austerity is terrifying. A poet is not a pure intellectual by virtue of any amount of meditation or abstractness or moralizing; the abstract thought of nearly all poets is mediocre enough, and often second-hand. It is better to go to the "De Anima" than to the "Purgatorio" for a theory of the soul. A poet like M. de Bosschère is an intellectual by his obstinate refusal to adulterate his poetic emotions with human emotions. Instead of refining ordinary human emotion (and I do not mean tepid human emotion, but human however intense—in the crude living state) he aims direct at emotions of art. He thereby limits the number of his readers, and leaves the majority groping for a clue which does not exist. The effect is sometimes an intense frigidity which I find altogether admirable.[16]

"Adulterate" is a forceful word: similar force is required to turn "frigidity" into a virtue. Both words indicate that emotions are ambiguous gifts or blows to be deflected. The difference between "ordinary human emotion" and "emotions of art" is not self-evident. What Eliot admires in "Homère Mare" is the bold designation from which every trace of human emotion has been excised. It is as if de Bosschère wrote poems from the usual resources of emotion and with the usual complement of adjectives and adverbs but removed those elements from the first draft. The result is a sequence of nouns linked by the simplest grammar. Each noun is surrounded by a space through which conventionally human associations may not pass: it is a condition of its being retained that it has given up all yearning for the plenitude of domesticity. De Bosschère anticipates Alain Robbe-Grillet and the Nouveau Roman. Homère travels, takes on the color of every place he visits, for the time being. He is never himself and never feels the loss of himself:

Pendant quatre saisons, Homère voyage
Et dans chaque ville il est un autre personnage;
Bleu sous le ciel bleu, gris à Londres,
Recueilli à Paris, perverti à Rome
Parmi l'ordre de la tombe des tombes.
Byron dans les îles, et Shakespeare encore
Dans la poussière d'hommes de Rome
Mais jamais il n'est Mare.[17]

As for the difference between ordinary human emotions and the emotions of art: words, in the poems Eliot cared for, had already come through, had evaded the claims of emotion to the extent of their achieved style. I am free to like or dislike de Bosschère's poems, but they are what they are; they are not evidence of his having failed to make them emotionally opulent. The intense frigidity that Eliot admired—and on occasion hoped to achieve—is the force of their

standing apart from the human emotions that might have been expected to lay a claim on them. De Bosschère writes about the appur-
tenances of ordinary life—house, garden, hearth, travel—but he presents his Homère as a man who preserves himself notionally intact by
lending himself to whatever invitations come along: his sensibility is
only on loan. Meanwhile no emotion is permitted to be importunate.
Reading de Bosschère's poem, we feel the pressure of all the emotions his Homère has set aside so that the nouns of his chosen life may
stand out boldly yet unassertively against those enticements. This
device would be even more necessary to sustain a life like the early
Eliot's, beset on all sides by panic and fright.

But there may also be an impersonal consideration. Blackmur has
argued, with Marianne Moore's poems as evidence, that it is characteristic of American literature "to present the conviction of reality
best by making it, in most readers' eyes, remote." He has in view
Poe, Hawthorne, Melville (in *Pierre*), Emily Dickinson, and Henry
James. In Moore's poems "life is remote (life as good *and* evil) and
everything is done to keep it remote; it is reality removed, but it is
nonetheless reality, because we *know* that it is removed."[18] Eliot's
reasons for keeping reality removed are likely to have been more
pressing than Moore's.

"Lune de Miel"

"Lune de Miel" is the early poem in which Eliot has most completely
resorted to this device: in that respect it prefigures his more system-
atic dealings with Gautier in "Burbank with a Baedeker: Bleistein
with a Cigar" and the other quatrain poems.

Eliot wrote a few poems in French at a time when he was writer-
blocked in English. The foreign language released him from the op-
pression of his own. Few readers have wanted to take the French

poems seriously, though Eliot held them in enough esteem to include them in his *Collected Poems*. Normally, "Lune de Miel" is interpreted as a relatively crude satire on the triviality of modern tourism and modern sex. At first sight, and perhaps later, this interpretation seems reasonable. The poem and the quatrain poems to which it points have something of the power of caricature that Eliot ascribed to Jonson, and even more of the tragic farce that he found in the last act of Marlowe's *Jew of Malta*. Eliot's honeymooners are lodging for the night in a bug-ridden hotel in Ravenna before setting off for Padua, Milan, Switzerland, and France. Eliot's procedure appears to be what Kenneth Burke called "perspective by incongruity," a silent form of judgment by which incompatible images are brought to bear upon each other: the result is a judgment that includes them both. So we have the ironic relation between "les Pays-Bas" and "Terre Haute"; between the Last Supper in Milan and the cheap restaurant— "Où se trouvent la Cène, et un restaurant pas cher." We have, brought together in one line, "la sueur aestivale" and (rhyming with "Ravenne") "une forte odeur de chienne." The couple are reduced, dismembered, to backs and knees and "quatre jambes molles tout gonflées de morsures." Only a few miles outside Ravenna there is

> Saint Apollinaire
> En Classe, basilique connue des amateurs
> De chapitaux d'acanthe que tournoie le vent.[19]

But the relation of the honeymooners to those lovers of acanthus capitals turned by the wind is a matter for interpretation: it need not operate entirely in favor of art historians and aesthetes. William Arrowsmith has noted that Eliot is alluding to a passage in *The Stones of Venice* where Ruskin writes of Byzantine sculptures and of "leaves drifted, as it were, by a whirlwind round the capital by which they rise."[20] But Eliot's allusion is complex: he recognizes Ruskin's splendor but also the dismal sense in which he represents Christianity diminished to its aesthetic quality. He thinks of Ruskin as cousin to Arnold, who assumed that he could retain of Christianity only its beauty, and yet be saved.

In the second stanza Eliot proceeds as if he were paying tribute to de Bosschère: "the important thing is not how we are to feel about it, but how it is." Not an adjective in sight:

> Ils vont prendre le train de huit heures
> Prolonger leurs misères de Padoue à Milan
> Où se trouvent la Cène, et un restaurant pas cher.
> Lui pense aux pourboires, et rédige son bilan.
> Ils auront vu la Suisse et traversé la France.

But then, in a powerful change of tone, Eliot turns back to Saint Apollinaire:

> Et Saint Apollinaire, raide et ascétique,
> Vieille usine désaffectée de Dieu, tient encore
> Dans ses pierres écroulantes la forme précise de Byzance.

It is a flourish of the grand style. The force of feeling, accrued from the earlier invocation to the church in Classe, is restrained in "raide et ascétique" and the parenthetical "Vieille usine désaffectée de Dieu," then asserts itself at the end of the line with "tient encore," is held back again by "Dans ses pierres écroulantes," only to take command with "la forme précise de Byzance," rhyming authoritatively with "France." The perspective of judgment is enforced by such incongruities that a reading of the poem as satire appears to be irresistible: satire, caricature, farce, the readiest means by which escape from human emotions may be effected.

But Arrowsmith's interpretation of the poem must be reckoned with. Tender toward the honeymooners, he takes them as pilgrims,

unconsciously turning toward the light of spiritual being. The bed-
bugs that bite them are brought into the same poetic field as the bites
in Dante's "Paradiso"—"Tutti quei morsi"—that "have power to
make the heart turn to God." Instead of reading the juxtaposed de-
tails as enforcing "perspective by incongruity," Arrowsmith takes
them as intersecting and therefore as making possible the striving of
the Many toward the One: "Thus in Eliot a *restaurant pas cher* is the
worldly counterpart of the Last Supper; an ordinary cocktail party
becomes a shadow play of the Communion. . . . Reality for [the
honeymooners] is just this misery of sensual repetition; the ideality to
which it unknowingly aspires is represented by the saint's hard, conceptual rigor. But, however diminished, that ideality—that unsatisfied craving for a completeness beyond themselves—*inheres* in them
just as the form of the basilica still *holds* (*tient*) in the crumbling
stones."[21] The point here, according to Arrowsmith, "isn't merely
the desperate opposition of lovers and saint, but the fusion implied by
their opposition." F. H. Bradley, on whose theory of knowledge and
experience Eliot wrote his Harvard dissertation, is called upon for
authority: "Where a whole is complete in finite beings, which know
themselves to be 'elements' and members of its system, this *is* the
consciousness in such individuals of their own completeness. . . . It
is the self-realization of each member . . . to be himself, he must go
beyond himself, to live his own life he must live a life which is not
merely his own, but which, none the less, on the contrary all the more,
is intensely and emphatically his own individuality."[22] Hence the aspiration, which Arrowsmith ascribes to the honeymooners, toward the
wholeness of spiritual unity, as if it were Christendom or the "mind
of Europe," which according to Eliot's description has not superannu-
ated Shakespeare, Homer, or the rock drawing of the Magdalenian
draftsmen.

I wish I could find this reading of "Lune de Miel" convincing;

it would be a relief, after living so long with the image of those wretched honeymooners extending their misery from Padua to Milan. But Arrowsmith's interpretation seems applicable to "Ash-Wednesday" rather than to "Lune de Miel." For one thing, the honeymooners do not know—are not allowed to know—that they are "elements" and members of a system. They are having a terrible honeymoon, which might have been improved if they had been able to lodge in clean hotels. In 1917, Eliot was in the punitive phase of his talent, still exasperated by much that he had experienced as an American tourist in Europe. After "Prufrock"—written in 1910–11 and published in 1915—he seems to have felt compelled to discover new feelings, harsher than those of "Prufrock" and "Portrait of a Lady." He had to get the quatrains into his system before getting their feelings out of his system for good. The good is in the tone of "Ash-Wednesday" and the Ariel poems, especially "Marina."

Meanwhile there was "Prufrock." In a lecture at the Library of Congress on January 23, 1956, Blackmur remarked that "the reason why 'Prufrock' is *now* a popular poem (though it was a very difficult poem for most people for its first twenty years of life) is that the analogies with which it is composed have had time to sink in."[23] In my case it was not that the analogies had sunk in but that the tunes, the rhythms, had proved enchanting. They intuited not the world I inhabited but a possible other world in which a dandy, self-possessed within the constraints of his nervous system, walked the streets attended by an overwhelming question. I wanted nothing more than this melodrama. Later I had trouble distinguishing Prufrock from Baudelaire's Constantin Guys—except that Guys did something, drew, painted—or from an irregular image of the dandy, close kin to Pater, Wilde, Beardsley, and Nabokov, princes of the town, traveling *incognito* the while. I saw him or his shadow everywhere. Listening to poets reading their poems, I saw him slide into the back row and wait for the reading, departing without fuss when the question period started: he had his own besetting question, there was no need of another. Surely he was at Stevens's reading when the large red man read "Le Monocle de mon oncle" and committed himself to a primitive desire: "I wish that I might be a thinking stone." A thinking stone didn't strike me as at all as resourceful as a pair of ragged claws scuttling across the floors of silent seas. As if that were not enough, Stevens asked: "Shall I un-crumple this much-crumpled thing?"[24] I felt as Humbert Humbert felt while he played tennis with Dolores in the pure air of Champion, Colorado, and an inquisitive butterfly passed, dipping, between them.

Voices

"The Three Voices of Poetry"

On November 19, 1953, Eliot delivered the eleventh annual lecture of the National Book League in London under the title "The Three Voices of Poetry." I bought the pamphlet—twenty-four pages—as soon as it appeared in Hodges Figgis's bookshop in Dublin. I was an assistant lecturer in English at University College, Dublin, busy preparing courses on Shakespeare, Webster, Jonson, and Sir Thomas Browne and, in the evening, going to concerts and trying my hand at music criticism. In spare time I was much occupied with Eliot's work in poetry, drama, and criticism. His distinction between the three voices held my attention: "The first is the voice of the poet talking to himself—or to nobody. The second is the voice of the poet addressing an audience, whether large or small. The third is the voice of the poet when he attempts to create a dramatic character speaking in verse; when he is saying, not what he would say in his own person, but only what he can say within the limits of one imaginary character addressing another imaginary character."[1] But Eliot did not leave the distinctions in that simple form. As the lecture went on, he presented the first voice as that of a poet released from any need to communicate: his sole desire is to rid himself of a burden.

> What you start from is nothing so definite as an emotion, in any ordinary sense; it is still more certainly not an idea; it is—to adapt two lines of Beddoes to a different meaning—a
>
>> Bodiless childful of life in the gloom
>>
>> Crying with frog voice, "what shall I be?"
>
> [The poet] is oppressed by a burden which he must bring to birth in order to obtain relief. Or, to change the figure of speech, he is haunted by a demon, a demon against which he feels powerless, because in its first manifestation it has no face, no name, nothing; and the words, the poem he makes, are a kind of form of exorcism of this demon. . . . [A]nd when the words are finally arranged in the right way—or in what he comes to accept as the best arrangement he can find—he may experience a moment of exhaustion, of appeasement, of absolution, and of something very near annihilation, which is in itself indescribable.[2]

"A kind of form of exorcism of this demon" is laborious, it has at least one "of" too many, but the labor is justified. The experience Eliot described is evidently as arduous as that of Confession, the Christian sacrament that the penny Catechism tells us must, to be valid, have four stages: contrition, confession, satisfaction, and absolution. In poetry, the process corresponds to the lyric, in which a poet communes with his "sole self."

Eliot darkens our understanding of the second voice by referring to "the poet addressing other people in either his own voice or an assumed voice." These situations should be differentiated. When Yeats begins "The Municipal Gallery Revisited" with the line, "Around me the images of thirty years," we are free to think that the voice we hear is Yeats's, but when Eliot begins "Gerontion" with an epigraph from *Measure for Measure* and the lines,

> Here I am, an old man in a dry month,
> Being read to by a boy, waiting for rain . . .

we do not think that the poet is speaking in his own voice. He is writing a dramatic monologue, imagining someone else speaking in the posited circumstances. Eliot may be doing this, too, in "New Hampshire":

> To-day grieves, to-morrow grieves,
> Cover me over, light-in-leaves;

unless we are prepared—I feel no such inclination—to identify "me" with the child Eliot. I don't think he is speaking in his own voice in "Whispers of Immortality"—

> Donne, I suppose, was such another
> Who found no substitute for sense . . .

even though I find the same sentence in *The Use of Poetry and the Use of Criticism:*

> Coleridge was one of those unhappy persons—Donne, I suppose, was such another—of whom one might say, that if they had not been poets, they might have made something of their lives, might even have had a career."[3]

The third voice is heard in the dramatic monologue. Most—but not all—of Eliot's poems are in this form, though not in Browning's manner. Eliot admired Browning's dramatic monologues: "Who can forget Fra Lippo Lippi, or Andrea del Sarto, or Bishop Blougram, or the other bishop who ordered his tomb?"[4] But when he wrote in this form, he showed no sign of wanting—as Browning evidently did—to get as much of the imagined life as possible into the words ascribed to the personage. In fact, he seemed to want to reduce his personages to ghosts or shadows. I'm not sure why. Leonard Woolf gives a possible explanation in an account of one of Eliot's visits: "During his visit Virginia one evening tackled him about his poetry and told him that 'he wilfully concealed his transitions.' He admitted this, but said that it was unnecessary to explain: explanation diluted facts. . . . What he wanted to do was to 'disturb externals'; he had had a kind of personal upheaval after 'Prufrock' and this altered his inclination, which had been to develop in the manner of Henry James.' "[5] If Eliot had wanted to disturb externals, he would have found no merit in setting up additional Browningesque characters: better to imagine them already disturbed or reduced. Presumably he could have imagined J. Alfred Prufrock as a complete character in a novel by Henry James—a Lambert Strether returned to America—but he chose not to. When he started writing for the theater he faced a different problem, that of imagining characters entirely separate from himself.

The third voice, in which the author of *Murder in the Cathedral, The Family Reunion,* and *The Cocktail Party* invents speech for imaginary characters, is easily distinguished: we are not likely to confuse what Celia says in *The Cocktail Party* with what Eliot would say in his own person. But three voices are not enough. Eliot's scheme doesn't allow for the nameless, undifferentiated voice we hear in "Burbank with a Baedeker: Bleistein with a Cigar":

Defunctive music under sea
Passed seaward with the passing bell
Slowly . . .

Maybe we can call this voice impersonal or omniscient narration, such that there is no point in asking who is speaking. It is not "the poet addressing other people in his own voice." If it is "the poet addressing other people in an assumed voice," then the poem is a dramatic monologue, but "Burbank with a Baedeker: Bleistein with a Cigar" isn't. Eliot's scheme should have allowed for styles of voicelessness, in which words appear as if from a printing press and without any sign of a continuously recognizable voice or an implied person who takes responsibility for them. Swift's *Tale of a Tub* is a case in point: we gain nothing by assuming that its words are those of Swift or of an anonymous Hack. They are words on a page, delivered with the taunting flourish of an anonymous pamphlet. Recourse to "voice" doesn't provide a comprehensive scheme of descriptions.

It's also strange that Eliot didn't allow for the voice of the Muse. The three voices are ascribed to the poet in his personal and historical capacity. In "Tradition and the Individual Talent" Eliot enforced a distinction between the man who suffers and the mind that creates, but he didn't clarify it. I assume that it is the same as the difference, a commonplace from Emerson to Harold Bloom, between psyche and pneuma—between the psychological or existential self and the poet through whom the wind of inspiration bloweth where it listeth. In *Winter Pollen* Ted Hughes has made such a distinction the main consideration in his understanding of Eliot. Eliot's silence on the issue is explained, I think, by his preoccupation with verse drama, work of the third voice. But he didn't throw much light on the question: in what sense, listening to Caliban, are we also hearing Shakespeare? What is Shakespeare's imagination, such that we attend to Caliban rather than to Shakespeare? Eliot's concern, at least in the early years, was more immediately linguistic: he regarded the writing of a play as a problem of language, how to find the right words for his characters. He evidently thought that he could deduce from the English language, given the resources of verse, characters sufficient for the purposes of the theater. In *Poetry and Drama* (1951) he acknowledged that he should have given more consideration to the characters, and that the problems involved in writing plays were not entirely problems of language.

I didn't notice at the time—nor did Eliot, apparently—that the whole vocabulary of "voice" is misleading. Even when we invoke the voice of the Muse, we give every style a quasi-personal form and we enforce a psychological or anthropomorphic explanation for every difference. It would be far better to have different styles predicated on something impersonal, to begin with, and to allow the personal factors to come in later. Wittgenstein provides a motto for this in one of his *Zettel:* "Like everything metaphysical the harmony between thought and reality is to be found in the grammar of the language."[6] The social correlative of this grammar would then be the "collective assemblage" described by Deleuze and Guattari in *A Thousand Plateaus:* it is the posited social authority for anything that can be uttered, but not in itself—or not yet—personal. No matter what you do with "voice," you can't fend off the question: whose voice, precisely?

None of this occurred to me as a problem in *The Elder Statesman.* That play affected my professional life. I read Latin and English for my B.A. degree at University College, Dublin, and I won a scholarship to do an M.A. in English. I could have done it either by taking further courses, sitting an examination, and writing a minor dissertation, an essay of about forty pages, or by writing a major dissertation of about three hundred pages on a scholarly topic. I chose the second method and wrote on the work of Charles Macklin, a late-eighteenth-century Irish dramatist and theater director who, like Arthur Murphy, Isaac Bickerstaff, Hugh Kelly, and several other writers at the time, left Ireland to seek his fortune in London. Macklin wrote nine plays, only three of which were published in his lifetime. He directed two productions, of *Macbeth* and *The Merchant of Venice,* that have entered into the history of Shakespearean theater in the eighteenth century. My dissertation was judged satisfactory, but I didn't see any possibility of publishing more than a chapter or two of it. At that time, I was a young man doing his best to get on in the academic world, and while I was under no pressure to publish a book or even scholarly articles—my colleagues disapproved of young men rushing into print—I wanted to write something. Poetic drama, or rather verse drama, was much in the air, largely because *Murder in the Cathedral, The Family Reunion,* and *The Cocktail Party* had put it there. For a few years it was widely thought that the future of serious theater (as distinct from Shaftesbury Avenue farces) depended on verse drama, particularly on Eliot and—though it seems hard to credit—on Christopher Fry.

There was also Yeats. I read the plays, but even in Dublin it was hard to see them performed. The Abbey Theatre, which Yeats helped to found, had long since turned away from his plays and given over the stage to peasant comedies and O'Casey's Dublin melodramas. I had to wait several years before seeing the Belfast Lyric Theatre, directed by Mary O'Malley, perform Yeats's Cuchulain plays in Sligo, and several more years to see James Flannery's productions of them at the Peacock Theatre in Dublin. I had already decided that Yeats's "plays for dancers" were remarkable and that something like a "total theatre," as Brecht envisaged such a thing, was to be found in the theory and practice of Yeats's *On Baile's Strand, The Only Jealousy of Emer, At the Hawk's Well, The Dreaming of the Bones, A Full Moon in March, Calvary, The Death of Cuchulain,* and *Purgatory.* In his memorial lecture at the Abbey Theatre in 1940, Eliot said that in regard to the verse play "Yeats had nothing, and we have had Yeats,"[7] a sentence good enough to justify my trying to write a book on the subject. Yeats's essays and Eliot's gave me enough theoretical lore to work with till I found a more useful theory of *poésie de théâtre* in Francis Fergusson's *The Idea of a Theatre* and his *Dante's Drama of the Mind.* For the practice of verse drama, I had Yeats, Eliot, Pound's *Women of Trachis,* Fry, Reuel Denney, and a number of more occasional dramatists to consider. Most of the book was already written when I heard that Eliot had a new play, *The Elder Statesman,* ready for the Edinburgh Festival. I wrote to him in the hope, frail indeed, that a text of it might be available. He was still changing it. The play opened on August 25, 1958. I went to Edinburgh, attended the first four performances, and wrote a chapter on the play from memory and a few notes. Through Fergusson's good offices, Princeton University Press published *The Third Voice,* my first book, in 1959. I was on my way, I thought.

But not into dramatic criticism. I soon realized that Fergusson, Eric Bentley, Kenneth Tynan, Vernon Young, Robert Warshaw, Stanley Kauffman, and many other critics had a feeling for theater and film that I could never acquire. When I wrote about a play—even one I had just seen on the stage—I made it sound like a long poem I had read and annotated. Besides, I couldn't afford to go to the theater often enough to repair my deficiency.

Toward the Poems

My immediate problem, after writing *The Third Voice,* was to come to terms with modern poetry. I was invited to teach two courses—Modern Poetry and Modern Drama—at the Harvard Summer School, and while I felt due misgiving about teaching a course in drama, I could not turn down the invitation. I was also given a fellowship of the American Council of Learned Societies to spend a year as a visiting scholar at the University of Pennsylvania writing a book—I called it *Connoisseurs of Chaos*—on nineteenth- and twentieth-century American poetry: roughly Whitman to Robert Lowell. I wanted to write the book, but I didn't know how to do it. It seemed to me impossible to present the history of modern poetry as one story and one story only. Some of the most influential critics tried to do that, and they ignored the diversity of the poems. It was as if they needed a hero and could not cope with more than one. Leavis's *New Bearings in English Poetry* made Eliot the crucial force, and presented in his vicinity Hopkins and Pound, but not Yeats, Hart Crane, or Stevens. In *The Well-Wrought Urn,* Cleanth Brooks took account of Yeats, but in *Modern Poetry and the Tradition* he interpreted virtually the whole story of English poetry since Shakespeare under Eliot's auspices and subject to his critical dispensation. It was significant, too, that F. O. Matthiessen's *Oxford Book of American Verse* and *The Achievement of T. S. Eliot* took Eliot as the major figure and disposed the other poets in relation to him. Later, Hugh Kenner's *Pound Era* presented modern poetry as the history of Objectivism from Pound, William Carlos Williams, and Marianne Moore to George Oppen and Louis Zukofsky. To get into that story a poet had to go to school with one of those masters, as Charles Tomlinson attended to Williams and Moore for a while. Even though Kenner wrote a book on Eliot—*The Invisible Poet*—he treated him as a special case, a symbolist, and therefore unassimilable to Objectivism, the only story worth telling. Being an associate of Pound's, Eliot had to be admired: he somehow made himself a great poet in an otherwise deplorable tradition. Donald Davie's *Thomas Hardy and British Poetry* and Philip Larkin's *New Oxford Book of Twentieth-Century Verse* took Hardy as the crucial figure after all, and claimed that the modernism of Eliot and Pound was a false trail. I respected the rhetorical power of these books, but I couldn't be convinced. It seemed to me that I should regard each of the big poets—Whitman, Dickinson, Hopkins, Hardy, Yeats, Eliot, Pound, Stevens, Williams, and Frost—as a largely independent master, and try to describe the poetic relations among them.

This was not easy in Eliot's case. Where to begin? It must count for something that he was an American poet who made himself a European—not, I think, an Englishman: there is a difference—but that seemed to be a matter of mainly biographical interest. One could draw lines of relation between him and Emerson, Hawthorne, Poe, Whitman, James, and Mark Twain, but "The Dry Salvages" and the "Landscapes" were the only poems that called for such annotation. The implied contexts of other poems, notably "Marina," were in part American, but not in such a way as to make them American poems. The fog in "The Love Song of J. Alfred Prufrock" and the name "Prufrock" may have come from St. Louis, but I couldn't believe that these origins mattered. I had to postpone the question of America. Meanwhile, Eliot was obviously an affiliate of Pound's program to "make it new," but the materials of his poetry were mostly old: Dante, Shakespeare, the Jacobean dramatists, the seventeenth-century poets and divines—Donne, Herbert, Andrewes—Poe, Beddoes, Tennyson, Swinburne, Lewis Carroll, and Edward Lear, and the poets of the 1890s, much as he affected to despise them. And then there were the French poets, especially Laforgue, Gautier, and Corbière. Eliot's relations to these writers, French and English, seemed to be opportunistic, he took what he needed from each of them and moved on to the next treasure trove.

Perhaps I could approach the poems the old-fashioned way by asking what they were about. I recalled Northrop Frye's remark that Eliot's early poems engaged a certain predicament, the excess of consciousness over being. That would explain how they differed from Browning's dramatic monologues, where there is no such excess. Browning takes pains to correlate consciousness and being: that is what a rounded character comes to. But Prufrock, Gerontion, and the several figures of the early poems are conscious far beyond any use to which they could put their consciousness. No wonder they turn aside from themselves in disgust.

There was also the question of Eliot's relation, as a poet, to a motive he repudiated as a critic: Art for Art's Sake. It may be thought absurd that I raise the question, but my masters raised it. Fergusson thought that Eliot was "deprived of any sympathetic connection with the world outside poetry" and that as a result he could "only mount to an ever narrower and less significant field of thought."[8] Blackmur conceded that Art for Art's Sake was "just around the corner, an awkward ghost," awkward because it was inherently out of place in Eliot's regimen. But he argued that Eliot had indeed a connection, sympathetic or not, with the world, "a connection all the more thorough for refusing to be lost in it."[9] That seemed persuasive, though it left me wondering why I needed persuading.

It is a question of the status of words. Is it their main duty to signify, to refer to things in a world at large deemed to be autonomous in whole and in every part? Have they an interest in conveying the impression that the given world is stable? Or may a writer declare "the absolute power of the word as a thing having life of its own and apart from its meaning?"[10] Elizabeth Sewell says in her book on Valéry that words are the mind's sole defence against being possessed by thought or dream. Surely in "The Love Song of J. Alfred Prufrock" the repetitions of phrase—"And indeed there will be time"—and the echoing of "all" throughout the poem protect Prufrock's mind from succumbing to the exorbitance of thought; just as they protect him from getting lost in a world other than his own. It was Yeats who wrote "Words alone are certain good." But it was Eliot, not Yeats, who acted on that principle as a poet, if equivocally as a critic.

In his essay on Swinburne, Eliot says—sounding for once like Pound—that "language in a healthy state presents the object, is so close to the object that the two are identified."[11] What can he mean? If the object is a cat sitting on a mat, it doesn't make sense to say that word and cat are identified. If the object is an esoteric experience, the experience may be inextricable from the words employed. Or the words may have an autonomous life and in that case the object is dissolved. As in Swinburne's poetry. Eliot goes on to say:

[Language and object] are identified in the verse of Swinburne solely because the object has ceased to exist, because the meaning is merely the hallucination of meaning, because language, uprooted, has adapted itself to an independent life of atmospheric nourishment. In Swinburne, for example, we see the word "weary" flourishing in this way independent of the particular and actual weariness of flesh or spirit. The bad poet dwells partly in a world of objects and partly in a world of words, and he never can get them to fit. Only a man of genius could dwell so exclusively and consistently among words as Swinburne. His language is not, like the language of bad poetry, dead. It is very much alive, with this singular life of its own. But the language which is more important to us is that which is struggling to digest and express new objects, new groups of objects, new feelings, new aspects, as, for instance, the prose of Mr. James Joyce or the earlier Conrad.[12]

In the end, Eliot distinguishes himself from Swinburne, but only in the end and by appeal to Joyce and Conrad. Up to that point, he has been laboring, not very successfully, to describe Swinburne's peculiar genius. The problem, which Eliot didn't want to recognize, is that Swinburne's genius is of a type akin to Eliot's own. Eliot's critical vocabulary, for once, is inflexible. There is no merit in claiming that "the meaning is merely the hallucination of meaning." The hallucination of meaning is another meaning, a more occult one, as in Eliot's early poems. I take the quoted passage to imply: "You may think that what I'm saying about Swinburne applies just as well to me. You may even think that the criterion I am applying—of language being so close to the object that the two are identified—is not fulfilled by my own poems. But it is. There is always an object in my poems, but it is a new feeling, a new aspect, I do not write Pure Poetry. In this respect I am with Joyce and Conrad."

I'm not taking the absurd position that Eliot's early poems are "merely verbal," whatever that may mean. But in those poems the use of language goes some distance toward giving words the independent life that Eliot ascribed to Swinburne's. Eliot's critical position on the issue was indeterminate: he often disapproved of writers whose gifts were similar to his own. As a critic, he felt it necessary to speak against the bias of his own poetic gift.

Meaning and the Auditory Imagination

In *The Use of Poetry and the Use of Criticism,* Eliot describes the "auditory imagination" as if it were necessarily active in poetry: "What I call the 'auditory imagination' is the feeling for syllable and rhythm, penetrating far below the conscious levels of thought and feeling, invigorating every word; sinking to the most primitive and forgotten, returning to the origin and bringing something back, seeking the beginning and the end. It works through meanings, certainly, or not without meanings in the ordinary sense, and fuses the old and obliterated and the trite, the current, and the new and surprising, the most ancient and the most civilised mentality."[13] In "From Poe to Valéry" he goes further and acknowledges "the incantatory element in poetry" which "because of its very crudity, stirs the feelings at a deep and almost primitive level."[14] Why? Presumably because the feelings of even the most refined person are to some extent crude. In the Conclusion to *The Use of Poetry and the Use of Criticism,* Eliot doesn't refer to the crudity of incantation but to its force. He agrees with the Abbé Bremond in finding some relation and more difference between mystical experience and the experience of writing poems: "I agree with Bremond, and perhaps go even further, in finding that this disturbance of our quotidian character which results in an incantation, an outburst of words which we hardly recognise as our own (because

of the effortlessness), is a very different thing from mystical illumination. The latter is a vision which may be accompanied by the realisation that you will never be able to communicate it to anyone else, or
even by the realisation that when it is past you will not be able to
recall it to yourself; the former is not a vision but a motion terminating in an arrangement of words on paper."[15] Even with this difference, Eliot's theory of poetry is a theory of inspiration, or at least it
takes care to make room for such a theory. The motion that termi-
nates in an arrangement of words on paper can't be resisted or chal-
lenged. Meaning, in any of its normal senses, must do the best it can:
it can't hope to insist on its privilege.

But the issue was a difficult one for Eliot. There is a discrepancy
between Eliot's poetry and his criticism at this point. In his major
essay on Dante, he claims that the differences between Dante's language and Shakespeare's make Dante easier for a foreigner: "Dante's
advantages are not due to greater genius, but to the fact that he wrote
when Europe was still more or less one. And even had Chaucer or
Villon been exact contemporaries of Dante, they would still have
been farther, linguistically as well as geographically, from the center
of Europe than Dante."[16] The language of Shakespeare or of any great
English poet "is his own language." The language of Dante is "the
perfection of a common language."[17] It follows that Dante's language
is free from the "opacity, or inspissation of poetic style throughout
Europe after the Renaissance." Hence the ease, the translucence of
Dante's style, and the fact that his allegory presents itself in clear
visual images: "Dante's is a *visual* imagination. It is a visual imagination in a different sense from that of a modern painter of still life: it is
visual in the sense that he lived in an age in which men still saw
visions. It was a psychological habit, the trick of which we have forgotten, but as good as any of our own. We have nothing but dreams,
and we have forgotten that seeing visions—a practice now relegated

to the aberrant and uneducated—was once a more significant, interesting, and disciplined kind of dreaming. We take it for granted that our dreams spring from below: possibly the quality of our dreams suffers in consequence."[18] Eliot might have said the same of Homer. What Homer gives us, according to Schiller, is "simply the quiet existence and operation of things in accordance with their natures."[19] Eliot did not propose to go back to Dante's Europe or even to his Florence. It was too late for that. One had to put up with the damage of many lifetimes, and with the inspissation of poetic style since the Renaissance. But Eliot retained his conviction that the conditions that issued in Dante's language were the best conditions for poetry that have ever obtained. Dante's visual imagination was the perfection of a once common but no longer available possibility. It might still be invoked as a criterion, especially where the most formidable poets were in question. In his first lecture on Milton, Eliot quoted a passage from *Paradise Lost* as evidence that in Milton generally "the complication is dictated by a demand of verbal music, instead of by any demand of sense." Warming to his theme, he argued that Milton's visual imagination was limited, and that the complications of his syntax were caused by a preponderance of the auditory imagination rather than by any attempt to follow "actual speech or thought." A comparison with Joyce followed, inevitably: two writers of musical taste and training, blind geniuses with "remarkable powers of memory perhaps fortified by defective vision." In both, and in *Paradise Lost* as much as in *Finnegans Wake,* we find "an auditory imagination abnormally sharpened at the expense of the visual."[20] Ideally, the visual and the auditory imaginations would have equal rights. Dante was always Eliot's exemplary writer for the visual imagination. In Shakespeare more than any other writer "the auditory imagination and the imagination of the other senses are more nearly fused, and fused together with the thought."[21]

But the question of sense and sound, eye and ear was difficult for Eliot, not just because Dante's conditions are no longer present but because Eliot's genius took the form of the auditory more than the visual imagination. The most recalcitrant issue was that of meaning. There is a strange paragraph in *The Use of Poetry and the Use of Criticism:*

> The chief use of the "meaning" of a poem, in the ordinary sense, may be (for here again I am speaking of some kinds of poetry and not all) to satisfy one habit of the reader, to keep his mind diverted and quiet, while the poem does its work upon him: much as the imaginary burglar is always provided with a bit of nice meat for the house-dog. This is a normal situation of which I approve. But the minds of all poets do not work that way; some of them, assuming that there are other minds like their own, become impatient of this "meaning" which seems superfluous, and perceive possibilities of intensity through its elimination. I am not asserting that this situation is ideal; only that we must write our poetry as we can, and take it as we find it.[22]

But on other occasions Eliot was severe on those poets who eliminated meaning in its ordinary sense. Even in the most purely incantatory poem, he maintained, "the dictionary meaning of words cannot be disregarded with impunity." As Poe disregarded it, in Eliot's view. In "From Poe to Valéry" Eliot contrasts Poe's use of the word "immemorial" —

It was night, in the lonesome October
    Of my most immemorial year

with Tennyson's "The moan of doves in immemorial elms." According to the OED, as Eliot noted, "immemorial" means "beyond memory or out of mind; ancient beyond memory or record: extremely old." None of these meanings is applicable to this use of the word by

Poe: "The year was not beyond memory—the speaker remembers
one incident in it very well; at the conclusion he even remembers a
funeral in the same place just a year earlier. [In] the line of Tennyson,
equally well known, and justly admired because the sound of the line
responds so well to the sound which the poet wishes to evoke . . .
immemorial, besides having the most felicitous sound value, is exactly
the word for trees so old that no one knows just how old they are."[23]
So Eliot convicts Poe of "an irresponsibility towards the meaning of
words."[24] But in "The Music of Poetry" he uses virtually the same
phrase not to indict the poetry of Edward Lear but to name one of its
pleasures: "His non-sense is not vacuity of sense: it is a parody of
sense, and that is the sense of it. 'The Jumblies' is a poem of adventure, and of nostalgia for the romance of foreign voyage and exploration; 'The Yongy-Bongy Bo' and 'The Dong with a Luminous Nose'
are poems of unrequited passion—'blues' in fact. We enjoy the music, which is of a high order, and we enjoy the feeling of irresponsibility towards the sense."[25] Perhaps the difference is one of genre.
Edward Lear and Lewis Carroll write Nonsense Poetry, Poe doesn't.
The theory we need, according to which all the earth is paper and all
the seas are ink, is given in Elizabeth Sewell's *The Field of Nonsense:* it
throws light on Lear and Carroll but none on Poe, whose poems of
incantation fulfill a different set of principles. What the evidence
shows is that the author of *Old Possum's Book of Practical Cats* was of
Lear's party and of Carroll's, but he was also susceptible to the poetry
of incantation—Poe's, Beddoes's, Tennyson's—and sometimes composed in that tradition while worrying about its irresponsibility toward the meaning.

There was also another kind of irresponsibility. Eliot enjoyed the
experience of not caring much what Pound said, but of admiring the
way in which he said it. He took the same liberty with Laforgue.

Laforgue and "Rhapsody on a Windy Night"

Eliot acknowledged, several times, his debt to Arthur Symons's *The Symbolist Movement in Literature,* which he read at Harvard in the second, revised edition of 1908. Years later he appreciated the book as "an introduction to wholly new feelings, as a revelation."[26] It is hard to say how seriously he took Symons's claim that in the literature of French Symbolism "the visible world is no longer a reality, and the unseen world no longer a dream."[27] But he was ready to believe that Symbolism was "an attempt to spiritualise literature, to evade the old bondage of rhetoric, the old bondage of exteriority."[28] In *Gaudier Brzeska: A Memoir,* Pound said, "There are two opposed ways of thinking of a man: firstly, you may think of him as that toward which perception moves, as the toy of circumstance, as the plastic substance *receiving* impressions; secondly, you may think of him as directing a certain fluid force against circumstances, as *conceiving* instead of merely reflecting and observing. One does not claim that one way is better than the other, one notes a diversity of the temperament."[29] It is the difference between the art of line and the art of color, between carving and modeling, as Adrian Stokes described them. Or between Cavalcanti and Petrarch, between Botticelli and Rembrandt, according to Pound's principles. Of course Pound preferred one set of values to the other; preferred carving to modeling, Cavalcanti to Petrarch. But it didn't trouble him that Eliot, by force of talent and disposition, was of the other party. Pound thought that the impressionist or symbolist way was best represented by Yeats, though later he decided that Eliot made more of the heritage of Symbolism than Yeats did. He thought that the second way, the "better tradition," was best embodied in Ford Madox Ford, but later he knew that Joyce had exceeded Ford in that way. In the end Pound believed that he himself and Wyndham Lewis showed the best possibilities of the second way.

The chapter of Symons's book that meant most to Eliot was the one on Laforgue. He marked this passage: "The old cadences, the old eloquence, the ingenuous seriousness of poetry, are all banished, on a theory as self-denying as that which permitted Degas to dispense with recognisable beauty in his figures."[30] Laforgue's poems showed Eliot "how much more use poetry could make of contemporary ideas and feelings, of the emotional quality of contemporary ideas."[31] The "imperative intimacy" a young writer may feel toward another writer— Eliot's theme in the fourth of his "Reflections on Contemporary Poetry"—seems to reflect his discovery of Laforgue's poems.[32] He paid tribute to that discovery by writing "Humouresque," a poem "after J. Laforgue," specifically after "Encore un livre," one of the "Locutions des Pierrots." Still, it was a somewhat histrionic gesture on Eliot's part to quote the first ten lines of "O géraniums diaphanes" in "The Metaphysical Poets" to illustrate "the essential quality of transmuting ideas into sensations, of transforming an observation into a state of mind."[33] It is not clear that this is what the lines do or that a comparison with Donne's poetry is valid:

> O géraniums diaphanes, guerroyeurs sortilèges,
> Sacrilèges monomanes!
> Emballages, dévergondages, douches! O pressoirs
> Des vendanges des grands soirs!
> Layettes aux abois,
> Thyrses au fond des bois!
> Transfusions, représailles,
> Relevailles, compresses et l'éternelle potion,
> *Angelus!* N'en pouvoir plus
> De débâcles nuptiales! De débâcles nuptiales![34]

The novel feature of those lines is their refusal of syntax. The poetry issues from nouns and past participles taken from different levels of being. The best way to read the lines is to let the words and their associations create a field of force, like an electrical circuit. By an act of divination we may infer that the poem is an anti-epithalamion; it is about marriage, childbirth, and the dread of both: "De débâcles nuptiales!" "Emballages, dévergondages, douches!" epitomize the stages of disappointment in marriage, from enthusiasm through sexual throes to disillusion. We divine a situation corresponding to the diction, and we add it to the line to make up for the missing syntax.

"Rhapsody on a Windy Night" seems to me Eliot's most Laforguian poem. B. C. Southam has associated it also and justly with Bergson's *Introduction to Metaphysics* and *Matter and Memory,* Charles-Louis Philippe's *Bubu de Montparnasse* and *Marie Donadieu,* and the urban poems of John Davidson. I'll quote the first stanza:

> Twelve o'clock.
> Along the reaches of the street
> Held in a lunar synthesis,
> Whispering lunar incantations
> Dissolve the floors of memory
> And all its clear relations
> Its divisions and precisions,
> Every street lamp that I pass
> Beats like a fatalistic drum,
> And through the spaces of the dark
> Midnight shakes the memory
> As a madman shakes a dead geranium.[35]

Laforgue's "géraniums" and "monomanes" gave Eliot the madman shaking a dead geranium, but in appreciating Eliot's lines one would pay even more attention to the rhyme of "drum" and "geranium," a rhyme even more effective—like the later rhyme of "comes" and "geraniums"—than Laforgue's internal rhyme of the trisyllabic words, "diaphanes" and "monomanes" or his rhyme of "opium" and "géranium" in "C'est, sur un cou." Laforgue's method is one of loose but not casual association: each exclamatory phrase marks an act of perception about which, he implies, nothing more specific need be said. One exclamation leads to the next by having one word call to another. "Diaphanes" calls to "monomanes," "géraniums" to "guer-royeurs," "sortileges" is echoed in its last two syllables by "Sacri-lèges," the alliteration pointing to the transition. If "emballages" means exotic wrapping paper, as on wedding presents, it gets its sheen from "dévergondages" and its dismal ending in "douches." Laforgue's diction, not his syntax-without-syntax, released Eliot. None of Eliot's poems proceeds by having one exclamation call to another. In "Rhapsody on a Windy Night" memory throws up a crowd of twisted things—and we hesitate over the bizarre propriety of "crowd" to refer to a branch on the beach and a broken spring in a factory yard—but Eliot delivers these images with Augustan firmness of purpose. It is not surprising that he gave up attending on Laforgue's poems after a year or two and turned toward Gautier and Corbière; he had learned the whole lesson. He continued to pay tribute to Laforgue for having helped him to discover his own voice by listening to a different voice in a foreign language.

The Limits of a Language

In the first canto of *Paradiso,* Dante, gazing upon Beatrice who is gazing upon the sun, speaks of an experience that lies beyond nature and in the same breath says that it is impossible to express such a thing: "*Trasumanar significar per verba / non si poria.*" ("Passing be-yond humanity may not be set forth in words.") Dante acknowledges the impossibility by going from Italian to Latin. We allude to such experiences, but we can't express them; there may be different kinds of failure, but each is absolute. There are experiences that lie so far beyond our nature that words have never been found for them: they belong to the good angels. There are also experiences that lie far beneath our nature: their words belong to the fallen angels. Our nature is in the middle. It is impertinent to assume that there are words for everything: if there were, music and silence would be redundant. There are moments in which language stands baffled, saying of whatever it has just said that that is not what it meant at all. Such moments are welcome because they tell against the idolatry of language to which we are all, in some moods, susceptible. Knowing that language has done so much, we find it hard to believe that its powers are not endless.

Idolatry of language marks an outer limit of my theme. I hope it is not necessary to take up residence there. The theme assumes a more palpable form if we think not of language as such but of particular languages. I refer to the situation in which a writer using a particular language feels that he has come upon a limit either of that language or of his own sense of it. He has made a raid on the inarticulate or the inexpressible and has returned with nothing much to show for his labor. He feels, with inevitable frustration, that the most he can do with his language is not enough. The language is intractable as if on principle.

It is sometimes maintained that a poem that proceeds by association and contrast naturally issues in the diversity of languages with which "The Waste Land" ends. Eliot wanted to transcend the limits of any single language so that he could gain for his poem at least an air of universal application. But there is more to it than that. Eliot was remarkably sensitive not only to associations and contrasts but also to transitions from one tone to another. His imagination, like his theology, was responsive to different levels of being, and to the significance of passing from one to another. In "Poetry and Drama" he said that "a mixture of prose and verse in the same play is generally to be avoided: each transition makes the auditor aware, with a jolt, of the medium." Such a mixture is justifiable "when the author wishes to produce this jolt: when, that is, he wishes to transport the audience violently from one plane of reality to another."[36] The jolt is similar to the one we feel in a poem when two different vocabularies are brought together, as in Emily Dickinson's phrase "a quartz contentment." Or in *Macbeth,* when the Latin flourish of "this my hand will rather / The multitudinous seas incarnadine" is stilled by the Anglo-Saxon "Making the green one red."

I'll come back to the ending of "The Waste Land." I'm also thinking of the several languages in Pound's *Cantos,* the flurry of Provençal at the end of *Purgatorio* 26, and the "Raphel" line in *Inferno* 31. That line is meant as gibberish, but it is probably another version of the "matter and impertinency mixed, reason in madness" of *King Lear.* These occasions are hard to compare. The Provençal lines ascribed to Arnaut Daniel, though composed by Dante, are a compliment by which one master allows another to speak in his own language rather than suffer the indignity of a swift assimilation to modern Italian. As for the single line permitted to Nimrod before he is suppressed: he is his own accuser, Dante says in Italian ("Elli stessi s'accusa"), presumably because he tries to communicate in his own tongue and finds it impossible, as a result of the confusion of tongues he caused at Babel. Whatever Nimrod's words mean to him, there is no evidence that they intend to accuse him. The linguist "per lo cui mal coto / pur un linguaggio nel mondo non s'usa" ("through whose ill thought one language only is not used in the world") could offer a justification of his actions by appealing to an extreme form of nationalism. The fact that the appeal would be incommunicable would point not to a defect in his program or even to an error of method but merely to consequences beyond his intention. It is charming that Dante's Virgil rounds upon Nimrod in strict Italian, a language which by definition Nimrod can't understand any better than Virgil can understand Nimrod's idiolect, though I assume that gestures of anger are universal and may be understood by everyone beneath the words. When Othello comes ranting to Desdemona in words as opaque to her as Nimrod's to Virgil, she answers: "I understand a fury in your words, / But not the words."

We generally neglect this form of understanding. We are so concerned to correlate words with sense and sense with words that we are sluggish in dealing with signs that come before, after, or beneath the words. Dante's Virgil is an impatient critic, though his morality is impressive. He should have attended to the fury in Nimrod's words, if it was fury, and not to the words. A good reader is patient. By patience I mean the attitude that William Carlos Williams brought to the foreign passages in Pound's early cantos: "As to the Greek quotations—knowing no Greek—I presume they mean something, probably something pertinent to the text—and that the author knows what they mean. . . . But in all salient places, Pound has clarified his outland insertions with reasonable consistency. They are no particular matter save that they say, There were other times like ours—at the back of it all."[37] Many of Pound's outland insertions say that there were other times, unlike ours and better. But Williams's patience was the proper start toward further recognitions. He respected the foreign elements in Pound's poem: he knew that they testified to perceptions and feelings that Pound wanted to retain in an insolubly foreign state rather than to have them dissolved in his sensibility or the reader's. It is a mark of Pound's imagination, more than of Eliot's in "The Waste Land" and the early poems, that the foreign elements keep themselves intact and autonomous. This doesn't quite hold for Eliot's dealings with Dante.

There are several reasons to account for a writer's recourse to a language other than his own. Luther's table-talk shows that he switched from German to Latin when the theme became severely intellectual or theological. In "Fragment of an Analysis of a Case of Hysteria," Freud breaks into French when he wants to invoke an attitude of intelligent worldliness in sexual matters. Eliot read poems in French to jolt his imagination into rhythms and feelings different from his own. He evidently felt, too, that no modern language was comparable to Dante's Italian for practicing the imagery of lucidity and spiritual vision. It was not just that Dante happened to possess an acute visual imagination. Some disciplines of perception are exercised more resolutely in one language than another. When the familiar compound ghost of "Little Gidding" says—

> From wrong to wrong the exasperated spirit
> Proceeds, unless restored by that refining fire
> Where you must move in measure, like a dancer . . .

—readers do well to recall the refining fire in *Purgatorio* 26, "Poi s'ascose nel foco che gli affina" ("Then he hid himself in the fire that purifies them"), the line quoted again at the end of "The Waste Land." But a good reader does well enough without the allusion. Eliot could not have managed without it. Dante showed him that certain perceptions, at home in Italian rather than in English, were possible and that he might pursue them, but Dante also made available disciplines and acknowledgments that came slowly to Eliot's temper.

I refer to the subjective and idealist character of Eliot's genius, and the obstacles in his sensibility he had to surmount before he could acknowledge motives radically different from his own. Bradley's philosophy mainly endorsed a sense of the isolation of the self that was congenital in Eliot. The convinced recognition of feelings different from his own and equal in privilege to his own was an experience Eliot had to decide to submit to. It speaks well for him that, taking his own feelings so seriously, he eventually went out of the way of his temper to respect the feelings of others. Going out of the way was a spiritual act. Eliot's plays were crucial to him if only as ascetic exercises in that discipline: there are passages in them which show how much native prejudice his sensibility had to give up. In his early poems, objects tend to lose their identity and to become functions of the consciousness that takes note of them. It is not only Prufrock who is shadowed by that exorbitance. Eliot's insistence on the impersonality of the work of art was a first step toward humility. It might have made a difference if he had studied Levinas rather than Bradley. What he needed as a poet was Dante's impartial imagination. It was not enough that he alluded to Dante. In an allusion, as in a translation of Dante's Italian into Eliot's English, there was always a risk of staining the translation with one's subjectivity, making Dante obey Eliot's measure.

Eliot discussed these matters by reference to tradition and classicism rather than to Otherness. He was the first person he had to convince. It was only by an immense effort of conscientiousness that a poet as subjective and idealist as Eliot could turn toward the diverse recognitions that constituted tradition, classicism, and impersonality. The effort corresponds in poetic terms to the acts of prayer that resulted in his conversion to the Anglican communion. It went against his grain, and that is its interest. The fragments shored against his ruins at the end of "The Waste Land" are given in their own languages not merely as selected instances of tradition expressing themselves in different voices but as voices testifying to their radical difference. It is not merely that "shantih" would be poorly represented by "the peace that passeth understanding," but that such peace is already too completely domesticated: it is a platitude of Christian culture and therefore indistinguishable from ourselves. It is still possible to be irritated by those foreign bits and to complain that they pointlessly disrupt the movement of a poem in English. Nabokov has a passage in *Tyrants Observed* where someone switches to French to complain of "the artificial *grasseyement* that would appear" in his former lover's speech "when she needlessly switched to French." But the foreign bits at the end of "The Waste Land" have the force of prayer: they are not self-indulgent. The changes of tone mark the occasions on which Eliot refuses the urgings of his talent, which would have him rest in the echoes and recesses of his own language.

A mild form of this refusal occurs when Eliot resorts to a word that exists in English but gets its full reverberation in another language. The reference in "Little Gidding" to "the spirit unappeased and peregrine / Between two worlds become much like each other" is a case in point. "Peregrine" is not an unobtrusive particle of English: that is its force. In the Rome of the Republic and the Empire, *peregrini* were citizens of any state other than Rome: they remained foreign in Rome. Astrologers say that a peregrine is a planet situated in a part of the zodiac where it has none of its essential dignity. Blackmur has noted that *Purgatorio* 13 has—

> O frate mio, ciascuna e cittadina
> D'una vera citta; ma tu vuoi dire
> Che vivesse in Italia peregrina

—"O my brother, each is a citizen of a true city, but you would say one that lived in Italy as a peregrine."[38] The force of Eliot's phrase is gained by passing from "unappeased"—a word that recalls its Latin origin without insisting on it—to "peregrine"—a word that lives fully in Latin and Italian and only as an echo of those in English.

Another example, also from "Little Gidding":

> And all shall be well and
> All manner of thing shall be well

When the tongues of flame are in-folded
Into the crowned knot of fire
And the fire and the rose are one.

It's debatable whether Eliot was wise to hand himself over to Dante here. "In-folded" draws attention to itself not only by its position at the end of the verse line but by its having only residual status in English. The dictionaries give it as an obsolete variant of "enfolded," and while it has a frail claim to separate existence, it isn't at home in the language. Its home is in *Purgatorio* 33, a passage that Eliot quoted in his major essay on Dante—

Nel suo profundo vidi che s'interna,
Legato con amore in un volume,
Cio che per l'universo si squaderna

—"In its depth I saw ingathered, bound by love in a single volume, that which is dispersed in leaves throughout the universe." "In-gathered" is the word given in the translation Eliot used, a slightly modified version of Philip Wicksteed's translation for the Temple Classics. When it becomes "in-folded," it holds itself aloof from the words surrounding it. Eliot is determined to rise to Dante's occasion, even at the cost of using a rare English word and forcing readers to pay it a special form of attention.

He has something different in mind in "The Waste Land":

Unreal City,
Under the brown fog of a winter dawn,
A crowd flowed over London Bridge, so many,
I had not thought death had undone so many.
Sighs, short and infrequent, were exhaled,
And each man fixed his eyes before his feet.

Baudelaire's swarming city in "Les Sept Vieillards"—"Fourmillante Cité"—may have caused Eliot to give the singular noun "crowd" a plural adjective, "so many," instead of the expected "so large." Baudelaire keeps his city swarming with individuals by calling it "cité pleine de rêves," since we dream separately. In the corresponding passage in *Inferno* 3, Dante emphasizes in "si lunga tratta / di gente"— "so long a train of people"—the collective extent of the crowd, not the individual cowards but cowardice itself, souls collectively lost in their character. "I had not thought death had undone so many." We have in this line a motif of peculiar salience in Eliot's poetry: it attends the predicament in which action is confounded, undermined, retracted. In the context of Dante and Eliot, the motif goes from La Pia's line in *Purgatorio* 5—"Siena mi fé, disfecemi Maremma" ("Siena made me, Maremma undid me") to Eliot's allusion in "The Waste Land"—

> Highbury bore me. Richmond and Kew
> Undid me

—and it reaches out to the lines from Heywood's *A Woman Killed with Kindness* that Eliot said "no men or women past their youth can read without a twinge of personal feeling."[39]

> O God! O God! that it were possible
> To undo things done; to call back yesterday . . .

The "Unreal City" passage is one of the most poignant in Eliot's poetry: it is a tone poem of extraordinary eloquence. The key signature is given in the first syllable, internally rhyming with the first syllable of the next line. The rhyme brings together two words of different valences: adjective and preposition, the adjective casting a Baudelairean shadow over the whole passage, the preposition maintaining the melody in a minor key. In the second line, first and last words are linked by assonance, "under" being echoed in "dawn."

The motif is continued in the "undone" of the fourth line. Again the valences of the end-rhyming of "so many" and "so many" are differentiated. The first is an adjectival phrase qualifying "a crowd," the comma keeping the phrase as an afterthought. The second is the object of its sentence, coming without hesitation: "I had not thought death had undone so many." The change to the passive voice in the fifth line, "Sighs, short and infrequent, were exhaled," reduces the breathing to the almost-zero of impersonality, the crowd, till the next line steadies the iambic pentameter of the lines to the tread of "And each man fixed his eyes before his feet." Not "on his feet." The few inches beyond his feet are needed for safety. The line restores the men to their dignity, short of presenting them as individuals. James Wood has noted the spirit of the passage: "the slow, lovely cortège of these lines."[40]

So far, Eliot has been "imitating" Dante and Baudelaire, according to a procedure he described in "What Dante Means to Me":

> Certainly I have borrowed lines from him, in the attempt to reproduce, or rather to arouse in the reader's mind the memory, of some Dantesque scene, and thus establish a relationship between the medieval inferno and modern life. Readers of my "Waste Land" will perhaps remember that the vision of my city clerks trooping over London Bridge from the railway station to their offices evoked the reflection "I had not thought death had undone so many"; and that in another place I deliberately modified a line of Dante by altering it—"sighs, short and infrequent, were exhaled." And I gave the references in my notes, in order to make the reader who recognized the allusion know that I meant him to recognize it, and know that he would have missed the point if he did not recognize it.[41]

The source of the altered line in *Inferno* 4—

Quivi, secondo che per ascoltare,

Non avea pianto mai che di sospiri

Che l'aura etterna facevan tremare

—is Dante's description of Limbus, the first circle of Hell, inhabited
by the souls of virtuous pagans, the unbaptized who live in darkness,
longing, and hopelessness: "Here there was no plaint that could be
heard, except of sighs, which caused the eternal air to tremble." The
previous line in "The Waste Land"—"I had not thought death had
undone so many"—translates Dante as directly as possible, but this
one veers from him. The passive voice—"were exhaled"—makes the
sighs abstract, but the adjectives "short and infrequent" give them
the mechanical quality of beings neither alive nor dead. In Dante the
sighs are generic, in Eliot mechanical.

The concept of chivalry, as René Girard has described it, clarifies
the relation between Eliot and Dante, and therefore between a language and the force that marks its limits. He is speaking of the relation
between Don Quixote and Amadis of Gaul: "Chivalric existence is
the *imitation* of Amadis in the same sense that the Christian's existence is the imitation of Christ." And further: "Chivalric passion
defines a desire *according to Another,* opposed to the desire *according to
Oneself* that most of us pride ourselves on enjoying."[42] In this connection a passage in Plato's *Republic* is salient. Plato distinguishes between
those things that can be judged quite adequately by our senses and
those that can't be judged by our senses without producing contradic-
tory conclusions. In these latter, the mind must intervene. In the first
case our senses meet familiar objects and are gratified by the familiarity. In the second, we meet not recognizable objects but what
Deleuze in *Proust and Signs* calls "encountered signs," which force us
to think. Our senses are confused, our minds are engrossed. I apply
the distinction to languages. We are at one with our native language,

suffused by its familiarity. We recognize the words at a glance or upon a whisper: they seem virtually indistinguishable from ourselves. It is possible to meet in our native language words and sentences strange enough to count as violent signs—the spirit unappeased and peregrine. But this is rare. Poets cultivate this violence, effecting estrangement between the words and ourselves, so that we are impelled to rise to each encountered occasion. Geoffrey Hill wants us to maintain this sense of estrangement even when the language is our own. "When you write at any serious pitch of obligation," he says, "you enter into the nature of grammar and etymology which is a nature contrary to your own," and he warns us against assuming "the concurrence of language with one's expectations."[43] The warning is justified, because we long to think of ourselves as being at home in our native language if nowhere else. In general we find "encountered signs" most completely in a foreign language. What we lose in intimacy we gain in the stimulation of living for a time among strangers, *peregrini*. That is one reason why a translation should in seeking perfect assimilation also take care to avoid it: the foreign elements should not be completely domesticated. Eliot might have found a better translation of "shantih" than "the peace that passeth understanding." Shree Purohit Swami and W. B. Yeats give it as "May peace and peace and peace be everywhere." But Eliot's instinct was sound: to leave the word as he found it in Sanskrit and let it acquire in time a certain radiance while retaining its secret. It holds itself aloof from him and from us.

[3]

"La Figlia che Piange"

I can't be the only reader who thinks that "La Figlia che Piange" is Eliot's most beautiful poem. It is also his most Virgilian poem, unless we regard "The Waste Land" as equally Virgilian and Dickensian.[1] "La Figlia che Piange" is not his greatest poem—"The Waste Land" is that—but it is the poem most gratifying in its diction and movement. Beautiful? Beauty? Irving Howe, good socialist that he was, felt that he had to defend himself when he conceived a great affection for ballet, especially for Balanchine's as danced by the New York City Ballet. He imagined Tolstoy denouncing him for reveling in Suzanne Farrell's and Peter Martins's dancing of *Chaconne*. But in the end he told Tolstoy that "there are kinds of beauty before which the moral imagination ought to withdraw, and that in my lifetime these kinds of beauty have been served well by Balanchine."[2] Good: even without debating the politics of beauty with Tolstoy, I intend to keep the word at hand. In *The Critique of Judgment*, Kant maintains that when you say that something is beautiful, you are exercising your taste; you are saying that you take pleasure in the thing without submitting it to any concept. That is what he calls free beauty, *pulchritudo vaga*. When you look at a range of mountains and declare it beautiful, you are not judging it by appeal to the concept of a mountain or of what an ideal range of mountains would look like. You are not even claiming that this particular range is the most beautiful of its kind. The judgment you offer is pure in the sense that it is not dependent on the concept of an ideal mountain range. You are bringing together, to form a single experience, the thing and the pleasure you take in it. But your judgment is not merely subjective or otherwise eccentric, it is "disinterested" because it is free of conceptual determination. That seems convincing to me. But the consequence that Kant draws from it is doubtful. He argues that a disinterested judgment can claim to be universal: everyone should take pleasure in that range of mountains. He speaks of "the *universal validity* of this pleasure."[3] But he seems to ground the claim on the conditions that make a conceptual judgment universal; as if the human capacity were the same in both cases but exercised differently, the aesthetic judgment being an extension of the conceptual one. The problem arises from Kant's prejudice in favour of representation: he doesn't allow for abstract or stylized art, and he thinks that music must be representational. "A natural beauty is a *beautiful thing;* an artistic beauty is a *beautiful representation* of a thing."[4] The representation is validated by the thing it represents. But suppose a painting doesn't represent a thing, or doesn't merely do that: think of Blake's "Pity" or nearly any painting by Jackson Pollock. There is no prior thing to be appealed to on cognitive or mimetic grounds.[5]

I can't see that much would be lost if the claim to universality were abandoned. The claim that a particular range of mountains is beautiful would depend on its local convincingness and would succeed or fail with those to whom it is addressed. Kirk Varnadoe could still persuade a fair number of people that a certain painting by Jackson Pollock is beautiful, even if some parents insisted that their ten-year-old child could paint one just as beautiful if only she had a large canvas, a stick, and several cans of paint in different colors. But Varnadoe would have to prepare the way, saying many things about modern art and about Pollock before coming to the particular canvas on a wall in the Museum of Modern Art. It wouldn't do just to say: "Isn't it beautiful?"

Many of Eliot's readers evidently think "La Figlia che Piange" a slight poem. B. C. Southam hasn't annotated it in *A Student's Guide to the Selected Poems of T. S. Eliot*. Christopher Ricks doesn't mention it in *T. S. Eliot and Prejudice*. None of the first generation of Eliot's major critics—Leavis, Empson, Blackmur, Richards, Tate, or Brooks—took much note of it. Eliot called it, in 1921, "the mildest of my productions," by comparison, presumably, with "Mr. Apollinax" and "Portrait of a Lady."[6] But I think its being a beautiful poem—leaving aside the superlative I used a minute or two ago—should count for something, and that Eliot's mildness is a quality of some interest.

To prepare the ground for an appreciation of "La Figlia che Piange," I should say a little about Symbolism and distinguish several forms of it. It is standard practice to point to Symons's *The Symbolist Movement in Literature* as a crucial book for Yeats and Eliot. Yeats seems to have paid most attention to its first chapters, Eliot to its last. Each took from the book only what he needed. Yeats needed to be assured that certain words had acquired, through long association, a bright halo of implication. Even when he felt it desirable to distinguish a symbol from an emblem, he remained Symons's pupil. He decided that a symbol differed from an emblem in being a gift of nature. The sun, the moon, caves, rivers, the ocean, and shells on the beach at Rosses' Point are given to us by nature and in that respect they lend themselves—or may be borrowed—to suggest a certain kinship between us and the world we live in. This sense of kinship has the authority of being derived from apparent gifts of nature or of God. Emblems are gifts of history and culture. Swords, statues, towers—

Thoor Ballylee—are works of culture which have gathered ancestral force in certain traditions: they can be invoked almost as if they had the authority of natural symbols, almost but not quite. Using such words in a poem, Yeats gains further indefinite degrees of reverberation for whatever he is saying; the authority of his statements doesn't arise from his charisma or even from the cogency of his argument. It is as if the symbol or the emblem came from afar and brought with it an unusually rich if indefinite reach of implication. Eliot didn't use symbols in that way. He needed words that were already in literature, parts of the literary tradition; or in the sacred books of religion. His use of them in a poem lays no claim to an ancestral affiliation between man and nature. Instead, it brings into the poem a trace or an echo of their old contexts, even when a reader discerns those vaguely or not at all. It is often enough to divine that a context of some majesty is being invoked, and to feel the pressure of that: we need not know the source of it. "And after this our exile," in "Ash-Wednesday," "Belladonna" and "Sweet Thames, run softly till I end my song," in "The Waste Land" enrich their poems without claiming to assume a relation between the world and the people who inhabit it. They alter the texture of the poem and amplify its feelings, but only because of the authority they gain from their earlier uses in literature.

Eliot used another device that may also be called symbolic. I have to approach it somewhat roundabout. Guy Davenport says:

> Psychology in the study of dreams defined the symbol as essentially opaque, a confusion rather than an epiphany of meaning. The darker the symbol, the richer it was thought to be, and ambiguity became a virtue in literature. . . . The symbols of the French *symbolistes* and their school from Oslo to Salerno, from Dublin to Budapest, were not properly symbols at all, but enigmas derived from the German doctrine of elective affinities among things and

from Fourier and Swedenborg. These symbols so-called in the sensibilities of Baudelaire and Mallarmé became an abstract art, paralleling the disappearance of intelligible images in the painting of Malevich and Kandinsky a generation later. You cannot interpret a *symboliste* symbol, you can only contemplate it, like a transcendentalist brooding on the word *nature*.[7]

Symons allowed for this by displacing the given world in favor of dreams and visions: so far as a symbol referred to anything in the world, it referred to it as loosely as possible: mainly it created a space for wandering intuitions. Yeats's early poems learned this lesson from Blake—who would not willingly have taught it—and from Swedenborg. Symons assured Yeats that in reaching for the old symbols he was being modern in Mallarmé's way. Interpretation in any strict sense was hardly required, it could be just as vague as the symbol it interpreted. It was enough that the symbol had an air of large-scale if imprecise sense.

Davenport's reference to the symbol as "a confusion rather than an epiphany of meaning" shows that he has Joyce in view to represent another procedure. For the first time since Dante, he argues, symbols became transparent on Joyce's pages:

> Joyce, who rethought everything, rethought symbolism. It must first of all be organic, not arbitrary or fanciful. It must be logical, resonant, transparent, bright. From Flaubert he had learned that a true symbol must be found in an image that belongs to the narrative. The parrot Loulou in *Un Coeur simple* acts symbolically to make us feel the devotion, loneliness, ecstasy, and inviolable simplicity of Felicité. . . . In Joyce a rolled up newspaper with the words *Gold Cup* and *Sceptre* among its racing news becomes a symbolic blossom around which two men, symbolic bees, forage. This is a deeper symbolism than more apparent ones in operation at the

same time: Odysseus among the Lotus Eaters, a spiritually lost Jew longing to return to Israel ("and the desert shall blossom like the rose"), a man psychologically a drone to his queen-bee wife, a man named Flower enacting the suffering of a saint named Flower (Anthony) and his temptations; and on and on. Joyce's symbols are labyrinths of meaning, but they are logical, and they expand meaning. They are, as mediaeval grammarians said, *involucra*—seed husks asking to be peeled.[8]

Like Pound, Davenport prefers to recognize images rather than symbols: his values, like Pound's and Hugh Kenner's, move between Imagism and Objectivism. He is uncomfortable with Symbolism and likes to distance it by calling it something else, as here, the deployment of enigmas.

Eliot is closer to the French symbolistes, even in Davenport's revised version of their procedures, than he is to Pound or to Davenport's Flaubert and Joyce. As a critic, he is remarkably responsive to uncanny moments in a poem or play, moments in which something extraordinary is going on but you can't say what: all you can do is stare. In "Dryden the Dramatist" he compares Shakespeare's *Antony and Cleopatra* with Dryden's version of it, *All for Love*. It is a standard comparison—Leavis and other critics have made it, but not as Eliot makes it. He compares two parallel passages. In *Antony and Cleopatra* when the soldiers burst in after Cleopatra's death, one of them says: "What work is here! Charmian, is this well done?" Charmian, who has applied an asp to herself and is about to die, says:

It is well done, and fitting for a princess
Descended of so many royal kings.
Ah, soldier!

In *All for Love* she says:

> Yes, 'tis well done, and like a Queen, the last
> Of her great race. I follow her.

Eliot comments:

> Now, if you take these two passages by themselves, you cannot say
> that the two lines of Dryden are either less poetic than Shake-
> speare's, or less dramatic; a great actress could make just as much,
> I believe, of those of Dryden as of those of Shakespeare. But con-
> sider Shakespeare's remarkable addition to the original text of
> North, the two plain words, "Ah, soldier!" You cannot say that
> there is anything peculiarly poetic about these two words, and if
> you isolate the dramatic from the poetic you cannot say that there
> is anything peculiarly dramatic either, because there is nothing in
> them for the actress to express in action; she can at best enunciate
> them clearly. I could not myself put into words the difference I feel
> between the passage if these two words, "Ah, soldier!" were
> omitted and with them. But I know there is a difference, and that
> only Shakespeare could have made it.[9]

Eliot doesn't interpret the two words, say what their purport is or
why the effect of them is uncanny. He contemplates them as if they
were a symbol, and leaves off. His genius as a critic consists in per-
ceiving that something extraordinary has been done. When he speaks
up for other values, it is because he wants to keep his symboliste
inclination under rebuke.

On Davenport's point about symbols and the disappearance of
intelligible images: Eliot's poems are not abstract, but they have an
impulse to abstraction. This impulse makes him equivocal in his dealing with intelligible images: he does not accept their authority or
confide his feeling to them. It also makes him thwart the indicative
bearing of words by generalizing, refusing to specify, refusing to grat-

ify a reader's desire to be rid of words and get back to the empirical world. It is as if he said: "I have to live among words, why should you be exempt from their importunity?" In the same spirit he believes that the ideal never coincides with the actual: if you allow the ideal to exert its claim upon you, you must be prepared to go beyond every punctual object of your care. No finite object deserves your entire love.

But Eliot's method differs from Yeats's. He does not allow the sense of a poem to gather to the volume and privilege of single words and phrases, as Yeats does: "O chestnut tree, great rooted blossomer." No single word, symbol or emblem, clinches Eliot's statements in the early poems. Invocations of the fire and the rose bring "Little Gidding" to an end, and are characteristic of the late poetry. But in the early poems Eliot distributes the symbolic value along the whole trajectory of the poem, and makes us respond to that. "La Figlia che Piange" is like Gregorian chant, where the energy is felt continuously in the rhythm and at every point along the line: it is not like a symphony by Mahler, which stirs the listener by alternations of assertion and withholding.

II

"La Figlia che Piange": the title is thought to refer to a stele of a weeping woman in a museum in northern Italy.[10] A friend mentioned it to Eliot and urged him to see it. In the late summer of 1911, Eliot was in Italy and tried to find it but failed. The experience may have provoked in him a sense of absence and presence, the presence of an absent thing or a lost person. The next words a reader meets are the epigraph: "O quam te memorem virgo . . . " It comes from the first book of the *Aeneid,* where Aeneas's mother Venus, disguised as a virgin huntress, meets him in the woods at Carthage and speaks to him. Aeneas answers: "O—quam te memorem, virgo? namque haud tibi voltus / mortalis, nec vox hominem sonat; o dea certe!" "By what name should I address you, maiden; for your face is not mortal, nor has your voice a human ring to it. Surely you are a goddess?"[11] (Eliot alluded to this episode again in a canceled passage of "The Waste Land.") Venus speaks to him about Dido, and finally, as she leaves for Paphos, Venus discloses herself to Aeneas and he recognizes her as his mother: "You too are cruel," he says. "Why do you mock your son so often with these vain shows?" "Quid natum totiens, crudelis tu quoque, falsis / ludis imaginibus?" "Why can't we join hands honestly, face to face?" The episode often reminds readers of two later passages in the *Aeneid*. In Book IV some months after Dido and Aeneas have become lovers, Jupiter sends him a message that he must leave and establish the city of Rome. Aeneas gets ready to leave, but Dido hears of his preparations and denounces him for abandoning her. She vows that "when cold death has severed soul and body, everywhere my shade will haunt you." The scene is comparable, as Kenneth Reckford has noted, to the one in Catullus 64 in which Ariadne gazes after her departing lover Theseus: "Immemor at iuvenis fugiens pellit vada remis" (line 58).[12] The second episode is in Book VI when Dido has killed herself and is now a shade in Hades. Aeneas meets her and tries to defend himself from her accusations. What he did, he was ordered to do. Dido starts to leave, and Aeneas tries to detain her: "Stay your step, do not withdraw from our view. From whom are you fleeing?": "siste gradum teque aspectu ne subtrahe nostro. / quem fugis? But Dido leaves, running back into the arms of her husband Sychaeus, without saying a word to Aeneas:

> illa solo fixos oculos aversa tenebat
> nec magis incepto voltum sermone movetur,
> quam si dura silex aut stet Marpesia cautes.

"She turned away, keeping her eyes fixed, and she no more changed her countenance as he started to speak than if it were set in hard flint or Marpesian rock."[13] ("The Hollow Men" speaks of "Eyes I dare not meet in dreams.") Eliot referred to this episode twice. In "What Is a Classic?" (1944) he said:

> I have always thought the meeting of Aeneas with the shade of Dido, in Book VI, not only one of the most poignant, but one of the most civilized passages in poetry. It is complex in meaning and economical in expression, for it not only tells us about the attitude of Dido— still more important is what it tells us about the attitude of Aeneas. Dido's behaviour appears almost as a projection of Aeneas' own conscience: this, we feel, is the way in which Aeneas' conscience would *expect* Dido to behave to him. The point, it seems to me, is not that Dido is unforgiving—though it is important that, instead of railing at him, she merely snubs him—perhaps the most telling snub in all poetry: what matters most is, that Aeneas does not forgive himself—and this, significantly, in spite of the fact of which he is well aware, that all that he has done has been in compliance with destiny, or in consequence of the machinations of gods who are themselves, we feel, only instruments of a greater inscrutable power.[14]

In "Virgil and the Christian World" (1951) he wrote:

> Aeneas and Dido had to be united, and had to be separated. Aeneas did not demur; he was obedient to his fate. But he was certainly very unhappy about it, and I think that he felt that he was behaving shamefully. For why else should Virgil have contrived his meeting with the Shade of Dido in Hades, and the snub that he receives? When he sees Dido he tries to excuse himself for his betrayal. *Sed me iussa deum*—but I was under orders from the gods; it was a very unpleasant decision to have imposed upon me, and I am sorry that

you took it so hard. She avoids his gaze and turns away, with a face as immobile as if it had been carved from flint or Marpesian rock. I have no doubt that Virgil, when he wrote these lines, was assuming the role of Aeneas and feeling very decidedly a worm.[15]

But Eliot doesn't allow for the possibility that Aeneas's feeling a worm was consistent with his also feeling that Dido might well have said a few words instead of turning herself to stone.

A symbol is a point of pressure within a particular context, such that the pressure is felt coming from other occasions, other contexts in nature, history, literature, religion, or mythology. It is as if the symbol were printed in italics. In "La Figlia che Piange" the pressure does not inhere in any single word but in the implied situation from first word to last: it is a force of implication issuing from the episode in the *Aeneid* and especially from the snub and the sense of it that is common to Aeneas and Virgil. When Dido leaves in silence, all we are told of Aeneas is:

nec minus Aeneas, casu concussus iniquo,
prosequitur lacrimis longe et miseratur euntem. (VI. 475–476)

The Loeb translator gives this as: "Yet none the less, dazed by her unjust doom, Aeneas attends her with tears afar and pities her as she goes."[16] But it might be made clearer that the doom is the one Aeneas feels that Dido has imposed on him, rather than the one he inflicted on her.

I take it that the implied speaker of "La Figlia che Piange" is not Virgil's Aeneas but Eliot's. Eliot has imagined a similar situation. The girl feels herself abandoned and speaks not a word: the main effort on the speaker's part is to change the scene and remove himself from the feelings in the case. Like Aeneas, he mostly feels a mixture of guilt, fatedness, and frustration.

We have a poem in three unequal stanzas, seven, nine, and eight lines, respectively: the lines are also unequal, running from as few as three to as many as twelve syllables till they stabilize themselves in the last three lines as regular iambic pentameters. The rhymes are irregular, linking in each stanza three, five, and three syllables, respectively. In the first stanza we are to suppose that the Dido-woman has been abandoned. Perhaps her lover has committed the further indignity of giving her flowers as a going-away present; or she has gathered them herself in keeping with the pathos of the situation. The speaker is directing her as if in a film; he is something of a dandy, too—"Clasp your flowers to you with a pained surprise."[17] Or he is a painter of pre-Raphaelite disposition, like D. G. Rossetti painting "La Pia de' Tolomei," disposing his model to express pathetic, picturesque, and in every respect aesthetic values. Her distress must be turned into poses and gestures. It is strange that despite the title of the poem we don't see her weeping. The stanza is governed by imperatives, enforced further by the placing of the verbs at the beginning of the lines: stand, lean, weave, clasp, fling, and (repeated again) weave. Only the fifth line has two imperatives, one at the beginning, one at the end of the line, and the next line has no verb at all. When the next imperative verb comes in the last line of the stanza, it is mollified by a slight postponement, before the repetition is itself repeated—"But weave, weave the sunlight in your hair." It is as if the film director were to tell the girl: in the midst of these instructions, whatever else you do, weave, weave the sunlight in your hair. The imperatives have a distancing effect, showing how much the feeling in the scene has to be controlled. But the last line releases the girl to her gesture.

The second stanza is different, reflective where the first was imperative. The speaker is distancing himself from himself, just as much as from the girl. He is directing himself, turning his own feelings into a gesture and a pose. "So I would have had him leave." He has divided himself into two, the film-director and the Aeneas-figure, "I" and "him." The distancing is effected by the change of grammar from the imperative to the conditional perfect, "would have had," "would have had," and "would have left." The violence of the abandonment, "As the soul leaves the body torn and bruised" and "As the mind deserts the body it has used," suggests the lover's guilt, commensurate with Dido's vow of vengeance in Book IV: "when cold death has severed soul and body," "cum frigida mors anima seduxerit artus." Ronald Bush has noted that either soul or body may be qualified as "torn and bruised."[18] The speaker is still directing the scene, hence the studied composure, the rhymes of syntax in the lines: so, so, so, and after three lines, some, some, and simple. After the shortest line, "I should find," the distancing gestures turn sinister, caught between affectation and opportunism. "Simple and faithless as a smile and shake of the hand" is Eliot's version of Laforgue's "Simple et sans foi comme un bonjour" from "La vie qu'elles me font mener." It also alludes to Aeneas's chiding of his mother: "Why can't we join hands honestly, face to face?" Such a joining would not necessarily mean what it seemed to mean. In "La Figlia" the Laforguian gesture may be affected, or it may recognize that there is no choice. The main effect of the conditional perfects is to slow the pace of the lines: the monosyllabic ponderousness of the arrangements—"So I would have had him leave"—and the arduousness of the repeated "have had" testify to the speaker's efforts to remove himself from involvement, and to the difficulty of doing so. Cynicism wins out in "Some way incomparably light and deft, / Some way we both should understand." "Both": girl and lover, the "I" and the "him" are one now. Understand as what? It is a moment of Jamesian hesitation before it resolves itself into Laforgue's worldly irony, entirely French.

The change in the third stanza is abrupt, from the conditional perfects to the simple past tense: like Dido, "she turned away." It is another distancing gesture, but one that allows what has passed to remain and to press upon the present, as it does in Book VI of the *Aeneid*. The pathos is in the repetition: "many days, / Many days and many hours." The repetitions in the first stanza, "Weave, weave" and "weave, weave," were incantations to charm the agony into peace: now it is too late for that. The only hope is to fix the girl in an enchanting image: "Her hair over her arms and her arms full of flowers." For the first four lines, director and lover are one, the Aeneas-figure, but they are divided again in the fifth—"And I wonder how they should have been together!"—and for the rest of the poem. It is a musical nuance by which the word "imagination" in "Compelled my imagination many days" persists to rhyme across five lines with "cogitations." The most distancing gesture is the retrospect of speculation: "And I wonder how they should have been together," an unstaged "have been" quite different from the staging of "So I should have had him leave." The last three lines have an air of quittance, the division between speaker-as-lover and speaker-as-film-director being complete:

> I should have lost a gesture and a pose.
> Sometimes these cogitations still amaze
> The troubled midnight and the noon's repose.

The irony on "lost" tells against the film director; the real loss is the one this loss only technically evades. The man should feel himself a worm. "Amaze" is amazing. It is a word of the spectacular and it keeps the director's self-protectiveness going while the need of self-protection is acknowledged. The past love is not past, so long as he has to control it by making it a thing of spectacle and astonishment. There may be a trace of Marvell's "The Garden"—"How vainly men themselves amaze," meaning bewilder or confound themselves. In the end, the poem reposes on reposeless repose.

III

"Poetry is not a turning loose of emotion, but an escape from emotion," Eliot said in "Tradition and the Individual Talent."[19] One way of escaping from an emotion is by finding a semblance of it somewhere else, preferably in such a poem as the *Aeneid*. Then you could imagine the experience afresh, and hope to consign the pain of it to another's lines. But I surmise that "La Figlia che Piange" did not start with feelings—guilt, self-disgust—from which Eliot was impelled to find relief in words. It has nothing to do with his first marriage or his decision, many years later, to leave Vivienne. Eliot wrote the poem in 1912, four years before his marriage. His early poems analyze feelings he didn't otherwise have; he found them in poems by other poets—Virgil, Dante, Laforgue, Gautier, and many more. I believe that "La Figlia" started with Eliot's sense of a possible poem that might be conjured from another poem, and then with an emotion of art, in which Eliot recognized the episode of Dido and Aeneas, like that of Ariadne and Theseus, as a fundamental story, one of the primary experiences of love-and-loss in a supreme articulation. Reimagining the experience, and changing it for reasons we can only guess, he made it become his own emotion in the end: he could not stop this from happening. I think he intended to write a Pure Poem for once, a poem entirely poetic, musical, and to yield to the twists and turnings made possible by the moods of English grammar. He would confine himself to the possibilities effected by a few gestures and poses, with repetitions to enhance the music, and as far as possible he would fend off extraneous considerations. Other emotions would not gain a hearing, even if they were his. They become his as the poem comes to recognize its formal destiny.

IV

Even those who admire the efforts made by theorists from Kant to Ruskin to keep the subject of Beauty open seem to appreciate Walter Pater's reluctance to discuss "beauty in the abstract":

> Many attempts have been made by writers on art and poetry to define beauty in the abstract, to express it in the most general terms, to find some universal formula for it. The value of these attempts has most often been in the suggestive and penetrating things said by the way. Such discussions help us very little to enjoy what has been well done in art or poetry, to discriminate between what is more and what is less excellent in them, or to use words like beauty, excellence, art, poetry, with a more precise meaning than they would otherwise have. Beauty, like all other qualities presented to human experience, is relative; and the definition of it becomes unmeaning and useless in proportion to its abstractness. To define beauty, not in the most abstract but in the most concrete terms possible, to find, not its universal formula, but the formula which expresses most adequately this or that special manifestation of it, is the aim of the true student of aesthetics.[20]

Manifestation of what? Normally, if required to be explicit about beauty and to show cause, we point to the harmony and reconciliation of the parts to the whole, as in "La Figlia che Piange"; the *sprezzatura* with which the poem moves from first word to last; the finesse with which it raises expectations and in the end fulfills them in an unexpected way; the convincingness of the rhythm, the command of word and phrase and cadence; the unnagging verve with which the poem solicits its space; the delicacy with which it allows its emotion to survive every attempt to refute it—as at the end where no merely personal claim is admitted but the whole space is suffused by the feeling the lines fend off:

Sometimes these cogitations still amaze
The troubled midnight and the noon's repose.

Or if we are convinced by Aquinas, we try to show in the poem the three qualities he thought necessary for beauty: integrity, proportion or harmony, and clarity (S. T. 1. 39,8). Is this enough to justify my saying that "La Figlia che Piange" is beautiful, even if I don't claim further that everyone should share my conviction that it is?

The main problem in talking about beauty is that it is not enough to satisfy a fully aesthetic demand. Adorno is clear on this limitation: "The idea of beauty draws attention to something essential to art without, however, articulating it directly. If artifacts were not in various ways judged to be beautiful, the interest in them would be incomprehensible and blind, and no one—neither artist nor beholder—would have reason to make that exodus from the sphere of practical aims, those of self-preservation and pleasure, that art requires by virtue of its constitution. Hegel arrests the aesthetic dialectic by his static definition of the beautiful as the sensual appearance of the idea. The beautiful is no more to be defined than its concept can be dispensed with, a strict antinomy."[21] It is a further problem that the long-supposed correlation between the true, the beautiful, and the good has lost much of its force. Beautiful images are regularly put to mundane use, as in TV advertisements where beautiful women recommend beauty products for the smile they promise. Or beauty is provided instead of more demanding images, as in the Merchant-Ivory films. Or it is used as the stuff of the "culture industry." The

Concorde is an image by Brancusi. There is no merit in being stiff about this, but it is part of the process by which modern liberal societies persuade us to feel that what we have to do is what we want to do, because it is inscribed in the nature of things and the nature of things is beautiful.

Adorno's answer to the problem of beauty and aesthetics is suggestive, if desperate. He proposes to cede the properties of beauty to the general culture and to alter correspondingly the claim for works of art. He would require works of art to put at risk the considerations that make them beautiful, by admitting the force and violence of truth that would disturb their poise. He points out that the values which Kant reserved exclusively to nature as sublime have increasingly entered works of art.[22] "The ascendancy of the sublime," Adorno says, "is one with art's compulsion that fundamental contradictions not be covered up but fought through in themselves: reconciliation for them is not the result of the conflict but exclusively that the conflict becomes eloquent."[23] But there is an equivocation in Kant on the question of the sublime and nature. Sometimes he implies that the sublime is not a property of nature but of consciousness, a vertigo of pain and pleasure induced by a sense of impossibility, contradiction, incommensurability, as in mathematics, the ideas of the finite and the infinite. But sometimes Kant finds the sublime in objects of nature that the mind can't represent, such that the mind must experience its defeat by objects in the world that are beyond its cognitive reach. And yet the mind finds the vertigo of this experience pleasurable in some occult sense. Adorno, thinking of modern art and modern music and setting his mind to comprehend them in their alpine reaches, resorts to the sublime as the mode of acknowledged impossibility. He then decides that the aesthetic experience must be based on that, rather than on the easier transactions of beauty. The decorum of taste yields to the recognition of the sublime as truth, "an alterity that eludes conceptual capture," as J. M. Bernstein puts it.[24] Adorno's *Aesthetic Theory* revises Kant in the light of modernist art, which has gone from beauty to the sublime, from taste to the force of truth: it represents "the moment of beauty it could have had" but has chosen to forgo.[25] Art provides a transformation of perception, a transformation that must be seen "not in the way that the truth of a statement is recognized, but in the way a face is recognized."[26] From fact to face; or, as in Adorno's *The Philosophy of Modern Music,* from Stravinsky to Schoenberg.

It is a desperate choice. I'm not sure we have to make it. As a value, beauty has not been entirely degraded, as Irving Howe recognized in going so often to Lincoln Center. The beauty of "La Figlia che Piange" is not refuted or shamed by the sublime of "The Waste Land." But this conclusion is too neat. There are moments in "La Figlia che Piange" which admit the turbulence of the sublime. The violence of "As the soul leaves the body torn and bruised"—whether we read "torn and bruised" as qualifying body or soul—becomes compulsive with the near-repetition, "As the mind deserts the body it has used." Grammatically, the lines are nearly identical, but the change from "soul" to "mind," the intensification of "leaves" to "deserts," and the spilling-over of "torn and bruised" on "used" disturb the Gregorian movement of the poem. The irony of "Some way incomparably light and deft" lets the reader take up a critical position, detecting the speaker, until the issues are released in the last three lines.

[4]

"Gerontion"

The poem was originally called "Gerousia," Greek for a consultative body or counsel of elders in Sparta. The definitive title means a little old man. The epigraph from *Measure for Measure* (III.i.32f.) should read: "Thou hast nor youth nor age, / But as it were an after-dinner's sleep, / Dreaming on both." William H. Marshall has noted that Eliot approved three emendations, only one of which has yet been made. Line 1, delete the final comma; line 35, read "And issues," making it clear that Eliot thought of "issues" as a noun going with "corridors" rather than a verb going with "deceives": this has been cleared up in the 1963 edition. Line 37—"when our attention is distracted"—add a final comma.[1] The emendations would bring the text back, in those particulars, to the version published in *Ara Vos Prec* (1919). Later texts have many variants. In line 8, "jew" was changed in the 1963 edition to "Jew." The belatedness of the change has incited some of Eliot's readers to enter it as evidence of his alleged anti-Semitism. In line 9, "juvescence" probably started as Eliot's mistake for "juvenescence," and has been retained for metrical preference and because the meaning—the Spring—is not much affected. Line 40: "or if still believed" appears in some printings, including 1963, as "or is still believed," a printer's error, I think, though it is grammatically feasible. Line 42: John Crowe Ransom pointed out that "Gives too soon / Into weak hands, what's thought can be dispensed with" is ungrammatical, and should read "what it's thought."[2] Line 52: "concitation," meaning rousing, stirring up, agitating, has been obsolete since the seventeenth century. The main textual change is in line 34: in the loose leaves the first word is "Nature," not "History." The first version would have made "Gerontion" a different poem, as you'll see if you recite lines 34 to 43 with Nature as their subject. Eliot may have been prompted to the change by reading the first two chapters of Joyce's *Ulysses:* in the first, Haines says to Stephen, "It seems history is to blame"; in the second, Stephen tells Mr. Deasy that "History is a nightmare from which I am trying to awake," and Deasy answers that "All history moves towards one great goal, the manifestation of God."

The main allusions are well known—Southam's *Guide* gives them in detail—but I'll refer to three of them. The first two lines are adapted from a striking sentence in A. C. Benson's *Edward Fitzgerald* (1905): "Here he sits, in a dry month, old and blind, being read to by a country boy, longing for rain." Blindness and longing were removed, presumably, lest the change to a first-person speaker bring a too urgent appeal for pity. The most sustained allusion comes from Chapter 18 of *The Education of Henry Adams,* the first paragraph about Washington in spring: "Here and there a negro log cabin alone disturbed the dogwood and the judas-tree, the azalea and the laurel. . . . No European spring had shown him the same intermixture of delicate grace and passionate depravity that marked the Maryland May. He loved it too much, as though it were Greek and half human."[3] George Monteiro has noted, too, that Chapter 21 of Adams's *Education* gave Eliot a purple patch for the poem's dying fall.[4] Adams describes how he came back from the South Seas with John La Farge: "Adams would rather, as choice, have gone back to the east, if it were only to sleep forever in the trade-winds under the southern stars, wandering over the dark purple ocean, with its purple sense of solitude and void."[5] The remaining allusions are clear enough: the Old and New Testaments, Dante, Shakespeare, Jonson, Lancelot Andrewes, *The Revenger's Tragedy, The Changeling,* Shelley, and Newman's *The Dream of Gerontius.* Even if they are ignored, the reading needn't be interrupted, except for one difficult passage:

And it is not by any concitation
Of the backward devils.

The devils seem to be evil spirits prompting Gerontion to backslide, and the backsliding is that of prying into history for excitement: the source is probably Dante, *Inferno* 20, where soothsayers and false prophets have their heads twisted backwards.

"Gerontion" has been sensitively read. Some early readers were troubled not by the words but by the gaps between them. Blackmur felt that Eliot hadn't quite "completed" the poem and had left the reader to complete it for him. Gerontion, he says, is "an ideal figure self-seen, self-dramatised in a series of rapid, penetrating statements." Each statement, separately, is intelligible and sums up a position in the drama, "but the material *between* the statements is not always forced into being; and several times the reader finds his breath inexplicably cut short."[6] In *Primitivism and Decadence* (1937) Yvor Winters was irritated by what he called "pseudo-reference" or "reference to non-existent plots": each of the figures named in the poem—Mr. Silvero, Madame de Tornquist, Fräulein von Kulp, and Hakagawa—"is denoted in the performance of an act, and each act, save possibly that of Hakagawa, implies an anterior situation, is a link in a chain of action," but we have "no hint of the nature of the history implied."[7] But in *The Anatomy of Nonsense* (1943), Winters, while still severe on Eliot's work generally, was evidently impressed by "Geron-tion." The poem, he said, "is the portrait of an individual from whom grace has been withdrawn, and who is dying of spiritual starvation while remembering his past; it is thus a prelude to 'The Waste Land,' a portrait of a society from which grace has been withdrawn and which is dying of its own triviality and ugliness."[8] This interpretation, or something like it, has been generally accepted. Ransom thinks that the poem is an old man's confession, addressed to Christ. Gerontion is an apostate—"I that was near your heart was removed there-from"—who has put the world before Christ. Now he is offering rea-sons and excuses, stricken in his tragedy, for having rejected Christ. "We remember that Eliot, his author, was just coming out of a period of poems, some of them in savage satire against the religious institu-tion, and others in which he was nostalgic for it."[9]

In *An American Procession,* Alfred Kazin brings Eliot and Adams together on the ground of "Gerontion": "Both suffered the inaccessi-bility of God. That is the deepest strain in 'Gerontion': it is easier for God to devour us than for us to partake of Him in a seemly spirit."[10] But Kazin forces the comparison of Eliot and Adams to the point of asserting that what Eliot valued was religion, not faith, and that he valued religion for the "culture" it leaves; so did Adams. Kazin ad-duced *Mont-Saint-Michel and Chartres* and "Buddha and Brahma" as evidence that for Adams "religion is culture rather than belief, reli-gion is literature that attests the unbelief Adams never denied and was even sardonically proud of."[11] Kazin is confusing Eliot with Matthew Arnold and forgetting that what Eliot deplored in Arnold was his willingness to accept high culture as a substitute for faith. Eliot in-sisted that there is no substitute. If you can't accept the grace of God to the extent of faith, then you must live without it. Culture is a minor consideration in the absence of belief.

The title of the poem is satiric: not Newman's Gerontius, a Christian terrified of dying but praying to be received into the presence of God, but a little old man—Adams by the way was short—ripe for satire. The epigraph that follows from *Measure for Measure* is mockery: the Duke, disguised, urges Claudio to adopt a perspective so lofty that his current interest in the fate of his life will appear of no account. But it gives the "figure" of the poem: "age" and "youth," constituents of reality, float adrift, removed at every moment by the unreality that Gerontion's ego enforces. Wasted, as Kazin says, by history in which he has played no part, Gerontion is transfixed between a real action he is not resolute enough to take and the vacant gesture that mocks it.

Eliot started work on "Gerontion" in 1917 and finished it by August 1919. If we read the other things he wrote at about the same time, including "Hamlet and His Problems," the review of *The Education of Henry Adams,* and "Tradition and the Individual Talent," we find him wrestling with an issue of personal insistence, the exorbitance of emotion to any object that supposedly provokes and justifies it. What corresponds to Hamlet's buffoonery is Gerontion's unmoored eloquence.

The problem of the exorbitance of emotion to any cause that may be invoked to justify it is endemic to Eliot's early poems. It required him to formulate further questions. What would "adequacy" entail in a relation between the inner and the outer world of experience? Is it possible to prescribe relations between the experiences we designate as knowledge, feeling, emotion, ideas, and images? The answers to these questions involved Eliot in elaborate philosophical definitions, most of them glosses on Bradley and Royce. Briefly: Eliot required that one's sentient experience be understood as a continuous development and refinement of feeling, on the assumption that feeling or immediate experience is what one starts from. Thereafter, consciousness, the construction of a subject, the discrimination of subject and object, emotions, ideas, and so forth should be construed as different stages in the history of one's feeling. The life of one's feeling should be continuous. The emotion attendant upon any occasion should enable one to understand it and therefore to survive it. It should not be "in excess of the facts as they appear": as they appear, I assume, to one's intelligence, which seeks, in any experience, coherence and comprehensiveness.

I agree with those who say that Adams is the most pervasive presence in "Gerontion," but not when they affirm, as Kazin does, that "the Adams whom Eliot reviewed with so much distaste could only have been the speaker in 'Gerontion.'" The poem discourages this precision by starting with two lines that couldn't be attached to Adams. It is not necessary to know that they refer to Fitzgerald: the only confirmation provided by reading Benson's book is such as to strengthen the sense, in the two lines, of spiritual lassitude. Fitzgerald's defect, according to Benson, was moral debility to the degree of disgrace: he wouldn't rouse himself to an interest in anything. His life documents the "gifts reserved for age," according to the list the familiar compound ghost of "Little Gidding" supplies, starting with

> the cold friction of expiring sense
> Without enchantment, offering no promise
> But bitter tastelessness of shadow fruit
> As body and soul begin to fall asunder.

Adams, too, was spiritually defective, though in ways that require a different description. In Eliot's review of the *Education*—"A Sceptical Patrician"—Adams is presented as a type of the New England mind: he is compared to George Wyndham, the English Romantic aristocrat on whom Eliot commented, in a review originally called "A Romantic Patrician," that he "had curiosity, but he employed it romantically, not to penetrate the real world, but to complete the varied features of the world he made for himself."[12] Adams was always busy, but "busy with himself." A great many things interested him, "but he could believe in nothing": "Wherever this man stepped, the ground did not simply give way, it flew into particles; towards the end of his life he came across the speculations of Poincaré, and Science disappeared, entirely. He was seeking for education, with the wings of a beautiful but ineffectual conscience beating vainly in a vacuum jar."[13] I don't know if the reader is meant to bother with Eliot's allusion to Arnold in that last sentence, or Arnold's reflection upon Shelley: it may be just a vivacity on Eliot's part. "His extreme sensitiveness to all the suggestions which dampen enthusiasm or dispel conviction may be responsible for what one feels in him as immaturity, indeed as a lack of personality; an instability." At this point Eliot comes to the question I've touched on, the ideal continuity of feeling. Adams is defective again: "For the immaturity there may be another reason. It is probable that men ripen best through experiences that are at once sensuous and intellectual; certainly many men will admit that their keenest ideas have come to them with the quality of a sense-perception, and that their keenest sensuous experience has been 'as if the body thought.' There is nothing to indicate that Adams's senses either flowered or fruited: he remains little Paul Dombey asking questions." Finally, Eliot made a brief contrast between Adams and Henry James, in James's favor, to enforce the point that "it is the sensuous contributor to the intelligence that makes the difference."[14]

The difference, to put it more explicitly than Eliot does, is that feeling, in James, was continuous: his ideas were distinguishable moments or phases of his feeling, inseparable from its life. Adams had an idea, and then he had another one, but his ideas were adrift from his feeling. He was like Tennyson and Browning, as Eliot described them in "The Metaphysical Poets": "Tennyson and Browning are poets, and they think; but they do not feel their thought as immediately as

the odour of a rose. A thought to Donne was an experience; it modified his sensibility."[15] Or, to try another contrast, Adams didn't have
the power that Eliot attributed to the later Yeats, of preserving the
liveliest emotions of youth "to receive their full and due expression in
retrospect"; "for the interesting feelings of age are not just different feelings: they are feelings into which the feelings of youth are
integrated."[16]

Suppose, then, we think of Gerontion as a figure compounded
mainly of Adams and Fitzgerald; a fragmented figure in whom ideas
have long since lost connection with the experience of smelling a
rose; spiritually febrile, vain enough to think that history must be
corrupt and the world incomprehensible upon no better evidence
than that his spiritual *anomie* requires these notions. Vanity, in such a
case, would issue in a self-regarding style, for which the readiest
examples are available in Jacobean smoke and sulphur, the revenge
plays of Webster, Chapman, Tourneur, and Middleton, and the Senecan speeches in Shakespeare. Nearly any smoke and sulphur would
do, if they provoked the vaunting eloquence that works as a substitute
for the action it should accompany and define.

The epigraph from *Measure for Measure* establishes a motif—that of
fracture and dissociation—that persists throughout the poem. A second epigraph with a similar emphasis appears in an early typescript
of the poem: two lines from *Inferno* 33—"Come il mi corpo stea /
Nel mondo su, nulla scienza porto" ("How my body stands in the
world above, I have no knowledge"). Fra Alberigo is saying that because he betrayed his guests, his soul was taken while he lived. So the
poem begins, with Benson's sentence transposed from third to first
person.

Lines 1–16: "Wasted by history in which he had played no part" is
Kazin's note on Adams and, unfairly I think, on Eliot. The speaker is
dissociated from whatever he would acknowledge as reality: an epic

style of it, indeed, the references to Thermopylae and cutlasses disengage the poem from its modern sources. Or even from its modern application. Not to have fought at either of the battles of the Marne would have much the same bearing. The lines mainly establish Gerontion's self-regard, especially in the elaborately suspended syntax between "Nor fought . . . " and "Bitten by flies, fought."

Line 16: "A dull head among windy spaces." Ronald Bush makes a telling point about wind, which he takes as the dominant element of the poem, a Dantesque cold wind, embodying "a ceaseless randomness which cannot find an end and yet cannot die." The point is fulfilled in the later reference "Vacant shuttles / Weave the wind." Bush's phrase, "Gerontion's windiness," connects the element and its corresponding rhetoric.

Lines 17–20: The Pharisees couldn't recognize the Messiah and demanded a sign. The first words of St. John's Gospel, developed in Lancelot Andrewes's sermon for Christmas Day 1618, testify to silence as the wordless Word. Eliot turned Andrewes's "the Word without a word; the eternal Word not able to speak a word" into the inspired "The word within a word . . . " "Juvescence" calls up its opposite, "senescence." "Came Christ the tiger": I like Ransom's gloss, that "the lamb who came to be devoured turns into the tiger when Gerontion has forgotten the lamb."[17]

Lines 21–32: The line from Adams's *Education* starts a Black Mass of images and figures. Bush treats these and other pseudo-references as dream-play, arising from Gerontion's guilt. I am content with that, especially as it accommodates the sacrilegious and blasphemous gestures—"to be eaten, to be divided, to be drunk / Among whispers." But I am more fully persuaded by Sherna Vinograd's argument about these figures. The question is: how are we to deal with Mr. Silvero, Hakagawa, and the rest, who apparently have lives that are given to us only in their shadow-play—caressing hands, bowing among the Titians, shifting the candles? Arrested gestures are sinister in Eliot's poetry—however poignant in "La Figlia che Piange"—but each is sinister in a different way. Self-awareness, egotism, the self-preoccupation that Eliot feared because he saw it in himself: it is easy to attribute such a motive to these figures, and to regard them as alike involved, with Gerontion, in the vanity of restlessness and curiosity. Vinograd's essay concentrates on the figures that inhabit the poem without disclosing themselves: they are drawn over into the drifting movement of the poem, in ways hard to account for: "Of course, any poem which subdues hard fact or sharp concrete image to its drift gives a sense of mastery to poet and reader. When, however, the poem's drift lies implicit somewhere between arbitrary image, symbol and an irony extended to the point of allegory, we move with the poem in the tension and terror of a world nearly but not wholly revealed."[18] Such a world would have the terrible, because specious, stability of the dreaming that holds it in place: we revert to Claudio's prison of self. "I have no ghosts," Gerontion complains or confesses: ghosts would be for him genuine possessions, authentic memories, integrities of spirit.

Lines 33–47: Up to this point, Gerontion is talking either to himself, musing the obscure, or to Christ. But he moves into a different tone, more discursive and argumentative, as if he accosted his conscience directly. If Christ is the one addressed from the start, he is still addressed, but the tone is more truculent. Now that it is too late to play a part in history, all that Gerontion can propose—like Adams—is to understand it, in the hope of escaping from it. Adams thought of understanding it in terms of unity and multiplicity, order and chaos. Gerontion, projecting his guilt upon history, resents it; he personifies History—"she"—the better to resent its force; and construes that force on the analogy of sexual power and the caprice with which women allegedly exert it. The motif of dissociation persists: nothing is given at the right time; "the giving famishes the craving"; we are not saved even by our virtues.

History in this passage is the modern substitute for the large meaning traditionally offered by religion: it includes ambition and vanity in a range of speculation from Hegel to Adams. It is the nineteenth-century project of replacing God by the secular interest of Progress. Nineteenth-century sages tried to establish History to take the place of Providence—or perhaps of Nature, if we think again of the first draft—and set about trying to discern its *Geist* as believers tried to deepen their faith in God. Eliot's view of that plan is consistent with his reference, in "*Ulysses,* Order, and Myth," to "the immense panorama of futility and anarchy which is contemporary history." To Gerontion, History seems as arbitrary as the most willful God—a rigmarole of false absolutes, a wilderness of mirrors: destiny is diminished to caprice. "These tears are shaken from the wrath-bearing tree," but also from Gerontion's Jacobean whispers and vanities.

Lines 48–60: The main difficulty is to construe "you" and "your." Ransom thinks that a silent listening Christ is intended. I don't see any need to give "you" and "your" an objective form. Gerontion can still be regarded as communing with his conscience, the communion now being more intense, more intimate. Eliot says, in his review of Adams's *Education,* that "conscience told him that one must be a learner all one's life." To be intimate with one's conscience is a quality of the New England mind; it involves the "fatal American introspectiveness," as Eliot said with Conrad Aiken in view.[19] Something along these lines is enough to give "you" and "your" their force.

It is in this passage of the poem that we smell the Jacobean smoke and sulphur. The passage as a whole recalls the self-justifying swagger of Othello's last major speech. Compare Gerontion's

> Think at last
> We have not reached conclusion, when I
> Stiffen in a rented house
with Othello's
> Set you down this;
> And say besides, that in Aleppo once . . .

The rhetorical brag in the stretching between "I" and "Stiffen" is just as assertive as Othello's claim—"besides"—upon the record of history. "Cheering himself up," Eliot called it, in "Shakespeare and the Stoicism of Seneca": "He is endeavoring to escape reality, he has ceased to think about Desdemona, and is thinking about himself. Humility is the most difficult of all the virtues to achieve; nothing dies harder than the desire to think well of oneself. Othello succeeds in turning himself into a pathetic figure, by adopting an *aesthetic* rather than a moral attitude, dramatising himself against his environment. He takes in the spectator, but the human motive is primarily to take in himself."[20] So, too, Gerontion cheers himself up by making words give him the splendor and the grand appearance that History has denied him. But there is a difference. Othello wants to see himself looking well-accoutered in pathos. Gerontion claims that it is his virtue that has destroyed him:

> I that was near your heart was removed therefrom
> To lose beauty in terror, terror in inquisition.

If he is talking to his conscience, the claim in "inquisition" is that his analytical scruple has defeated him, it has cut him adrift from the sensuous power of his old life. He then gets petulant:

> I have lost my passion: why should I need to keep it
> Since what is kept must be adulterated?

So the poem moves toward its end.

Lines 61–75: Not as easy as they seem. "These," the first word, may refer to the five senses Gerontion has just been listing. But that doesn't work well with the divergence between "membrane" and "sense":

> These with a thousand small deliberations
> Protract the profit of their chilled delirium,
> Excite the membrane, when the sense has cooled,
> With pungent sauces . . .

Better to take it as saying: "these large deliberations, and a thousand small ones, are the sorts of things I go in for to keep me going." Gerontion is explicating the "concitation" he disavowed ten lines back. This last section represents the moment in which he detects himself and his self-dramatization, as if to say, "Well, what difference does my posturing make, I'm not fooling anyone, not even myself." This change of mood leads naturally enough into the subtly modified tone of—

> What will the spider do,
> Suspend its operations, will the weevil
> Delay?

—the delay being mimed across the line-ending. Otherwise put: "What does all this matter? Those who have something to do will do it. Even the insects have more talent for conviction than I have. The spider will keep going about his self-protective business: the weevil will keep on worming into the corn."

> De Bailhache, Fresca, Mrs. Cammel, whirled
> Beyond the circuit of the shuddering Bear
> In fractured atoms.

Who these figures are is less to the point than what happens to them. The phonetic trajectory of "whirled," "circuit," and "Bear" sends them, as Kenner has remarked, into the void. The void is the place where those go who are ignored by History: it is the secular name for Hell. The Bear comes from Chapman's *Bussy D'Ambois*—he found it in Seneca's *Hercules Aeteus*—where the dying Bussy calls on his fame to tell the heavens that he is coming:

> fly where men feel
> The burning axletree, and those that suffer
> Beneath the chariot of the snowy Bear.

No astronomical fact requires "shuddering." It may refer, as Southam suggests, to the other bear, the animal whose orgasm is said to last nine days. Johannes Fabricius has argued that the Bear "signifies *the Terrible Mother,* the frightening experience of the *maternal;* as the archetypal Mother imago further serves to symbolize the unconscious, 'the shuddering Bear' ('Gerontion') may express an unruly and dangerous mental state."[21] More immediately, the shuddering comes from the "whirling," the vortex:

> Gull against the wind, in the windy straits
> Of Belle Isle, or running on the Horn.

A reversion, this, to the epic grandeurs and pretensions with which the poem begins—a mariner's Thermopylae—and a desperate gesture to fend off History's dire intentions:

> White feathers in the snow, the Gulf claims,
> And an old man driven by the Trades
> To a sleepy corner.

Fitzgerald's Stoicism; Adams's, or anyone's, desire to let go. The last lines are hardly necessary:

> Tenants of the house,
> Thoughts of a dry brain in a dry season.

"Thoughts" is a word of poor repute in Eliot; it is quite distinct from "thinking," because it marks the moment at which the mind, wearied, is prepared to settle for the easy victory of ideas rather than continue to explore its feeling.

That Henry Adams is one of the ghosts of the poem can hardly be doubed: much of Gerontion's feeling is continuous with Adams's sense, in the *Education,* that "Chaos was the law of nature; Order was the dream of man." But it is my impression that Yeats, just as much as Adams, represented for Eliot the egotism and vanity the poem tries to repudiate.

On July 4, 1919, Eliot reviewed, with memorable distaste, *The Cutting of an Agate.* He maintained that Yeats was "not 'of this world,' *this* world, of course, being our visible planet with whatever our theology or myth may conceive as below or above it." Yeats's mind was "in some way independent of experience." It was a mind "in which perception of fact, and feeling and thinking are all a little different from ours." There was no difference, Eliot maintained, between dream and reality in Yeats's work: they were identical, because each was equally independent of experience. "His remoteness is not an escape from the world, for he is innocent of any world to escape from; his procedure is blameless, but he does not start where we do." Eliot insisted that Yeats's mind was "extreme in egoism, and therefore crude." The defect of that mind was not, in Eliot's view, that it was inconsistent, illogical, or incoherent, but that the objects upon which it was directed were not fixed: "as in his portraits of Synge and several other Irishmen, we do not seem to get the men themselves before us, but feelings of Mr. Yeats projected."[22] In 1934, Eliot included Yeats in the parade of heretics surveyed with notable asperity in *After Strange Gods,* and he deplored the fact that "so much of Yeats's verse is stimulated by folklore, occultism, mythology, and symbolism, crystal-gazing and hermetic writings."[23] Eliot's opinion of these stimulants was no higher in 1934 than in 1919, when he wrote "A Cooking Egg" and reflected upon the instruction to be received from Madame Blavatsky in the Seven Sacred Trances. He thought Yeats's supernatural world "the wrong supernatural world," not a structure of spiritual significance but "a highly sophisticated lower mythology summoned, like a physician, to supply the fading pulse of poetry with some transient stimulant so that the dying patient may utter his last words."[24] Where Yeats should have bowed his head in humility and penitence before a divinely revealed body of truth, he merely indulged himself in "dissociated phases of consciousness."[25] The revelations given in those states could neither be confirmed nor denied. Eliot thought Yeats's procedures mostly vain, blatant examples of egotism.

If we hold in our minds, while reading "Gerontion," not only Eliot's sense of Adams but his sense of Yeats, we come upon a crucial force within the poem—Eliot's sense, at once exhilarated and appalled, of the availability of words to provide us with specious worlds in which we may sink to rest. As a critic, he associated the glamour of this desire with Seneca as distinct from Greek tragedy. In *Twelfth Night,* Viola says: "They that dally nicely with words may quickly make them wanton." Eliot was susceptible to that dallying and to those words, and to the character of language that created them. I have glanced at his dalliance and referred to his erotic companions, Poe, Tennyson, Swinburne, and Mallarmé. His genius, in the early poems, was neo-Jacobean: it enforces itself again in the Sweeney of "Sweeney Agonistes" and the Harry of *The Family Reunion.* Am I saying, or avoiding saying, that Eliot's native genius was that of a sophist? E. M. Cioran says of the sophists that "having ceased to be *nature,* they live as a function of the word." Style, "transforming itself into an autonomous principle, becomes fate." Further: "To produce a 'perfect' work, one must be able to *wait,* to live within that work until it supplants the universe."[26] Eliot's genius was not immune to these extravagances. It is implicated in every ostensibly negative "placing" of Gerontion. When Gerontion says

> I an old man,
> A dull head among windy spaces . . .

the confession is far more histrionic than if he had said "I am an old man, / A dull head among windy spaces." The latter version would have conformed not only to standard syntax but to the world such syntax acknowledges: it would have lodged itself in the world. The version we have on Eliot's page has the sonority of a sophist, living within the rhetoric until it supplants the world. But the poem includes a diagnosis of the sophistry in which it takes pleasure. "Gerontion" recognizes that mere words have to be redeemed, style submitted to the Word of God, for which silence is the only decent analogy. Thereafter, the words, purified, can participate in a correspondingly authentic world, verifiable by experience. If the words are not submitted to the Word of God—if they persist in being their mere selves—they remain signs of our egotism, and Yeats's work is—to Eliot, not to me—their example. The egotist can indulge himself only in explosions of eloquence, arbitrary because irresponsible—

> whirled
> Beyond the circuit of the shuddering Bear
> In fractured atoms.

—exciting the membrane with pungent sauces but coinciding with no respectable truth.

"Gerontion" forces a certain moral disposition to give itself away and registers the Senecan thrill of doing so. This is a complex issue. One of Eliot's qualities as a poet was his trust in his own experience: if an image lodged in his mind, he never disowned it. In *The Use of Poetry and the Use of Criticism* he refers to the lines about "the circuit of the shuddering Bear," acknowledges their origin in Seneca and their reappearance in Chapman: "There is first the probability that this imagery had some personal saturation value, so to speak, for Seneca; another for Chapman, and another for myself, who have borrowed it twice from Chapman. I suggest that what gives it such intensity as it has in each case is its saturation . . . but with feelings too obscure for the authors even to know quite what they were."[27] Eliot then wondered why, for all of us, certain images recur, charged with emotion, rather than others. He did not attempt an answer: such images, which he spoke of as memories, "may have symbolic value, but of what we cannot tell, for they come to represent the depths of feeling into which we cannot peer."[28] But Eliot didn't say what is true of his sensibility, that such images are unquestionable. They are more authoritative in his poetry than any law. If the image from Chapman comes into the composition of "Gerontion," it is accepted as a gift from the Muse, even if it were to usurp the context in which it appears. It speaks to the Senecan thrill of being among words. The part it plays in the economy of the poem is harder to specify, except that it delivers some of the neo-Jacobean melodrama.

The disposition I have referred to is what Eliot, in "Shakespeare and the Stoicism of Seneca," calls *bovarysme*—the notion is Jules de Gaultier's—"the human will to see things as they are not." What made the poem possible was the capacity of certain styles to create semblances of worlds other than the one we commonly know, and to enforce those semblances against every rival consideration. But Eliot, as I have argued in several contexts, was not a disinterested critic of that capacity. As a poet, he was addicted to such styles, especially to the style of lurid incantation which he found just as compelling in Poe and Tennyson as in Donne, Webster, and Chapman. As a poet, Eliot yearned for the ease of mind, the release of spirit, in styles that sent him drifting beyond empirical provocations. "Gerontion" gains its resonance from his determination to detect a luxuriant impulse in himself, while releasing it. He forces it, against the pressure of equivocation and the bias of his genius, to disclose itself.

"Burbank with a Baedeker: Bleistein with a Cigar"

I n the Introduction to *The Oxford Book of Modern Verse* (1936), Yeats called Eliot a satirist. Admittedly, he was nearly tone-deaf to Eliot's poems. Nor did Eliot take the trouble to see what Yeats's poems were up to till publication of *The Tower* made him open his eyes. Still, Yeats's Introduction is bizarre:

> Eliot has produced his great effect upon his generation be-cause he has described men and women that get out of bed or into it from mere habit; in describing this life that has lost heart his own art seems grey, cold, dry. He is an Alexander Pope, working without apparent imagination, producing his effects by a rejection of all rhythms and metaphors used by the more popular romantics rather than by the discovery of his own, this rejection giving his work an unexaggerated plain-ness that has the effect of novelty.

"Rhythmical flatness," Yeats says, and in "The Waste Land" "amid much that is moving in symbol and imagery there is much monotony of accent," whereupon he quotes four lines of parody that snap shut upon the sexual routine they indict:

When lovely woman stoops to folly and
Paces about her room again, alone,
She smooths her hair with automatic hand,
And puts a record on the gramophone.

Refusing to put the early Eliot "among those that descend from Shakespeare and the translators of the Bible," Yeats thinks of him as satirist rather than poet. "Only once does that early work speak in the great manner," and Yeats quotes the last two stanzas of "Sweeney among the Nightingales," the only stanzas that Yeats himself might have written:

The nightingales are singing near
The Convent of the Sacred Heart,

And sang within the bloody wood
When Agamemnon cried aloud
And let their liquid siftings fall
To stain the stiff dishonoured shroud.

In "The Hollow Men" and "Ash-Wednesday" there is, Yeats says, "rhythmical animation," a quality that "two or three of my friends" attribute to "an emotional enrichment from religion," but "his religion compared to that of John Gray, Francis Thompson, Lionel Johnson in 'The Dark Angel,' lacks all strong emotion; a New England Protestant by descent, there is little self-surrender in his personal relation to God and the soul."[1] A few parsimonious sentences about *Murder in the Cathedral* follow, enabling Yeats to move on to a more congenial figure, Ezra Pound.

In his early years in London, Eliot was often regarded as a sophisticate, witty in a mordant way, bleak in a New England way, and sharp as a vulture. But it should have been clear by 1936 that the early poems characteristic of his genius were impressionist, symbolist, and receptive in Pound's designation. Like Joyce's *Portrait of the Artist as a Young Man,* Eliot's early poems practice what Fredric Jameson has called "strategies of inwardness," devices to take the harm out of an opaque objective reality by transforming its constituents into private styles and gestures. Joyce's sentences change Dublin into Stephen's sensibility, leaving only as much of the city as is compatible with the exchange. In 1920, when *Ara Vos Prec* was published, Eliot barely knew the nature of his talent. He thought it might be what the little world of London said it was, and only hoped to think better of it by thinking of it differently. A few days after the little book appeared, he felt bound to insist to his brother Henry that the poems were serious. Presumably he thought they might continue to be mistaken for bits of music hall or farce: "Some of the new poems, the Sweeney ones, especially 'Among the Nightingales' and 'Burbank' are intensely se-rious, and I think these two are among the best that I have ever done. But even here I am considered by the ordinary Newspaper critic as a Wit or satirist, and in America I suppose I shall be thought merely disgusting."[2] The quatrain poems in *Ara Vos Prec* were attempts to do something along the formal lines of Gautier's *Emaux et Camées,* a direc-tion recommended to Eliot by Pound. Putting forward Gautier's poems and Corbière's to correct the laxity into which free verse had fallen, Pound was also recommending his own poems. Eliot already knew Gautier's but hadn't given them "any close attention."[3] The quatrains indicated a turn from Laforgue to Gautier and Corbière, though such turns are never decisive: a poet doesn't disown an affilia-tion that has meant something to him. What Eliot most admired in *Emaux et Camées* was Gautier's syntactical variety, a quality to be emu-lated instead of Laforgue's exclamatory breathlessness. The qualities that Pound approved of—he called them hard, crystalline, and so forth—kept Eliot's poetry from sinking too deeply into auditory recesses. There were local considerations, too. The fact that Gautier wrote "Variations sur le Carnaval de Venise" made it nearly inevitable that Eliot would write "Burbank." Gautier's stanza form "gave the impetus to the content," as Eliot reported.[4] The problem was: how to find appropriate feelings to go with the form. Eliot couldn't just take over Gautier's feelings. In fact, his quatrain poems are more incisive than Gautier's and more diverse in their objects of attack: loose princesses, capitalists, American tourists, Jews in the history of Venice, Sir Alfred Mond, Madame Blavatsky, degenerate waiters, the Anglican Church, Grishkin with her Russian eye, Apeneck Sweeney, and Rachel *née* Rabinowitz.

"Burbank with a Baedeker: Bleistein with a Cigar" has come in for rebuke on grounds of anti-Semitism: it takes up a lot of space in Anthony Julius's *T. S. Eliot, Anti-Semitism, and Literary Form* (1995). I'll leave consideration of Eliot's social and cultural criticism till later.

When I started reading Eliot, as a student in Dublin, the question of his alleged anti-Semitism was rarely adverted to. In *Rebecca's Vest*, Karl Miller confirms that this was true for English readers of his generation. I don't recall that the big critics in England and America—Leavis, Tate, Blackmur, Ransom, Burke—ever raised the issue. Nor do I recall that Christian readers complained about "The Hippopotamus." Readers of that generation thought that Eliot was by native gift a satirist and that he must be allowed to have things to attack. I've been looking up a selection of fairly recent commentaries on "Burbank"—as I'll call it for short, even though Christopher Ricks disapproves of the economy and wants the title in full—and on the poems up to "The Waste Land" to see to what extent critics since the Holocaust have agreed in denouncing the early poetry. I haven't counted heads or selected a jury, but I find six clearly marked positions.

According to (1), Eliot has no case to answer for "Burbank" because, as Robert Crawford says, "the poem is funny, but at everyone's expense."⁵ According to (2) he has no case to answer because the implied point of view in "Burbank" is not Eliot's. Guy Davenport holds:

> Eliot makes us see Venice through the eyes of his puppets, carica-
> tures of vapid, rich, Jewish tourists (" . . . Bleistein's way: / A
> saggy bending of the knees / And elbows, with the palms turned
> out, / Chicago Semite Viennese"). [He] places the blank modern
> mind, which sees nothing in Venice but international society (Lady
> Volupine, Sir Ferdinand Klein), in so degraded a position that it is a
> "lustreless protrusive eye / . . . stares from the protozoic slime"
> and reproduces the way such a mind explains to itself "Time's
> ruins": "The rats are underneath the piles, / The Jew is under-
> neath the lot." Or where it cannot explain in projections of its own
> vicious conception of men and history, it asks inadvertently perti-
> nent questions: "Who clipped the lion's wings / And flea'd his
> rump and pared his claws?" At a level that engages with Venetian
> history and in a tone removed from Eliot's wit, [Pound's Canto]
> XXV inspects what Burbank and Bleistein could not see, and notes
> in the margin that this kinship of poems ought not to be missed.⁶

According to (3) Eliot has no case—or a very weak one—to answer because he has already internalized his animosity against Jews: he is his own Jew. Karl Miller is thinking of "Dirge" rather than of "Bur-bank," but I'm sure he includes "Burbank" in this comment:

> In a draft of the poem the word "man" appears instead of "Jew,"
> and there are other such indications, elsewhere in his poetry, that
> Eliot was his own Jew, that the Jew could serve him both as a type
> of the distressed human being and as a figure for some distressing
> part of his nature—wandering, free-thinking, heretical, frightful.
> But this does not mean that his nature could not tolerate the famil-

iar simplex anti-semite who when he thought about Jews thought about noses and gold. The discouraging ironies that can be found here are not confined to what Eliot thought and wrote on these occasions: they must also have been present, at this time, for those who chose to look, in the docility of his readers.[7]

According to (4) Eliot has little or no case to answer for "The Waste Land" because whatever anti-Semitic feelings he had were normal for the pre-Holocaust time. Empson, reviewing the original drafts of the poem, argued that the main theme was a dreadful relation between son and father, much of it carried out "by exultantly rancorous parodies, describing the rich London Jews rotting under water." These parodies seemed to Empson "better poetry than the few bits which have been quoted from his youthful sex-fun poems. . . . The rejected passages of Jew-baiting are still deeply involved in the final poetry." These passages don't trouble Empson much: "I am not inclined to pull a long face about this. A writer had better rise above the ideas of his time, but one should not take offence if he doesn't, and the surprising thing is that Eliot and Pound were so careful to take the Jew-baiting passages out." Empson notes that Eliot's father "continued to be a staunch Unitarian while going into business." The difference this makes is: "Unitarians describe themselves as Christians but deny that Jesus was God, whereas Eliot was beginning to feel a strong drag towards a return to the worship of the tortured victim. Now if you are hating a purse-proud business man who denies that Jesus is God, into what stereotype does he best fit? He is a Jew, of course; and yet this would be a terrible blasphemy against his family and its racial pride, so much so that I doubt whether Eliot ever allowed himself to realise what he was doing. But he knows, in the poem, that everything has gone wrong with the eerie world to which the son is condemned."[8] According to (5) "Burbank" is strong evidence of Eliot's prejudice against Jews, at least while he was writing the poem. Ricks has argued that Eliot did not "estimate the difference between the dramatized hallucinatory clarity of 'Sweeney among the Nightingales' and the melodramatized (that is, irresponsibily diffused) animus of 'Burbank with a Baedeker: Bleistein with a Cigar.' " Ricks quotes a passage from Eliot's "Wilkie Collins and Dickens" about Collins's novella *The Haunted Hotel: A Mystery of Modern Venice:* "What makes it better than a mere readable second-rate ghost story is the fact that fatality in this story is no longer merely a wire jerking the figures. The principal character, the fatal woman, is herself obsessed by the idea of fatality; her motives are melodramatic; she therefore compels the coincidences to occur, feeling that she is compelled to compel them. In this story, as the chief character is internally melodramatic, the story itself ceases to be merely melodramatic, and partakes of true drama."[9] Ricks maintains that since "Burbank with a Baedeker: Bleistein with a Cigar" has no "chief character," "there is no position from which to gain purchase upon whether anyone is 'internally melodramatic,' while at the same time there is an obdurate emphasis on fatality and on the fatal woman."[10] Unlike "Sweeney among the Nightingales," "Burbank with a Baedeker: Bleistein with a Cigar" is not dramatized, so its "multiplicity of partial dramatizations" gives Eliot a license he seldom claimed. The poem is licentious, Ricks argues, because it allows Eliot to vent his animosity against Jews without taking responsibility for doing so. It is "the work of a poet here compelling coincidences to occur."[11] Forty pages later Ricks speaks of the "muddy roiling of feelings at large" in the poem.[12]

According to (6) Eliot is in this poem guilty as charged. "Burbank," argues Anthony Julius, "resonates with anti-Semitic scorn."[13] Eliot has indulged himself, Giorgio Melchiori maintains, in "a rabid and irrational form of anti-Semitism."[14] "I fear," Tony Tanner says of

"Burbank," "this is a piece of pre-Holocaust anti-Semitism which cannot be blinked away."[15]

I don't intend going through these six attitudes and pronouncing upon each. What they mainly show is the range of respectable judgments available on the anti-Semitic aspect of the poem. No one ought to feel ethically superior. The main issue is: who is speaking this poem? Is it Eliot in his own voice and person and on his own responsibility? Is it Eliot the impresario, forcing some blank modern mind to reveal its deficiencies? Is the speaker Mr. Impersonality, familiarly known as God? Is the poem a dramatic monologue? Unfortunately it isn't, Ricks answers: if it were, we would have the distressing sentiments folded into the chief character and there made available to be reckoned with, as in "Gerontion." We could examine the sentiments in relation to the fallible or disabled person who utters them. Lacking the dramatic character, we are in a mess of melodrama.

The problem with this argument is that those of Eliot's early poems which are not dramatic monologues have their own adequate principle of organization. The main principle is what McLuhan called "juxtaposition without copula," a discovery by nineteenth-century painters that they could establish on canvas two or more points of force—blobs of different shape and color—and have them set up potent but unspecified relations within the frame. When I look at the painting, I intuit such relations without trying to turn them into discourse: it is sufficient that I feel their force. In Brussels last year I went to an exhibition of paintings by Paul Delvaux. One of them, "L'appel," juxtaposes a Grecian temple, naked or near-naked priestesses, and a skeleton. In "Leda," the naked Leda kneels, holding with tenderness Zeus in the form of a swan: the background has telegraph wires and a modern church. Other paintings by Delvaux feature, in seemingly arbitrary juxtaposition, a railway station, naked women, a fully clothed man, and other objects never seen together on land or sea. Looking at the paintings entailed subordinating the objects painted to the formal relations that Delvaux prescribed for them. The conventions of realistic portraiture and landscape-painting were invoked in detail only to be refuted at large, in the whole composition. Each painting became a field of force without official syntax, a closed system resistant to translation. In "Whispers of Immortality," Eliot nearly had the poem written as soon as he had put Webster, Donne, and Grishkin in the same field. Blackmur thought the procedure "almost a formula: Sweeney and Agamemnon; Grishkin and Donne—all 'expert beyond experience.' " Or: Burbank, Bleistein, Princess Volupine, and Sir Ferdinand Klein, none of them expert beyond experience. But Blackmur qualifies his account of the procedure. It's not quite a formula. What remains outside the formula is "the necessity of making the opposition itself, as well as the images opposed, intelligible."[16] The question is then: what are the relations between Burbank, Bleistein, the Princess, and Klein? Are these figures related by similarity, contrast, or some other consideration?

Each of them is reflected upon, but not equally or for the same reasons. Burbank "falls" with the Princess, but hardly falls in love with her. If the god Hercules means sexual vitality, the assignation in the small hotel was not a success. His having a Baedeker shouldn't count against him. Eliot owned one in London. And Burbank is redeemed at least to the extent of having a worthwhile thought in the last stanza. The Princess is loose, there is nothing to be said for her as she hands herself on from Burbank to Klein. Bleistein is a stereotyped Jew, moneyed, a primitive intelligence staring at Canalettos. Klein is also a Jew, ennobled by a British monarch in return, presumably, for financial services rendered to the party in power. They are all four assembled in Venice, in varying degrees of fallenness, the city itself in decay.

Each of these characters, except Klein, is "placed" by being associated with other figures from myth or literature. Eliot's procedure is another version of juxtaposition without copula, the "mythical method" he praised in *Ulysses*. Burbank is diminished by comparison with Hercules. The Princess has to put up with intimations of Cleopatra in her barge, though the one burning on the water all the day is also Aurora. Bleistein is a Shylock reduced still further to the protozoic slime. Sir Ferdinand is not compared or contrasted with anyone; he is sufficiently low to be entertained by the Princess, unfresh from her recent assignation.

If we were to agree with Guy Davenport that the vantage point in the poem isn't Eliot's, we would reduce our difficulties; we would see the four characters appropriately set down in Venice, doing the few things they do in a city sufficiently diminished to provide a scene for these activities. If we don't agree with Davenport and we insist on finding the feelings and prejudices on show Eliot's, then we have to consider the status of those impulses. Most of the feelings in the poem are unconscious or spontaneous; appropriately, since that is what prejudices are. Gadamer has defined prejudice as "a judgment that is given before all the elements that determine a situation have been finally examined."[17] He also points out that there are legitimate as well as illegitimate prejudices, "if we want to do justice to man's finite, historical mode of being."[18] If I accept someone's authority and go along with his judgment of a particular issue because he knows more about it than I do, I act on a legitimate prejudice. If I abide by a tradition, I hold to a legitimate prejudice. As Gadamer says: "The validity of morals . . . is based on tradition. They are freely taken over, but by no means created by a free insight or justified by themselves."[19]

The feelings in Eliot's poem include animosity against Jews involved in the decay of Venice, and against the other types deprecated—American tourists, promiscuous princesses, and so forth.

Eliot didn't need Laforgue to instruct him in the power of unconscious images; or Laforgue's main authority, Hartmann's *Philosophy of
the Unconscious.* His own poetics of inspiration and incantation meant
that he would not disown unconscious images and stirrings. Yeats
said: in dreams begins responsibility. But it is a long way from that
beginning to the ethical responsibility we take or refuse to take. The
purpose of "Burbank" is to bring these unconscious impulses to the
light of day and form, thereby making them take responsibility for
themselves. The poem moves between Laforgue and Gautier, between unconscious images acknowledged as such and their conscious
ends pressed eventually into existence by the formality, the syntax, of
the stanza. The process by which this is done explains Eliot's recourse
to allusions, which are extraordinarily diverse even by his standard.[20]
The allusions to Ariosto, Canaletto, Mantegna, Shakespeare, Marston, Byron, Gautier, Ruskin, Browning, Wilkie Collins, Henry
James, and Pound: what can these be except points at which other
feelings, similar and different, in regard to the rise and fall of Venice,
have already become conscious? Allusions in Pound normally say:
there have been other times, similar and different. Allusions in Eliot
normally say: there have been other feelings, similar to and different
from mine, and these too have been brought to light and some degree
of order. Eliot's discursive prose is quite another issue, because it is
supposedly free from the drag of unconsciousness.

Who is speaking the poem? The more I read it, the more I become
convinced that it is the epitome of a Jamesian novel, though not *The
Aspern Papers* or *The Wings of the Dove,* his fictions of Venice. It is
Jamesian in the sense that it is governed by the conventions of *style
indirect libre:* third-person narration, subject to the constraint that the
vocabulary used—the diction—is the one the character focused upon
would use if he or she were managing the narrative. In *Joyce's Voices,*
Kenner calls this device the Uncle Charles principle, on the strength

of the chapter in *A Portrait of the Artist as a Young Man* in which Uncle
Charles is said to "repair to his outhouse but not before he had
creased and brushed scrupulously his back hair and brushed and put
on his tall hat."[21] It is third-person narration, but the key words are
Uncle Charles's. If you were to ask him how he started his day, he
would tell you that he repaired to his outhouse, a salubrious place,
and that he lit his pipe, finding his brand of black twist "very cool
and mollifying." Impersonal narration is concentrated upon Uncle
Charles and yields to his diction. Is this the case in "Burbank with a
Baedeker: Bleistein with a Cigar"?

The poem begins with fragments of prose strung together to
steady themselves eventually into a sentence: the gondolier's "tra-la-
la," a Latin tag from Mantegna's painting of the martyrdom of St.
Sebastian, a few clauses inaccurately quoted from *The Aspern Papers,*
an outburst from *Othello,* a phrase from Browning's "A Toccata of
Galuppi's," and stage directions from a masque by Marston. Southam
has suggested that the epigraph may be a joke, like Corbière's "Epi-
taphe," although he notes, too, that all the fragments, except the last,
"have a connection to Venice."[22] Then we have the narrative of Burbank and Princess Volupine in the first three stanzas, a sexual conjunction with appropriate references to the god Hercules "that had
loved him well" and the summer dawn on the water. The next three
stanzas present Bleistein, though it's not certain that the "lustreless
protrusive eye" staring "from the protozoic slime / At a perspective
of Canaletto" is his: it could be anyone's. But the Jewish references
are enforced in the next stanza—

On the Rialto once.
    The rats are underneath the piles.
The Jew is underneath the lot.
    Money in furs.

Whose perceptions are these? Burbank's, by my reading. The whole poem concentrates on him and yields to what he sees and thinks and says to himself. This doesn't make it a dramatic monologue, but it establishes the vision in the case—and the prejudices—as Burbank's, not Eliot's. I disagree with Ricks: we can, I think, gain a purchase on the poem by interpreting it as Burbank's story, in much the same way as James gives the managing of *The Ambassadors* to Lambert Strether and incriminates him in the story. The eyes that are turned on the scene are his: we watch him as he watches the other characters.

Most of the debate about "Burbank" has turned on the question of anti-Semitic prejudice. Few critics have remarked how fine the poetry is, especially the last two stanzas:

> The boatman smiles,
> Princess Volupine extends
> A meagre, blue-nailed, phthisic hand
> To climb the waterstair. Lights, lights,
> She entertains Sir Ferdinand
>
> Klein. Who clipped the lion's wings
> And flea'd his rump and pared his claws?
> Thought Burbank, meditating on
> Time's ruins, and the seven laws.

It is Eliot's early version of the grand style, as good in that way as the last stanzas of "Sweeney among the Nightingales." The distant rhyme of "Klein" and "declines," eight lines back, the first words in their respective lines, has the exactly judged degree of insistence. The dividing of his name across the line ending has the effect of mocking the Princess: she would call her new lover "Sir Ferdinand," possessively, and let the "Klein" await its turn. "Lights, lights" recalls Brabantio in *Othello* trying to save his daughter from sexual ruin: it is too late for any guardian of the Princess to protect her virtue. The superbly delivered questions, "Who clipped the lion's wings / And flea'd his rump and pared his claws?" depend on the rapidity of the sentence with its three equal parts. And then we have Burbank, saved for this meditation. "Inadvertently pertinent questions," Davenport calls them. Surely not inadvertently.

[6]

"The Waste Land"

The publication of the first drafts of "The Waste Land" has not greatly eased the difficulty of reading the poem. It appears—though Empson disputes this, as we'll see—that the poem issued, however circuitously, from the unhappiness of Eliot's first marriage. The poem, it is worth saying against a common opinion, has nothing to do with the alleged breakdown of Western civilization or any other Spenglerian excruciation. Certain lines in the first drafts were written before 1915 and waited for a provocative opportunity to take part in a composition. We hardly know what to make of the relation between marriage and poem, unless it prompts us to say that the dominant feeling in the poem is not universal despair but particular guilt, and that the specific movement of feeling through the words corresponds, however obscurely, to the act of penance. Some readers of "The Waste Land" feel that Eliot is saying: "God, I thank thee that I am not like the rest of men, extortioners, unjust, adulterers, or even like this small house-agent's clerk." But this sense of the poem is unworthy, false to its spirit as a whole, though there are a few passages that support it. The area of feeling which the poem inhabits is that of guilt, fear, dread; the presence of disgust, including self-disgust, is not surprising. The first drafts show that the poet's original sense of his poem made it, even more than the final version, a medley of dissociated voices. Calvin Bedient has argued that every word in the poem is attributable to one voice, but to sustain the argument he has to posit the voice as that of God or some other figure of omniscience. That isn't much help. It still strikes me as a poem of different voices, heard, overheard, voices off, voices on. Pound's criticism tightened the poem but did not otherwise alter its movement. One characteristic of the poetry remains. Eliot's poems often try to escape from the emotional condition that incited them, not by willing its opposite but by working through a wide range of alternative conditions. The poems find safety and relief in numbers. One mood is answered not by another, equal and opposite, but by a diversity of moods. It is the diversity that saves. The medley of poems that became "The Waste Land" was designed, it appears, with this diversity in view. The movement of the poem is such as to make an act of penance possible. Diversity, number, and allusion are the auspices under which the poem proceeds.

This sense of the poem is related to our recognition of its character as a distinctively American work. Specifically, it is, in Hawthorne's terminology, a romance. In the Preface to *The House of the Seven Gables,* Hawthorne distinguished between romance and novel. The novel aims at minute fidelity to the probable, but the romance, claiming "a certain latitude," proposes to present "the truth of the human heart" under circumstances "to a great extent of the writer's own choosing or creation."[1] There has always been an implication, in later comments on the romance, that it is the form of fiction most congenial to those feelings for which social correlatives are not available, or, if available, seriously inadequate. The romance, in Hawthorne's sense, holds a special position in American literature and is particularly serviceable to the writer who feels his imagination driven back upon its own resources. One of the tenable generalizations we make about English literature is that its position is not desperate in this regard. English writers generally think themselves ready to establish their feelings in a particular setting and to let them develop and take their chances there. They declare a certain confidence in representing the life of feeling in terms of man, nature, and society. Nearly everything is allowed to depend upon the relation of people to the society in which they live, the relation of person to person and to place. We say that English literature is personal, meaning that it is social, historical, and political. We do not say this of American literature. The question of locality is important to American writers, not least to Hawthorne in *The House of the Seven Gables,* but in American literature generally, and especially in the literature of the nineteenth century, a shadow falls between person and place. The feelings in the case are rarely entrusted to that relation, or indeed to any other: there is an impression that such feelings cannot hope to be fulfilled in those relations. There is a remainder of feeling which cries for release in dream, nightmare, and fantasy. "The Waste Land" is best understood as an American romance.

It may be useful to recall Eliot's sense of American literature. He rejected the assertion that there is an American language distinct from English: in his view, both languages use the same notes, even if the fingering is sometimes different. He was not of Mencken's party, or William Carlos Williams's, in that argument. As for the literature, he registered New England as a moral presence, a regiment in the army of unalterable law, but he was not intimidated by it. He reflected on the complex fate of being an American when he read Hawthorne and, still more, Henry James, who embodied one of the great possibilities consistent with that fate. In an essay on James he wrote that "it is the final perfection, the consummation of an American to become, not an Englishman, but a European—something which no born European, no person of any European nationality, can become."[2] Of the relation between Eliot and Whitman it is enough to say that Whitman is audible, for some good but more ill, in the third section of "The Dry Salvages," tempting Eliot into false grandeurs of reach and tone. Of Mark Twain, Eliot said that he was one of those writers who discover "a new way of writing, valid not only for themselves but for others,"[3] but I cannot recall any occasion on which Eliot's poetry moved in Twain's direction, despite "the river with its cargo of dead negroes" in "The Dry Salvages." The question of his relation to Poe is more interesting, because it is strange that he should have taken any interest in such a writer. In fact, he did not admire Poe's poems, he thought them adolescent things; Poe had never grown up. But his work, fruitless in the English and American traditions, entered the sensibilities of great French poets and especially of Baudelaire, Mallarmé, and Valéry. Eliot was interested in this event. There is almost a suggestion that Poe had somehow achieved the final perfection of an American by becoming a European.

The interest of American literature, especially literature since Emerson, arises from the sense of American feeling as making a new start, every day, with little or nothing regarded as capital saved from yesterday. The world is all before the American writers. These writers naturally think of making everything new, they do not feel oppressed by previous achievement. Emerson encouraged them to be independent. American writers burn their bridges behind them, relegating the previous, as James said in *The American Scene* of his compatriots generally, to the category of wan misery. If "The Waste Land" is written by an American who set out to make himself a European, its chief labor toward that perfection is the assumption of the burden of history. The allusions in Eliot's poem show not the extent of his learning but the gravity of the whole enterprise, the range of those responsibilities he is ready to accept in such a cause.

What most of the allusions say is: "there have been other times, not utterly lost or forgotten; we ourselves were not born this morning."

We may press the argument a little further. If English literature is preoccupied with the relations between person, place, and time, it acts by a corresponding syntax of prescribed relations. The first result is that the chief function of one word is to lead the mind to the next. No detail in *Middlemarch* is as important as the entire network of relations, word by word, sentence by sentence: the reader's mind is not encouraged to sink into the recesses of a word, but to move forward until the prescribed affiliations are complete. The modesty with which one word sends the reader's mind running to the next is the verbal equivalent of dependency in a given society, as one person accepts his enabling relation to another. A sentence marks a social responsibility, accepted. But the modern revolution in such American poems as "The Waste Land," "Hugh Selwyn Mauberley," "Paterson," "The Maximus Poems," and "The Changing Light at Sandover" depends on a different sense of life and a different syntax. One's first reading of these poems leaves an impression of their poetic quality as residing in their diction: the animation of the verse arises from the incalculable force of certain individual words or phrases that stay in the mind without necessarily attracting to their orbit the words before or after. The memorable quality of those phrases seems to require a clear space on all sides. The relations that the words of an American poem enact are not prescribed or predictive but experimental. Around each word is a space or a void in which nothing is anticipated, nothing enforced. Every relation must be invented, as if the world had just begun. Harold Rosenberg has argued that this is the chief characteristic of modern French poetry, though he offers a different explanation. "Lifting up a word and putting a space around it has been the conscious enterprise of serious French poetry since Baudelaire and Rimbaud"; and a little later he speaks of "the space around words necessary for consciousness."[4] In Eliot's early poems an American is trying to make himself a Frenchman, perfecting himself in the creation of Jules Laforgue; an enterprise capable of producing, in the long run, the magisterial achievement of making himself a European. The space around the words is necessary for an isolated consciousness, and it puts at risk the continuity of relations, as between one person and another. In Eliot, consciousness is the most available form of virtue: to be conscious is to be as near as possible to being holy, an affiliation that causes great difficulty in the plays and makes *The Family Reunion* and *The Cocktail Party* spiritually bleak. But the words surrounded by empty space receive a corresponding halo of significance, they compel the imagination not by their relation but by their loneliness. Such words take unto themselves a force of radiance, an exceptional power that Eliot in the later plays ascribes to saints and martyrs. Martyrdom is Eliot's favorite version of the Sublime.

II

There is a passage in *Writing Degree Zero* where Roland Barthes offers virtually the same distinction between what he calls classical language and modern language. In classical language the meaning is continuous, linear, it is always deferred until the end. So the mind, like the eye, runs along beside the words, and the movement is gratifying. But in modern poetry it is the word "which gratifies and fulfills like the sudden revelation of a truth." The word has lost its prescribed relations, but for that very reason it has acquired a magical power, become complete in itself, a revelation in its own recesses. Giving up its dependency, the word acquires Sibylline presence; it stands there like Rilke's archaic torso of Apollo. It is a mark of such words that we cannot read them, but they read us, they affront us by presenting their significance in relation to themselves. Barthes says of such words that they "initiate a discourse full of gaps and full of lights, filled with absences and overnourishing signs, without foresight or stability of intention, and thereby so opposed to the social function of language that merely to have recourse to a discontinuous speech is to open the door to all that stands above Nature." Classical language "establishes a universe in which men are not alone, where words never have the terrible weight of things, where speech is always a meeting with the others." Modern language presupposes a discontinuous Nature, "a fragmented space, made of objects solitary and terrible because the links between them are only potential." I would say that the links between them must be invented and are then fictive rather than pre-scribed or agreed: they have the freedom of fiction and, paying the price, the loneliness of being arbitrary. Such words, since they cannot be continuous with nature, must be above or below it, two conditions equally desolate. They are exceptions deprived of a rule. These words become names because of their oracular power, but what they name cannot be defined; they are like Stetson in "The Waste Land," whose chief quality is that he does not answer, though he instigates, the questions addressed to him. Stetson is the name of an interrogation, but he is under no obligation to reply. "The Waste Land" is the name of another interrogation, and its words are less answers than hints and guesses. Barthes says of these modern words generally—"words adorned with all the violence of their irruption, the vibration of which, though wholly mechanical, strangely affects the next word, only to die out immediately"—that they "exclude men: there is no humanism of modern poetry."[5] Stetson is not related to his interroga-tor or to London or even to Mylae; he is an oracle who stirs a nervous quiver of interrogation, and dies in a line from Baudelaire.

Classical language, then, is a system organized on the assumption that nature is continuous; hence the primacy of syntax. Classical poems stand in apposition to a seamless web of relations that we agree to call nature: when the web is domestic we call it society. The poems testify to those webs by enacting them in miniature. Long poems are valued as an extended ritual, offered to nature in the grandest terms, a celebration of prescribed relations. Readers may still be surprised, because they do not know at any moment which of the indefinitely large number of relations the writer will enact, but they know that one of them will be invoked. Each word is faithful to the others. But in modern poems, according to this distinction, the words are independent and therefore vulnerable. They live upon their acoustic value. In "The Waste Land" we respond to the words and phrases with a sense of their exposure: they are at one memorable and void. They are not obscure, we know what the dictionaries say of them and, mostly, where they come from. But they are Sibylline because of the darkness between them: they challenge us to provide them with a continuous syntax and they mock our efforts to do so—that was not what they meant at all. The whole poem looks like the subplot of a lost play; what is lost is the main plot, nature as a significant action. The attempt to specify the form of "The Waste Land" is doomed because the form is not specific, it is not—to use Blackmur's word— predictive. The poem cries for its form: what it shows forth in itself is not form but the desperate analogy of form, tokens of a virtual form which would be valid if there were such a thing. What holds the several parts of the poem together is the need, at once the poet's and our own, to keep life going, including the life of the poem in the dark spaces between the words. The problem is not that the poem lacks form but that it has a passion for form, largely unfulfilled, and—to make things harder—the memory of lost forms. Those lost forms would not answer the present need, even if they could be recovered: this is what Blackmur meant by saying of Eliot's early poems and "The Waste Land" that "they measure the present by living standards which most people relegate to the past."[6] What is present and vivid to us in the poem is the cry for form, the loud lament of that disconsolate chimera, and the cry is so pure that it almost makes up for what is merely lost. If the poem proliferates in little forms, it is because these are variations on an absent theme, a theme of which only the variations are known. The variations are recited from many different sources, and with increasing urgency toward the end, the sources being older versions of form, present now as broken images. In their bearing upon the reader, these images tell upon his conscience, forcing him to live up to the exactitude of the poem and to reject false consolations. If the poem is to be read as prologomena to penance, it is also, in its bearing upon the reader, an incitement to scruple.

So Blackmur on another occasion spoke of Eliot's task as a poet: "he has in his images to remind reason of its material, to remind order of its disorder, in order to create a sane art almost insane in its predicament." He has "to make a confrontation of the rational with the irrational: a deliberate reversal of roles."[7] But in fact Eliot had to make a double confrontation, the violence going both ways. He had to confront the rational with the irrational, with what is below nature, and the images used for this violence are mostly those he associated with Conrad's hollow men and "Heart of Darkness." In the passage that Eliot wanted to use as the epigraph to "The Waste Land" before he came upon Petronius's Sibyl, Conrad's Marlow says of Kurtz: "Did he live his life again in every detail of desire, temptation, and surrender during that supreme moment of complete knowledge? He cried in a whisper at some image, at some vision,—he cried out twice, a cry that was no more than a breath—'The horror! the horror!'" The confrontation of the rational with the irrational is propelled by the assumption that complete knowledge is possible and its horror inescapable. So I have always believed that the reader of "The Waste Land" ought to take Tiresias seriously as the name of such a possibility, and such a horror. But the other confrontation is equally valid: the irrational is confronted with the rational in all those ways for which, in the poem, the rational imagination is represented by Shakespeare, Spenser, St. Augustine, and, in the first version, by a passage from Plato's *Republic* that Pound deleted: "Not here, O Ademantus, but in another world."[8] The line comes from Book IX where Glaucon says that the city which has been described is merely verbal, it does not exist anywhere on earth, and Socrates answers, "Well, perhaps there is a pattern of it laid up in heaven for him who wishes to contemplate it and so beholding to constitute himself its citizen."[9] The contemplation of the City of God is also complete knowledge, above nature, its sublimity compelling to the citizen, and its finality asserted in the repeated Sanskrit word with which the poem ends. Tiresias would see the City of God as clearly as the Unreal City, its malign counterpart. So the poem moves between "Heart of Darkness" and "heart of light." Words stand between reason and madness, touched by both adversaries.

We need an authoritative example; from Section III of "The Waste Land," "The Fire Sermon":

But at my back in a cold blast I hear
The rattle of the bones, and chuckle spread from ear to ear.

A rat crept softly through the vegetation
Dragging its slimy belly on the bank
While I was fishing in the dull canal
On a winter evening round behind the gashouse
Musing upon the king my brother's wreck
And on the king my father's death before him.
White bodies naked on the low damp ground
And bones cast in a little low dry garret,
Rattled by the rat's foot only, year to year.
But at my back from time to time I hear

The sound of horns and motors, which shall bring
Sweeney to Mrs. Porter in the spring.
O the moon shone bright on Mrs. Porter
And on her daughter
They wash their feet in soda water
Et O ces voix d'enfants, chantant dans la coupole![10]

It is useless to ask of that passage such questions as the following: who is speaking, what is the point of the narrative, whose white bodies lay naked on the ground? Such questions assume that there is a world without words to which Eliot's words pay tribute; as, in common usage, the word "box" acknowledges the existence of a certain object that does not depend upon a word for its existence. A reader determined to give some kind of answer might say, to the first question: Tiresias, but he somehow includes Buddha, Ferdinand Prince of Naples, Ovid, and Verlaine. And to the second he might say: Well, the narrative is merely ostensible, we are not meant to think of it as a story, the words in that order make a psychological landscape in the reader's mind, which is at once subject and object; it has to do with Eliot's theory of the objective correlative or Santayana's theory of the correlative object. And the answerer might say to the third question: The king my brother and the king my father, I suppose, but again the point is verbal and atmospheric rather than denotative. Questions more in accord with the nature of the passage would include the following: what is going on, when "rat's foot" is preceded by the punning rhyme "rattled"? What is going on when a particular "zone of consciousness"—to use Kenner's phrase again—is occupied by fragments from Ovid, Verlaine, the Grail Legend, Australian popular song, Marvell, *The Tempest,* John Day, and Middleton? Why does the passage suddenly change its tone at that first insistent rhyme, "year" with "hear"? Why are we given "wreck" instead of "wrack" in the quotation from *The Tempest?* These questions are not likely to set anyone's heart astir, but they are in accord with Eliot's poem because they do not call another world in judgment upon the words. The questions keep strictly to language, and in this respect they follow the rhetoric of the poem. Symbolist poetry yearns for a world governed by the laws of Pure Poetry; internal laws, marking internal liaisons between one word and another, without any reference to nature as a court of appeal. In such a world, time takes the form of prosody. Meaning is not something out there in the world waiting silently to be companioned by the right words. As Blackmur said of a poem by Marianne Moore, "the parts stir each other up (where Keats put stirring things in sequence) and the aura of agitation resulting, profound or light as it may be, is what it is about."[11] In the passage from "The Fire Sermon" no effect is allowed to escape from the words. The images, figures, and rhythms make together a setting that we are not encouraged to leave or transcend. It is permissible to say that the speaker here and throughout the poem is Tiresias, but that is like saying that something is the speech of God—it merely replaces one problem by another. The words of the sermon are not completed by our conceiving for their speaker a personal identity. It is more useful to imagine a possible state of feeling which is secreted in the words. The best way to read the lines is not to ask that each phrase give up its meaning, as if that meaning were then to replace the words; but to ask what quality of force and detonation the phrases share. The particular quality may be found to attach itself to a state of feeling which cannot be given in other terms. Not a seamless narrative, but a set of lyric moments, each isolated for consciousness.

It is customary to say that the explanation for this use of language is to be found in the works of F. H. Bradley and in Eliot's thesis *Knowledge and Experience in the Philosophy of F. H. Bradley.* I quote a few sentences in which Eliot summarizes Bradley's argument (kinship between Eliot's prose and Bradley's has been noted). "It is only in immediate experience that knowledge and its object are one." "We have no right, except in the most provisional way, to speak of *my* experience, since the I is a construction out of experience, an abstraction from it; and the *that's,* the browns and hards and flats, are equally ideal constructions from experience, as ideal as atoms." "The only independent reality is immediate experience or feeling." " 'My' feeling is certainly in a sense mine. But this is because and in so far as I am the feeling." "Experience is non-relational."[12] These sentences refer to Bradley's general philosophical position but more especially to certain passages in his *Essays on Truth and Reality,* including this one: "Now consciousness, to my mind, is not original. What comes first in each of us is rather feeling, a state as yet without either an object or subject. . . . Feeling is immediate experience without distinction or relation in itself. It is a unity, complex but without relations. And there is here no difference between the state and its content, since, in a word, the experienced and the experience are one."[13] In Eliot's version, "feeling is more than either object or subject, since in a way it includes both." Furthermore, as Eliot says: "In describing immediate experience we must use terms which offer a surreptitious suggestion of subject or object. If we say presentation, we think of a subject to which the presentation is present as an object. And if we say feeling, we think of it as the feeling of a subject about an object. . . . It may accordingly be said that the real situation is an experience which can never be wholly defined as an object nor wholly enjoyed as a feeling, but in which any of the observed constituents may take on the one or the other aspect."[14] Perhaps this is enough to suggest what Eliot means when he speaks of the "continuous transition by which feeling becomes object and object becomes feeling." The language of "The Fire Sermon" is surreptitious in the sense that its objectivity is merely ostensible. The rat creeping through the vegetation has only as much to do with animal life as is required to incite a certain feeling in the presumed speaker at that moment. The rat has crept into the words and lost itself there; what transpires in the words is a certain feeling, in this case more subject than object. The meaning of a phrase, a line, a word in "The Fire Sermon" is every impression that attaches itself to those sounds under the pressure of consciousness—an assertion which reminds us that the famous Chapter XIV of Bradley's *Essays on Truth and Reality* is called "What is the real Julius Caesar?" The real "Waste Land" is a sequence of those impressions, incited by the sequence of words: the impressions are different for each reader.

There is nothing unorthodox in this, from the standpoint of a philosophical idealist. It would be possible to quote Susanne Langer or Cassirer just as relevantly as Bradley. It is also orthodox Symbolism, of the kind that Valéry treats in "Analecta, Tel Quel II," where he says that "the self flees all created things, it withdraws from negation to negation: one might give the name 'Universe' to everything in which the self refuses to recognize itself." The self refuses to recognize itself in any part of the objective world, so called, until the world is transformed into subjective terms, every apprehended object become subject. But the self is always willing to recognize itself in language and emblems, because they are human compositions. Thinking of Eliot's poem, one might give the name "language" to that alone in which the self recognizes itself. Recognition may be willing or desperate: willing if we emphasize the luxury of the words, the gypsy phrases and cadences, the impression that a man who passes his entire life among such words is the happiest of men; desperate, if we emphasize the allusions, and Eliot's need of them, the accepted weight of responsibility, those fragments shored against his ruins. The allusions are Eliot's insignia, and they have this further point: they give his sensibility other ground than itself, ground in history, literature, religion, revelation, through the words, the ground of our beseeching.

For while the self flees every created thing and refuses to recognize itself anywhere but in words, it needs something besides itself. Perhaps language is enough. In a chapter on solipsism from his dissertation Eliot writes: "The point of view (or finite center) has for its object one consistent world, and accordingly no finite center can be self-sufficient, for the life of a soul does not consist in the contemplation of one consistent world but in the painful task of unifying (to a greater or less extent) jarring and incompatible ones, and passing, when possible, from two or more discordant viewpoints to a higher which shall somehow include and transmute them."[15] In "The Waste Land" Eliot calls this higher perspective Tiresias: "we are led to the conception of an all-inclusive experience outside of which nothing shall fall," he says in the thesis on Bradley.

A year after the publication of "The Waste Land," Eliot reviewed Joyce's *Ulysses* and proposed a distinction which depends on the idea of greater and lesser perspectives. In this distinction between two methods of fiction, "narrative method" is based on the commonly accepted separation of subject and object. The personal equivalent is the notion of a literary character, cut out from his surroundings and endowed with certain qualities. The medium is words, but most of them are common, and they are placed in accepted arrangements. Books based on these arrangements are called novels, so the novel as a form of art came to an end, according to Eliot, with Flaubert and James. (He later repudiated this obituary, by the way.) The "mythical method," on the other hand, is based on immediate experience, the primacy of feeling, the idea of subject and object melting into each other beyond positivist redemption, and at last transcended in a quasi-divine perspective, Tiresias in "The Waste Land," the Homeric archetype in *Ulysses*. But we should not identify Tiresias with the ultimate form of consciousness. It is necessary to think of language (Valéry's "Saint Langage" in "La Pythie") as issuing from a perspective grander even than Tiresias's, since Tiresias can see the world only as one alienated from it: he does not give or sympathize, he does not participate in the suffering and transformation of "What the Thunder Said." It is necessary for the poem, and for poetry, to go beyond the phase of consciousness which Eliot calls Tiresias. The "going beyond" has no name; it is the action of the poem. Instead of common words in common places there is language, construed now as a great treasury of images and figures and, increasingly in Eliot, identified with the Word of God. Using language in this way, it seems natural to have Ferdinand Prince of Naples, the Phoenician sailor, the one-eyed seller of currants, and all the women in the world becoming Tiresias. For Eliot, as for Bradley, there is no question of a Wordsworthian liaison between man and nature. The only part of Bradley's *Appearance and Reality* that Eliot chose to quote in his notes to "The Waste Land" disengages itself from any such hope. In Chapter XXIII, Bradley says that "we behave as if our internal worlds were the same." But we err:

> Our inner worlds, I may be told, are divided from each other, but the outer world of experience is common to all; and it is by standing on this basis that we are able to communicate. Such a statement would be incorrect. My external sensations are no less private to myself than are my thoughts or my feelings. In either case my experience falls within my own circle, a circle closed on the outside; and, with all its elements alike, every sphere is opaque to the others which surround it. . . . In brief, regarded as an existence which appears in a soul, the whole world for each is peculiar and private to that soul.[16]

Our first impression here is wonder that such a view of the mind's predicament could ever have produced from Bradley's pupil a major poem. But the second impression is better, that for such a poet language is the only possible home: either language or that metalanguage we call silence. But we are in danger of confounding the pupil with his master. Just as Bradley cleared himself of a charge of solipsism by arguing in *Appearance and Reality* that "we can go to foreign selves by a process no worse than the construction which establishes our own self,"[17] so Eliot cleared himself of a charge of philosophy by becoming a poet; that is, by attending to all the affiliations of words, including their old hankering after objects. Against the persuasion of his idealism, there are the deep persuasions of Virgil, Dante, Shakespeare, Dryden; and there is eventually the persuasion of Christian belief in which time is redeemed and the higher dream is made flesh. Perhaps these are the necessary qualifications to make while returning to the poem. Without them, we are in danger of turning the poem into a set of more or less interesting ideas; forgetting that to Eliot, as to Bradley, "a mere idea is but a ruinous abstraction"; forgetting, too, that it was Eliot who praised Henry James for possessing a mind so fine that no idea could violate it.

With the passage from "The Fire Sermon" in front of us again, we see that what came first was not an idea but a feeling, "a state as yet without either an object or subject." The nearest expressive equivalent is rhythm, at this stage not yet resolved in words. In "The Music of Poetry," Eliot reported that in his own experience "a poem, or a passage from a poem, may tend to realize itself first as a particular rhythm before it reaches expression in words, and . . . this rhythm may bring to birth the idea and the image."[18] An account of our passage would be a blunt affair if it did not point to the changes of rhythm as among the chief moments, where the echo of Marvell's "To His Coy Mistress" imposes a new and deeper tone upon the verse; and from there until the line from Verlaine the transitions become more abrupt. Eliot remains true to the original feeling by remaining true to its rhythm. The words, when they are found, maintain a double allegiance: they are required to define the rhythm of the first feeling, and they must also allow for the melting of one experience into another.

The first consequence is that, to a reader skeptical of idealist assumptions, many of these lines appear willfully arch and secretive: they appear to go through the motions of grammar and syntax without committing themselves to these agencies. They are neither one thing nor the other, neither wholly subject nor wholly object: without proposing themselves as paradoxes, they are paradoxical. A further result is that, in verse of this kind, incidents drawn from whatever source cannot have the status they would have in a novel or another poem. In the *Metamorphoses,* Ovid tells of the rape of Philomela by King Tereus of Thrace. Eliot recalls the story in "A Game of Chess." Trico's song in Lyly's *Alexander and Campaspe* has the lines:

Oh, 'tis the ravished nightingale.
Jug, jug, jug, jug, tereu! she cries.

Matthew Arnold's "Philomela" is one story, John Crowe Ransom's is another—the story is diversely told. How it appears in the mind of God, there is no knowing; what is the real Philomela is a hard question. How it appears in the inordinate mind of Tiresias is given in "The Waste Land":

Twit twit twit
jug jug jug jug jug jug
So rudely forc'd.
Tereu. . . .

Here are the twit of the swallow, the Elizabethan nightingale-call and, by curious association, the word for "slut," a fine phrase of justice from Middleton's *Game of Chess,* and lastly the simple vocative "Tereu." Ovid's story is given, indeed, but only the gist of it, the story insofar as it survives transposition into the inclusive consciousness of

Tiresias. In that strange place, one image melts into another; hence Eliot's idiom of melting, transition, becoming, and deliquescence.

It is easy to think of Eliot as he thought of Swinburne: "only a man of genius could dwell so exclusively and consistently among words." In Swinburne, as in Poe, words alone are certain good. But it is well to qualify that report by adding another, from "The Music of Poetry," where Eliot speaks of the poet as occupied with "frontiers of consciousness beyond which words fail, though meanings still exist." In some respects language is omnipotent, in other respects it is feeble. Cioran says that "the indigence of language renders the universe intelligible"—which accords with Nietzsche's claim that there's no point in getting rid of God if we retain Grammar.[19] In his poems, Eliot tries to transcend the limits of language by appeal to St. John of the Cross and to the English mystical writers; in his plays, by invoking miracle, "the way of illumination." Tiresias is the Unidentified Guest until he too is transcended in Celia. The effort of the plays is to allow people to live by a holy language, however limited that language is in other respects. Language, the ancient place of wisdom, is sustained by conscience and consciousness, as in *Four Quartets*. That is why, at last, "the poetry does not matter." The procedures of "The Waste Land," which were enabled by the force of language itself, are transposed into the idiom of characters acting and suffering. Transitions and perspectives, entirely verbal in "The Waste Land," take more public forms in the later poems and plays, the forms of personal action, chances, and choices. The frontier of consciousness is not the place where words fail but where self dies, in faith, making the awful surrender. Bradley is not repudiated, but he is forced to accommodate himself to the Shakespeare of *A Winter's Tale* and *The Tempest:* that is one way of putting it.

It is characteristic of Eliot's language in "The Waste Land" to effect an "absence in reality," and to move words into the resultant vacuum. At first, the words seem to denote things, *sensibilia* beyond the lexicon, but it soon appears that their allegiance to reality is deceptive, they are traitors in that respect. So far as the relation between word and thing is equivocal, so far also is "objective" reality undermined. The only certainty is that an absence in reality has been effected by the words, and now the same words are enforcing themselves as the only presences. Seamus Heaney has pointed to a similar privileging of words in Paul Muldoon's poetry: it is a poetry that "insists on its proper life as words before it concedes the claims of that other life we all live before and after words."[20] In this way the words acquire the kind of aura, or the kind of reverberation, which we feel in proverbs; with this difference: proverbs appeal to our sense of life, an inherited wisdom in our sense of things; Eliot's words appeal to primordial images and rhythms that can be felt, though they cannot well be called in evidence. I cannot explain this use of language except by suggesting that if the common arrangements of words issue from the common sense of time, Eliot's arrangements issue from a quarrel between time and value. I assume that value is a way of breaking the chain of time, one thing after another. Eliot is using words as if their first obligation were neither to things nor to time. Philip Wheelwright has called this kind of imagination "archetypal," the imagination "which sees the particular object in the light of a larger conception or of a higher concern." Nearly everything in Eliot's language arises from the pressure he exerts, upon himself in the first instance and thereafter upon the reader, to register the force not oneself that makes for truth. We are urged beyond the divisions of subject and object to a state compounded of both; beyond the divisions of time and eternity to a point of intersection in which the double obligation is felt; beyond the divisions of speech and silence to the "word within a word," as speechless and eloquent as the Christ child. I am not maintaining that the word "rat" in "The Fire Sermon" has ceased to observe all relation to a rodent, but that the word is a double agent; it accepts the friction between reality and language but it does not give full allegiance to either party. The word points beyond individuality and even beyond species to an indeterminate form of verbal life in which the thing denoted is inseparable from the feelings of which the word itself is the embodiment. On one side stands the world of things; on the other, a rival world of dissociated forms, Platonic cities. Between them stands the individual word, maintaining a secret life.

Eliot's problem is easy to state. He must accept the fact that words are no longer deemed to contain a changeless truth; they are read as signs, pointers, stimuli. But he has to use words when he talks to us, so his formal and linguistic procedures are designed as desperate expedients to drive us out of ourselves and beyond our common selves. We are driven toward the recognition that truth is embodied in the Word of God, the Logos of revelation; that the world of facts and appearances is merely nature in fragments, not the abiding City of God; that beyond every specific act of knowledge there is "that supreme moment of complete knowledge," certified as form, pattern, perfection. The poem does not proceed by juxtaposing one word, one image, against another but by setting against mere words, local and natural, the "higher viewpoint" that shall somehow include and transmute them. Against the heap of broken images, there is every token of revealed order, "the heart of light, the silence." The unreal city is made real as the City of God. Every claim we insist upon is answered by "the awful daring of a moment's surrender." Eliot ascribes to the Word of God, and to that alone, what the entire tradition of Romantic poetry has ascribed to the imagination, the inclusive power that transcends the divisions of subject and object, self and nature, by establishing itself as the unity beyond every division. The spirit killeth, the letter giveth life. Ultimately, and despite the peacemaking efforts of Wordsworth and other poets, the Romantic imagination finds in nature merely a heap of broken images, useful only because they indicate the conditions of fracture which the imagination alone can confront. Eventually, the Romantic imagination gives up the effort to make peace between self and nature, and ends the war by a decision in its own favor. Henceforth, imagination is to be the ground of our beseeching. To Eliot, this resolution is merely the latest form of heresy, the "egotistical sublime" of pride, first of the deadly sins, the vanity of ignorance and egoism which the Eliot of *After Strange Gods* denounced in Lawrence, Hardy, and Yeats. It is the aim of Eliot's poetry to make our delusions uninhabitable. The reason why "the poetry does not matter" is that something else, the love of God and the love of people in the light of that love, is what alone matters. The weight of Eliot's poetry is therefore represented by one line in "The Waste Land": "Shall I at least set my lands in order?" The words can be recited with different emphases: on *I* or *at least* or *my,* but in any version they point beyond themselves to a spiritual perspective which alone makes sense of them and redeems their human limitations. This is the work of "The Waste Land," "Ash-Wednesday," and *Four Quartets:* to establish the Word that is true because it is not our invention, against the reduction of Logos to Lexis that has been effected upon the sole authority of the human will. Or, as the epigraph to *Four Quartets* quotes from Heraclitus: "We should let ourselves be guided by what is common to all; yet, although the Logos is common to all, most men live as if each of them had a private intelligence of his own."[21]

III

I should say something more about the poem in light of Empson's *Using Biography* (1984) and Valerie Eliot's edition of the first volume of Eliot's *Letters* (1988). Empson maintains that the marriage to Vivienne did not go wrong till 1926 or 1927. There are letters in the autumn of 1921 that show Eliot not only devoted to her but dependent on her company. But there was still a lot of unhappiness in the household, from many causes: money troubles, interminable illnesses of husband and wife, bad nerves in both, exhaustion, Vivienne's affair with the goatish Bertrand Russell—even though Eliot may have been party to it in the beginning and in any case was too much of a gentleman to object or to remove the tempter. Eliot was not yet ready to add to the "torment / Of love unsatisfied" the violence of "The greater torment / Of love satisfied." That came with "Ash-Wednesday." But he was moving in a grim direction.

Empson disliked Symbolism so much that he was reluctant to believe that it could result in a good poem, but he admitted with "The Waste Land" in view that Symbolism had "scored a few resounding triumphs, such as this." Still, he wanted to find in the poem the attributes he valued: a good story, characters, themes, and enough motive to keep these going. He thought that Pound's revisions and excisions were designed to reveal a theme till then latent—London, a city that had survived one war but couldn't be expected to survive another, being in the hands of international financiers. Thinking of London led Empson to say that Eliot was imitating Dickens, as the original title—"He Do the Police in Different Voices"—acknowledged. Like a novel by Dickens, "The Waste Land" is a loose assemblage of characters and voices. The bits that Pound cut out were passages in which Eliot failed to get the voices right—he hadn't really listened to Boston roisterers and Cape Cod fishermen. But the poem as it stands is Dickensian, predicated on London and, in the middle of that, the more immediate theme of father and son. Eliot's father was so disgusted by his son's decision to stay in England and marry an Englishwoman that he cut her out of his will. In April 1923 Eliot wrote to John Quinn: "Owing to the terms of my father's will any property coming to me is in trust, and reverts to my family on my death—instead of being left outright, as to my brother and sisters. Thus my wife can get no benefit from my inheritance in the event of my death. My father disapproved of my residence in England."[22] Disapproved of his marrying an Englishwoman, Empson thinks. Eliot married Vivienne Haigh-Wood on June 26, 1915. His father died on January 7, 1919. His mother could have mitigated the provisions of her husband's will, but didn't. In the poem, Eliot's immediacies of rage and resentment are displaced, sent off to seek disguised forms of themselves in the motif of father and son in *The Tempest*. The effect, it seems to me, is to modify the Dickensian emphasis and to turn much of the feeling of the poem toward Shakespearean motifs of late romance and Wagnerian procedures of music-drama: the poem seems not an epitome of *Dombey and Son* but a music-drama that recalls *The Tempest* and *Parsifal*.

One letter seems to endorse my emphasis on Eliot's recourse to higher perspectives, in "The Waste Land," to control such immediacies of rage and disgust. On September 19, 1927, Eliot wrote to Mary Hutchinson, who had sent him a story to read: "The only fault I find . . . is . . . that you had got thoroughly *inside* the feelings, but hadn't quite got out again. I like to feel that a writer is perfectly cool and detached, regarding other peoples' feelings or his own, like a God who has got beyond them; or a person who has dived very deep and comes up holding firmly some hitherto unseen submarine creature. But this sort of cold detachment is so *very* rare—and *stupid* detachment is so much the rule, that it may be only a particular taste."[23] Eliot assumes that Mary Hutchinson will know what he means by stupid detachment. I'm not sure that I do. Maybe it means indifference become habitual, no longer subject to scrutiny when it is called upon. Cold detachment, the right kind—as in De Bosschère's poems—refuses to capitulate to one's feelings, or to anyone else's, but presumably it pays attention to the claim a particular feeling makes, even though the adjudication submits it in the end to the most stringent critical perspective. "Those are pearls that were his eyes."

IV

I am assuming agreement that "The Waste Land" is fundamental to our sense of modern literature. It is the poem we call in evidence when we propose to show how the modern imagination enlarges its role in the play of experience: this is how the imagination makes a virtue of the necessity under which it labors. Eliot's way of dealing with experience, the tension caused by the force with which he invents and transforms it: our sense of these things is crucial to our reading of the poem. But if he is to invent and transform his experience, as well as merely receive it in the form of chances and events, he must intervene in the process of feeling before the feelings engaged are organized by forces beyond his control: he must grasp the impulses of feeling before they have been congealed by the bureaucracy of institutions or organized into the formulae of thoughts and ideas. There is a passage in Valéry's "Propos sur l'Intelligence" in which he refers to the conscientiousness with which a man "oppose l'esprit à la vie." Eliot's way of doing this is by invoking a *vie antérieure,* a net of impulses which can be grasped long before they have been caught in a grid of public codes. There is a sentence in *The Criterion* (XII, p. 471) where Eliot praises the Hemingway of "The Killers" and *A Farewell to Arms* for "telling the truth about his own feelings at the moment when they exist." It is the chief labor of Eliot's early poems to find a language for his feelings at the earliest stage of their emergence: if he can fasten upon them then, he has a good chance of holding on to them. The dramatic monologue is a deflection into other feelings, so that he may understand them sufficiently to control his own. I assume that this is what is going on, rather than any effort to describe something utterly separate from himself, in these unforgettable lines:

> A woman drew her long black hair out tight
> And fiddled whisper music on those strings
> And bats with baby faces in the violet light
> Whistled, and beat their wings
> And crawled head downward down a blackened wall
> And upside down in air were towers
> Tolling reminiscent bells, that kept the hours
> And voices singing out of empty cisterns and exhausted wells.

Vivienne Eliot combing her hair as if she were playing the violin, the bats from *Dracula,* all sorts of images; but if the whole passage sounds like a dream, it is because dreams consist of unofficial impulses active at a stage long before their official reception as thoughts, emotions, ideas. In normal usage language intervenes in the process of feeling too late to do anything more than apply to the aged thing called a thought its official label, so that it may be easily transported from one place to another. At that stage most of the damage to feeling has been done, and the rest is done by assimilating these thoughts to the public structure of attitude and convention which constitutes that "life" to which the poet's spirit can only oppose itself.

If this is true, the next phase of Eliot's art is to draw those early impulses toward their ideal form: this is where the notion of the highest possible perspective comes in, and it is roughly speaking a relation of existence to essence, particle to principle, the City of London seen in the light of its ideal or archetype, the City of God. Sometimes this is done by exerting upon an apparently simple sentence a degree of pressure capable of moving it toward transformation, as "What shall we do tomorrow?" (line 133) leads immediately to "What shall we ever do?" The procedure is an act of faith, and often a desperate contrivance: the City of God cannot be visited merely by one's wishing to go there, it can be approached or conceived only as a meaning absolutely beyond one's self. The energy required is a force of conscience and humility. In Eliot's early poems the approach is made by reaching through sensory events toward a principle deemed to supervise them. Valéry provides a reasonable idiom for this process when he says, of the poets who succeeded the French symbolists, that "they opened again, upon the accidents of being, eyes we had closed in order to make ourselves more akin to its substance."[24] From accident through substance to principle or essence: a direction rather than a formula.

"These fragments I have shored against my ruins": an early version of this line, superseded but never deleted in the manuscript, reads, "These fragments I have spelt into my ruins," implying, as Kenner has argued, "that the protagonist has visited the Sibyl of Virgil, whose oracles, like those of Madame Sosostris, were fragmentary and shuffled by the winds."[25] Or in any case bits of language, unanswered questions, oracular echoes, diction without syntax. "Ruins" is strong enough to carry whatever weight we care to put on it. A passage from Georg Simmel is helpful at this point. He is considering the aesthetic of ruins in landscape and he says that a ruin gives an impression of peace because in it the tension between man and nature has resulted in a consoling image of a purely natural reality. The erection of the building was an act of the human will, while its present state results from the force of nature: the power of decay draws things downward. But nature does not allow the work to fall into the amorphous state of its raw material: it retains the work of man to the extent of assimilating it to a purely natural order. "The ruin is easily assimilated into the surrounding countryside because, unlike a house or a palace, it does not insist upon another order of reality."[26] The implication of a ruin is that everything has returned to a natural unity in which man's work is not humiliated or merely set aside. But the ruin in language presents a different case. These fragments are broken from an original transparent language, the language before Babel destroyed its empire and established the thousand nationalisms of speech. The notion of an original Adamic language is the secular counterpart of an equally original Logos, the "word within a word" of Eliot's "Gerontion," the "word unheard, unspoken" of "Ash-Wednesday." The corresponding unity is the essence approached through the existence of the particular poetic form, the poem we are reading. What lies beyond Tiresias is the form of the poem which contains his name and his experience. The ruin in language differs from the ruin in landscape because nature has taken no part in bringing it about; Babel is the work of human pride alone, a Fall if in some respects a fortunate one. So the impression of peace in a ruin in landscape is replaced, so far as the ruin in language is in question, by an impression of guilt, frustration, and pathos. The only release from this impression is the partial consolation of seeing words aspire beyond their condition to create the very form by which their fragmentary state is judged.

[7]

The Music of "Ash-Wednesday"

When I was teaching at University College, Dublin, my more-than-equal and opposite number at Trinity College was the English poet and critic Donald Davie. He was a few years older than me and better established in the profession. For one thing, he was a graduate of Cambridge University and was set, after several years in Dublin, to go back to Cambridge as a university lecturer in the English faculty and a fellow of Gonville and Caius College. We were not intimate friends. He was morally intimidating, with a touch of the commissar about him. He used the word "infidel" more freely and more deliberately than I supposed it had ever been used since the seventeenth century. But he was never frivolous, he was grave all the way through. We were friends enough to meet in his rooms at Trinity to read poems and talk about poetry, and I felt myself honored by his company. I had no special theory of poetry apart from my sense of the miscellany of poems, brought into some degree of order by the conventions of literary history.

Davie had a few favorite notions. One of them was that there were three useful analogies for the understanding of poetry in general and modern poetry in particular. Poetry was like theater, as in Yeats; like music, as in Eliot; and like sculpture, as in Pound. Davie hadn't much to say about Yeats or the theater, but he was always ready to talk about Eliot and Pound, especially about Pound. He regarded Yeats and Eliot as major writers but also as forces to be suspected, adepts of different versions of Symbolism. Yeats's version kept his poems and plays out of the world by preventing him from looking hard at anything. Like Pound and Robert Lowell, Davie maintained that Yeats couldn't see anything, dazzled as he was by the symbol he held up as a veil or projected as a cloud before it. "Another emblem there!" Eliot's poems and especially *Four Quartets* worked to the limit of possibility and decorum the resources of modern French poetry from Laforgue to Valéry, but this attribute made him a dangerous force in English and American poetry. It was in Valéry's poems that the Paterian aspiration of the arts toward the condition of music was most arduously pursued. Eliot was Valéry with the difference of being an American from St. Louis. Davie thought that French Symbolism was a beguiling distraction for poets who wrote in English. He hoped that *Four Quartets* would bring it to an end. The most serious defect of Symbolism was that it had one preoccupation: itself, its linguistic processes, the charm of fulfilling itself in verbal music. Taking up a phrase of McLuhan's, Davie maintained that Eliot's poems fulfilled "the symbolist procedure of 'juxtaposition without copula,' the setting down of images side by side with a space between them, a space that does not need to be bridged."[1] Whatever merits might be claimed for the procedure, Davie hoped that it would be superseded by a poetry of "urbane and momentous statement," as he said in *Purity of Diction in English Verse,* neo-Augustan rather than neo-Romantic or post-Romantic. Pound was the master to be followed.

Davie took Hugh Kenner as his guide to Pound's poetry. He was convinced by Kenner's *The Poetry of Ezra Pound* and his book on Wyndham Lewis that the proper direction for English and American poetry was Poundian. *The Pound Era* had not yet appeared, but its advocated "line" from Pound through Vorticism to the Objectivism of Zukofsky and Oppen could be anticipated. Sculpture was the analogy to be pursued. But Davie took up a distinction between the main impulses of sculpture. Adrian Stokes's books and Pound's *Gaudier-Brzeska* clarified for him the moral difference between carving and modeling. In modeling, the material to be worked on, indeed the whole world, is deemed endlessly malleable, like clay in one's hands: it has no character, no rights, in itself. But the carver feels that "the form he wants is already present in the marble" and that it is his privilege "to make what is already there reveal itself."[2] Pound was a carver. Poetry under the sign of carving "has to do with a reality which is as fully and undeniably *out there,* as certainly other than us and confronting us, as is the block of marble where it lies in the quarry before the sculptor." Davie urged poets who engaged with the world through its natural and physical forms to think of themselves as exploring "the same reality as the sciences explore, but with different categories and different instruments." When the reality to be engaged was metaphysical, such poets should claim "to be exploring the same reality as religion or ontology." Davie attacked the assumption, which he ascribed to Symbolism, that physical or metaphysical reality *out there* could be turned into "a psychological reality *in here,* inside the artist's head."[3] It is only in Prufrock's mind that fog behaves as a cat behaves or that an evening is like a patient etherized upon a table. Davie didn't agree that the poem is justified to the extent to which it explores the peculiarities of Prufrock's mind. Later, he presented the difference between Eliot and Pound as a difference in their sense of language: "As compared with Pound, Eliot presents himself as pre-eminently a rhetorician, a man who serves language, who waits for language to present him with its revelations; Pound by contrast would master language, instead of serving language he would make it serve—it must serve the shining and sounding world which continually throws up new forms which language must strain itself to register."[4]

I should not give the impression that in the shining and sounding city of Dublin Davie merely kept on reciting the moral superiority of poetry as carving over the immorality of Symbolism, poetry as modeling, and poetry as music. But he held to that position in his poetry and criticism.

In *Articulate Energy* (1955), Davie took up the issue of poetry as music. He believed, with Fenollosa and Pound to sustain him, that the crucial factor in poetry is syntax. Purity of diction is a major consideration, but a difference of syntax is more comprehensive because it indicates the way a poet stands toward the world. Modern poetry assumes, he argued—with Eliot chiefly in mind—"that syntax in poetry is wholly different from syntax as understood by logicians and grammarians."[4] Davie repudiated that assumption and spoke up for logicians and grammarians, but he had to admit—as Empson did—that a few good poems had been achieved under its direction. He conceded that poetry as music is not merely a modern aberration: it is close to what he called "subjective syntax," which pleases "by the fidelity with which it follows the 'form of thought' in the poet's mind." His main examples were Coleridge's "Dejection" and "This Lime-Tree Bower My Prison": "How can a bower of lime-trees be a prison? And even as [Coleridge] begins to show how this can be, he proves that it cannot be, since the imagination cannot be imprisoned; and the poet goes on to acknowledge, at the end of the poem, that the prison is no prison, and the loss no loss. The syntax, continually finding new stores of energy where it has been affirmed that no more is to be found (the sentence, once the main verb has been introduced, seems ready to draw to a close), mimes, acts out in its own developing structure, the development of feeling behind it."[5] Syntax as music is like subjective syntax: it pleases "by the fidelity with which it follows a 'form of thought' through the poet's mind *but without defining that thought"* (Davie's emphasis).

In a chapter of *Articulate Energy*, Davie takes into consideration Susanne Langer's *Philosophy in a New Key*. He was impressed by the book, and by Sir Herbert Read's claims for it. He quoted Langer's judgment that "what music can actually reflect is only the morphology of feeling": hence some sad and some happy conditions "may have a very similar morphology." Langer continues: "Music at its highest, though clearly a symbolic form, is an unconsummated symbol. Articulation is its life, but not assertion; expressiveness, not expression. The actual function of meaning, which calls for permanent contents, is not fulfilled; for the *assignment* of one rather than another possible meaning to each form is never explicitly made."[6] Davie remarks that in poetry it is not so easy as it is in music "to articulate without asserting; to talk without saying what one is talking about": "But, as is well known, this difficulty was circumvented by the use of the objective correlative, the invention of a fable or an "unreal" landscape, or the arrangement of images, not for their own sakes, but to stand as a correlative for the experience that is thus the true subject of a poem in which it is never named. It is true that Mr. Eliot, who put the expression 'objective correlative' into currency, speaks as if the function of the correlative is to define, better than by naming, the experience, the feeling, for which it stands. But in the light of Mrs. Langer's distinction, we have to say that it defines the morphology of the feeling, not its distinctive nature."[7]

It seemed to me that Davie had got both Langer and Eliot wrong. Morphology is the branch of biology that deals with the form and structure of organisms without consideration of their function. Davie misinterprets Langer: he thinks she said that all symphonies are the same. She didn't; she said that a symphony doesn't mime or trace the lineaments of a particular feeling but articulates its structure.

One structure differs from another just as much as one feeling from another: morphology is the level of consideration on which the difference is registered. There is no merit in trying to distinguish the "morphology of the feeling" from its "distinctive nature." Its distinctive nature is recognized in its morphology. For similar reasons, Davie writes as if one of Eliot's poems must be the same as another. But Eliot's theory of the objective correlative doesn't entail this: "The only way of expressing emotion in the form of art is by finding an 'objective correlative'; in other words, a set of objects, a situation, a chain of events which shall be the formula of that *particular* emotion; such that when the external facts, which must terminate in sensory experience, are given, the emotion is immediately evoked."[8] A set of objects, a situation, a chain of events isn't the same as Davie's "fable or an 'unreal' landscape, or the arrangement of images." I take Eliot's "formula of that *particular* emotion" to coincide with Langer's "morphology." I wish I knew more securely what Eliot means by "which must terminate in sensory experience." Presumably he has in mind a reader's experience or an audience's: the chain of events must come home in the form of sensory experience—not merely in the belatedness of discursive or conceptual terms—to anyone who pays attention. In the essay on *Hamlet* and again in the one on Tourneur, Eliot is trying to find a relatively impersonal way of saying that a particular emotion should not be allowed to exceed the situation that provoked it. The idea he arrives at is a triangular one. Instead of trying to express the emotion directly and at once, a poet or dramatist should turn aside from it and imagine "a set of objects, a situation, a chain of events" and so forth: "The cynicism, the loathing and disgust of humanity, expressed consummately in *The Revenger's Tragedy,* are immature in the respect that they exceed the object. Their objective equivalents are characters practising the grossest vices; characters which seem merely to be spectres projected from the poet's inner world of nightmare, some horror beyond words."[9] Not that Tourneur shouldn't have written *The Revenger's Tragedy* as he did. The play is "a document on humanity chiefly because it is a document on one human being, Tourneur; its motive is truly the death motive, for it is the loathing and horror of life itself." Further: "To have realized this motive so well is a triumph; for the hatred of life is an important phase—even, if you like, a mystical experience—in life itself."[10] But the triumph is consistent with Tourneur's immaturity, his failure to submit his feelings to the discipline by which their morphology might be registered. Morphology is the higher perspective in which a feeling, desire, or passion may be understood. Tourneur did not put himself to the ethical labor of understanding his feelings; he sought only to express them. As in a successful dramatic monologue, the feelings are experimental, acts of discovery, rather than self-expression. Davie seemed to me to have misread Eliot.

As an example of syntax as music, Davie chose the first lines of "Gerontion":

> Here I am, an old man in a dry month,
> Being read to by a boy, waiting for rain.
> I was neither at the hot gates
> Nor fought in the warm rain
> Nor knee deep in the salt marsh, heaving a cutlass,
> Bitten by flies, fought.[11]

"In terms of the prose-sense of this passage," Davie says, there is no need for the second "fought":

> The word, coming where it does, has the further effect of acting out through syntax the dwindling and the diminution, the guttering frustration and waste, which is the arc of feeling here being presented. The verb, energetic in meaning, and in the active voice,

is held up by the three phrases ("knee deep in the salt marsh, heaving a cutless, bitten by flies"), and this postponing of the issue builds up a tension which the verb would, in the ordinary way, resolve with all the more vigorous *éclat,* in a powerful reverberation. But this it cannot do, having been negated from the first by that "nor" from which it is now so far removed. Hence it has the effect almost of parody, of a shrill and cracked vehemence.[12]

But if Gerontion is an imagined character, personage, or persona, rather than T. S. Eliot, the syntax of the passage becomes "dramatic" rather than "subjective" and should escape Davie's censure. "Poetic syntax is *dramatic,*" he says, "when its function is to please us by the fidelity with which it follows the 'form of thought' in some mind other than the poet's, which the poet imagines."[13]

The second example of syntax as music that Davie quotes in *Articulate Energy* is the opening passage of "Ash-Wednesday":

Because I do not hope to turn again
Because I do not hope
Because I do not hope to turn
Desiring this man's gift and that man's scope
I no longer strive to strive towards such things
(Why should the agèd eagle stretch its wings?)
Why should I mourn
The vanished power of the usual reign?[14]

Davie hadn't much to say about that passage, except to mark how elaborately the lines are interwoven by end-rhymes and by similarities of grammar and syntax. Syntax works like rhyme to establish a further relation of likeness. For once, Davie wasn't explicit, but he seemed to think that an interweaving as pronounced as this is like music because it keeps all the relations within the passage, it doesn't let any force of reference escape from the lines to a world outside. He disliked any poem that traced the movement of thought in the speaker's mind without further defining the thought. To define a thought, he insisted, you have to show its relation to an intellectual structure as well established as the palpable world in which it appears. He considered syntax as music a devious procedure, as if its adepts were trying to circumvent the authority of statements and concepts. I still recall how his face became grim when he conceded that Eliot was a great poet. The greatness was of a kind that Davie deplored.

Davie's brief comment wasn't much help to me in reading "Ash-Wednesday," and as I was a young man seeking all the help I could get, I looked abroad and found more light in I. A. Richards, F. R. Leavis, and Eliot himself. Kenner's *The Invisible Poet* had not yet been published.

II

Richards regarded "Ash-Wednesday" as "better poetry than even the best sections of 'The Waste Land.' " His reason was that the poem shows "still less 'dread of the unknown depths' " than "The Waste Land" does.[15] He had in mind, and quoted, the passage in *Lord Jim* about the wisdom of submitting oneself to the sea, the destructive element. In *Coleridge on Imagination* he has two pages on "Ash-Wednesday," mainly concerned with the process of reading the poem and avoiding the distraction of settling for a conceptual meaning. He didn't believe that the meaning of a poem was a statement to be formulated at the end or in addition to the experience of reading it. The meaning and the experience are one and the same. Richards urged on the reader a "receptive submission, which will perhaps *be reflected* in conjectures but into which inferences among these conjectures do not enter." His attitude was much the same as Eliot's, in the

preface to his translation of St.-Jean Perse's *Anabase:* there is "a logic
of the imagination as well as a logic of concepts." Any obscurity in
Anabase "is due to the suppression of 'links in the chain,' of explana-
tory and connecting matter, and not to incoherence, or to the love of
cryptogram." Further: "The justification of such abbreviation of
method is that the sequence of images coincides and concentrates
into one intense impression of barbaric civilization. The reader has to
allow the images to fall into his memory successively without questioning the reasonableness of each at the moment; so that, at the end,
a total effect is produced."[16] Not that the sequence in *Anabase* is entirely one of images: it includes exclamations and rhetorical flour-
ishes. "Fais choix d'un grand chapeau dont on séduit le bord. L'oeil
recule d'un siècle aux provinces de l'âme. Par la porte de craie vive
on voit les choses de la plaine: choses vivantes."[17] But the sequence
ought to be received—this is Eliot's point—as if it were a sequence of
images, each of them self-possessed, decisive.

Richards illustrated his way of reading "Ash-Wednesday" by not-
ing the differences between the opening lines of the first and the last
sections of the poem:

> Because I do not hope to turn again
> And
> Although I do not hope to turn again
> in their joint context and their coterminous sub-contexts, will
> come into full being for very few readers without movements of
> exploration and resultant ponderings that I should not care to at-
> tempt to reflect in even the most distant prose translation. And yet
> these very movements—untrackable as they perhaps are, and unin-
> ducible as they almost certainly are by any other words—are the
> very life of the poem. In these searchings for meanings of a certain
> sort its being consists. The poem is a quest, and its virtue is not in

anything said by it, or in the way in which it is said, or in a meaning which is found, or even in what is passed by in the search. For in this poem—to quote two lines from Coleridge's "Constancy to an Ideal Object" which is a meditation on the same theme—as in so much of the later poetry of Mr. Yeats,

> like strangers shelt'ring from a storm,
> Hope and Despair meet in the porch of Death!

And though from their encounter comes

> Strength beyond hope or despair
> Climbing the third stair

there is no account, in other terms than those of poetry, to be given of how it comes.[18]

I found Richards's reference to "Constancy to an Ideal Object" helpful, not because it named a theme the poem shares with "Ash-Wednesday"—Hope and Despair meeting in the porch of Death—but because Coleridge equivocates between saying that the ideal object is identical with the beloved woman and that it is not. In the end, trying to answer the question—is the Ideal Object nothing?—he shifts the terms altogether:

> And art thou nothing? Such thou art, as when
> The woodman winding westward up the glen
> At wintry dawn, where o'er the sheep-track's maze
> The viewless snow-mist weaves a glist'ning haze,
> Sees full before him, gliding without tread,
> An image with a glory round its head;
> The enamoured rustic worships its fair hues,
> Nor knows he makes the shadow, he pursues![19]

Coleridge says much the same as Wordsworth in "Tintern Abbey"—"both what we half-create and what perceive"—but he looks on the gloomy side of it. In "Dejection" he allows for the brighter side—"O lady we receive but what we give." The speaker in "Ash-Wednesday" is not an enamoured rustic, but he rejoices, "having to construct something / Upon which to rejoice." He knows he has to make the shadow he pursues.

Leavis admired "Ash-Wednesday" for different reasons than Richards did. The poet was preoccupied, he said, with the problem of sincerity: "He had to achieve a paradoxical precision-in-vagueness; to persuade the elusive intuition to define itself, without any forcing, among the equivocations of 'the dreamcrossed twilight.' The warning against crude interpretation, against trying to elicit anything in the nature of prose statement, is there in the unexpected absences of punctuation; and in the repetitive effects, which suggest a kind of delicate tentativeness. The poetry itself is an effort at resolving diverse impulses, recognitions, and needs."[20] The ironical function in the self-dramatization of the opening lines I have quoted—"Because I do not hope to turn"—is, Leavis says, "an insurance against the pride of humility; a self-admonition against the subtle treasons, the refinements, of egotism that beset the quest of sincerity in these regions."[21] The characteristic rhythm of "Ash-Wednesday" has "certain qualities of ritual; it produces in a high degree the frame-effect, establishing apart from the world a special order of experience, dedicated to spiritual exercises."[22]

The last emphasis was what I needed. "Ash-Wednesday" is in a sense out of this common world, as if it were written within parentheses or seen under glass, but it refuses merely to dissociate itself from the world. Its main impulse is to commit itself to the reality it contemplates, without disowning the sensuous memories and desires that officially count as obstacles. Eliot must do what he ascribes to Lancelot Andrewes rather than to the somewhat vulgar Donne: "Andrewes's emotion is purely contemplative; it is not personal, it is

wholly evoked by the object of contemplation, to which it is adequate; his emotion is wholly contained in and explained by its object. . . . Donne is a 'personality' in a sense in which Andrewes is
not: his sermons, one feels, are a 'means of self-expression.' He is
constantly finding an object which shall be adequate to his feelings;
Andrewes is wholly absorbed in the object and therefore responds
with the adequate emotion. Andrewes has the *goût pour la vie spiri-
tuelle,* which is not native to Donne."[23]

The question of rhythm, to which Leavis referred, called for further thought: it raised the issue of distance. In Eliot's poems the
experiences invoked are presented not immediately or directly but as
if in a later light, a higher perspective, or subject to a final cause. He
must bear in mind that they might have to be renounced in favor of
larger, more spiritually exacting considerations. The pleasure of the
words persists only because it can't in good faith be denied. The
solution is to present movements of desire as if they were embodied
in a ballet or transformed into a piece of music. In "The Music of
Poetry" Eliot says, "I believe that the properties in which music
concerns the poet most nearly, are the sense of rhythm and the sense
of structure. The use of recurrent themes is as natural to poetry as to
music. There are possibilities for verse which bear some analogy to
the development of a theme by different groups of instruments; there
are possibilities of transitions in a poem comparable to the different
movements of a symphony or a quartet; there are possibilities of
contrapuntal arrangement of subject-matter. It is in the concert
room, rather than in the opera house, that the germ of a poem may be
quickened. More than this I cannot say."[24] But the music is not the
kind that waits to be fulfilled, as a libretto waits on the composer.
Eliot distinguished two kinds of "music" in verse: "One is that of the
lyrics of Shakespeare or Campion, which *demand* the kindred music of

the lute or other instrument; a few songs of Shelley's, such as 'Music, when soft voices die,' and many songs of Burns and Heine make the same demand. . . . Donne's is the second kind of musical verse: the verse which suggests music, but which, so to speak, contains in itself all its possible music; for if set to music, the play of ideas could not be followed. His poems are poems to be read aloud, *not* sung."[25] So also with "Ash-Wednesday," which contains in itself all its possible music and would not gain by receiving the attention of a composer.

III

"Ash-Wednesday" was published in London on April 24, 1930, and in the United States the following September 26. Three of its six sections had already been published as separate poems with titles pointing to Dante and Cavalcanti. The first section was published in spring 1928 as "Perch 'io Non Spero," the first words of a *ballata* by Cavalcanti: the second appeared in December 1927 as "Salutation," probably a reference to the *Vita Nuova* iii, where the poet is greeted by the Lady "with a salutation of such virtue that I thought then to see the world of blessedness." The third section was published in autumn 1929 as "Som de L'escalina," the words addressed to Dante as he climbs the third part of the stairway on the Mount of Purgatory, at the top of which is the Garden of Eden. Then Eliot evidently sensed, as he did after the publication of "Burnt Norton," that musical analogies would make it possible for him to take the three sections as movements of a poem of larger range by adding three further cognate sections. He sent Leonard Woolf a typescript of the poem which at that point had five sections, each with a title from Dante or Cavalcanti.[26]

Ash Wednesday, the first day of Lent in the Christian calendar, marks a period of prayer, fasting, and penance—"dust thou art and

unto dust shalt thou return"—that ends with Good Friday, Holy Sat-
urday, and Easter Sunday. The Lenten weeks are a period of atone-
ment, mindful of the forty days and nights that Christ spent in the
desert. It is also the period during which, as I recall from my early
years in Warrenpoint and Dublin, we Roman Catholics are under
obligation to make a good Confession—that adjective having on the
lips of the Christian Brothers nearly as much emphasis as the sacramental noun—in preparation for the taking of Holy Communion:
"Bless me, Father."

There is no point in trying to name the germ, the embryo, from
which "Ash-Wednesday" or any of its constituent poems emerged.
Eliot went out of his way to articulate the rhythm without asserting
anything. The best he could hope for might be, in words from "Little
Gidding," to arrive where he started "and know the place for the first
time." The first impulse, the rhythm or germ, is his private business
and must remain so. But I'll risk the indelicacy of saying this. Suppose
a man, recently converted to Christianity, wished on Ash Wednesday
to join with his fellow Christians in the ceremonies of Lent. Suppose,
too, that he felt a scrupulous hesitation, however vague or diffused:
there is the fear of duplicity, of false humility, of appearing to deny the
world in ways he can't bring himself to. He might find himself separating body and soul to a degree merely officious. I assume that when
Eliot spoke of the rhythm or the germ he meant what F. H. Bradley
meant by "feeling," the first inner stir, which is felt long before it has
reached any of the stages we call an emotion or an idea. From the
moment of "firstness" it begins to nudge itself toward articulation,
however rudimentary. In Eliot's case, a few arbitrary words, long
before the orders of grammar or syntax came into play, seem to have
encouraged development. The ethical correlative of this stirring, I
imagine, is the possibility of achieving difficult sincerity, so that the

soul may take part in the rituals and sacraments of the Christian community in good faith.

Appropriately, then, Eliot's poem resorts to three fields of diction: (1) religious texts, the Old and New Testaments, rituals of Catholic devotion, sermons of Lancelot Andrewes, the litany of the Blessed Virgin, the "Hail Mary," and especially the Reproaches ("Improperia") of Good Friday—"Ash-Wednesday" is in communion with Herbert's "The Sacrifice" and with Pascal ("Teach us to sit still."); (2) texts from European literature, especially Dante, Cavalcanti, and Shakespeare; and (3) the common worldly language of reference and appreciation, but inclined toward generalization and away from specification or singularity—"the vanished power of the usual reign." The speaker is free to resort to any of these three for critique, irony, or acknowledgment.

The poem is a dramatic monologue. Eliot's implied speaker is a figure placed between being and absence, "between dying and birth," more than a wraith but less than a person, a voice to which we are discouraged from attaching further bodily attributes. We can't even be sure that he's old, despite "Why should the agèd eagle stretch his wings?" The voice may be entirely textual, an emanation from the English language in the Christian and Latin phase of its history. As in an examination of conscience, the speaker is not working toward a spiritual conclusion: ideally, there is no end to such an analysis, least of all the felicity of having reached a self-edifying conclusion. But the examination differs in this respect from the one prescribed by the Christian Church for its members: to achieve difficult sincerity, the speaker can't be content to divide himself into body and soul and deny the body's appeal. He must act justly toward the world, body, desire, and time; not only toward God, the Church, spirit, soul, and eternity. He is in the confessional, speaking to a priest in darkness:

> Wavering between the profit and the loss
> In this brief transit where the dreams cross
> The dreamcrossed twilight between birth and dying
> (Bless me father) though I do not wish to wish these things
> From the wide window towards the granite shore
> The white sails still fly seaward, seaward flying
> Unbroken wings

According to Northrop Frye, the dreams are "the dreams of waking consciousness, memory, and dream proper, all of them animated by desire, all of them having no end but death."[27] Well, yes, but in the dark of the confessional the speaker must tell as much truth as he knows and can bring himself to say, including the secular truth of pleasure and memory. The clause—"though I do not wish to wish these things"—indicates that the things must be irresistible if they survive the discouragement of the repeated verbs: it is far more difficult to rid oneself of those never-to-be-forgotten pleasures than the gift and scope disavowed in the first Section by another doubled verb—"I no longer strive to strive towards such things." And so it should be, else the spiritual voiding achieved in the Confessional is spurious. It is the compelling quality of the sensory experiences, forcing themselves upon the penitent's examination of conscience and being acknowledged there, that makes "Ash-Wednesday" a telling as well as a confessing poem. The poem ends, as it should, with the prayer: "And let my cry come unto Thee." But in the meantime there are the cries of other occasions, as in "The white sails still fly seaward, seaward flying." Davie might find this last phrase unnecessary, and it would be if semantics were king, but here the perception turning back upon itself becomes a caress of acknowledgment and exhilaration, with energy propelled from "towards" in the previous line: "From the wide window towards the granite shore." A similar gesture in the third poem gives us "Blown hair is sweet, brown hair over the mouth blown," and in the fourth poem "White light folded, sheathed about her, folded." The certitude of the cadence in these lines is an acknowledgment of values that the penitent is not obliged to renounce, unless renunciation must be so drastic as to include life itself.

The dictions I have isolated work, in the poem, to achieve a critical perspective beyond any one of them, just as a symphony or a string quartet as an achieved form is beyond the workings of the individual instruments it accommodates. The perspective can hardly be called anything but Language, a force of expressiveness prior to any particular expression it allows. Reading "Ash-Wednesday," we need to have such an abstraction in mind, if only to account for the distinctive style that exerts critical pressure upon the intimations of worldly gratification in the passages I have quoted. It is the style that, more than any other factor, makes it possible to think of "Ash-Wednesday" as the redemption of "The Waste Land" and "The Hollow Men." How to describe it? It is as if the first two dictions—the liturgical and the literary—were combined in one, and in that guise stood aside from the worldly pleasures, not to shame them but to submit them to more exacting discriminations. The style I refer to is judicial, hieratic, responsive to the sundry of the world but free of its blandishments:

> But the fountain sprang up and the bird sang down
> Redeem the time, redeem the dream
> The token of the word unheard, unspoken
>
> Till the wind shake a thousand whispers from the yew
>
> And after this our exile[28]

The tone of this passage corresponds to absolution. If the poem is an examination of conscience leading to a good Confession, absolution can take the form only of a distinctively poised presence within language itself.

IV

I may be able to clarify this by quoting a passage from a poem I've mentioned, Valéry's "La Pythie," and a comment on it by Elizabeth Sewell:

> Honneur des hommes, Saint LANGAGE,
> Discours prophétique et paré,
> Belles chaînes en qui s'engage
> Le dieu dans la chair égaré,
> Illumination, largesse!
> Voici parler une Sagesse
> Et sonner cette auguste Voix
> Qui se connâit quand elle sonne
> N'être plus la voix de personne
> Tant que des ondes et des bois![29]

We are to imagine Language, an abstraction to begin with, become a god in the flesh. Sewell translates the lines into prose:

> Honour of men, sainted LANGUAGE, discourse prophetic and adorned, fair chains in which the god lost in the flesh is content to be taken, illuminations, bounty! There speaks a Wisdom, here sounds that august voice which, when it sounds, knows itself to be not more the voice of a person than that of the waters and the woods.[30]

In her commentary, Sewell says:

> At first sight it seems almost an irrelevance, but when one looks into it, it is clearly the only answer Valéry could give—though not

perhaps the only one that could be given. Words are the mind's one defence against possession by thought or dreams; even Jacob kept trying to find out the name of the angel he wrestled with. Words made into poetry, the prophetic ornamented discourse, carefully chained lest too much freedom should let in the powers of darkness—these will effect such resolution as can be achieved between the logical and the irrational functions of the mind. . . . But apart from this, see how curiously this verse runs: there is the word, sanctified, a god in the flesh, the true light and glory, coming into the world—it is impossible to set it down like that and not be instantly reminded of the opening of St. John's Gospel. . . . This time it is "Au commencement était le verbe," in the beginning was the word, and it is Valéry quoting it and saying "But the word is nothing else than one of the most precise names for that which I have called mind" (esprit). Mind and word are almost synonymous in a great many uses.[31]

Words and mind, synonymous: it is a bias congenial not only to Valéry but to Eliot. I think Eliot allowed words a slight degree of priority and therefore of privilege before assenting to a relation amounting on the happiest occasions to identity. Lost in the flesh, he is content to be taken in the chains of language; or if not content—since he often complains that the words are not right or not sufficient—he can't think of any other chains in which to be held. His poems let the ordinary world in only because, language being discursive, it can't be kept out. Leavis's phrasing—"establishing apart from the world a special order of experience, dedicated to spiritual exercises"— applies to nearly all of Eliot's poems, not only to "Ash-Wednesday." This prejudice of Eliot's sensibility did not satisfy the Poundian Davie: he wanted to think of the self in anyone as a distinct configuration of energies, not entirely verbal; then of language as an instrument, a means, and in that respect as a gift of God; and likewise of the world, external, palpable, sounding and shining.

V

I'll quote the opening of the second poem:

> Lady, three white leopards sat under a juniper tree
> In the cool of the day, having fed to satiety
> On my legs my heart my liver and that which had been contained
> In the hollow round of my skull. And God said
> Shall these bones live? shall these
> Bones live? And that which had been contained
> In the bones (which were already dry) said chirping:
> Because of the goodness of this Lady
> And because of her loveliness, and because
> She honours the Virgin in meditation,
> We shine with brightness.[32]

Exegesis is not required, though it may be supplied by reference to the *Purgatorio,* Grimm's fairy tales "The Juniper" and "The Singing Bone," the Book of Ezekiel, and other sources. These allusions have force—to cite Blackmur—as "a constant reminder of the presence of the barbaric, of other and partial creations within our own creation."[33] But we may have the reminder without the sources. Taken as it stands, the passage is like a tapestry of strangely imperturbable presences. Kenner describes it as "dreamily static like an invention of the Douanier Rousseau's."[34] The lines have patience enough for local precisions—"the bones (which were already dry)"—but they don't find further singularities necessary. Two lines have between them "because" three times, rehearsing a motif from the opening poem: "Because I do not hope to turn." The verbs stand remote from immediacy: "dissembled," "proffer," "recovers," "withdrawn." It is poetry as music in Davie's sense, because it pleases by the fidelity with which it follows a "form of thought" through the speaker's mind but without defining that thought. What we meet is a mind saying things, the saying and the thinking being identical: it is a mind thinking rather than thoughts being uttered. The poetry is also poetry as music in Langer's sense, because the assignment of one rather than another possible meaning to each constituent is not explicitly made. Opacity is not in question; we move without hesitation or distress from one indeterminacy to the next, not stopping to ask what precisely the posterity of the desert is or the fruit of the gourd. But the passage is not mellifluous, nor does it make undue concessions to the Christian readers it may be supposed mainly to address. Anglican *einfühlung* is not appealed to. The propriety of the passage is in the cadence, the distinctive movement of a mind conscious of itself and conscious, too, of its obligation to the Lady, the Beatrice figure, and of the Virgin to be approached indirectly through the Lady who honors her in meditation.

VI

Not surprisingly, the attribute of Eliot's work that Davie regarded as most insidious was its susceptibility to incantation and the "auditory imagination." We avoided quarreling about it only because I couldn't think of any arguments that would persuade him. He was exasperated by this part of the ninth chorus from *The Rock:*

Out of the sea of sound the life of music,
Out of the slimy mud of words, out of the sleet and hail of verbal
    imprecisions,

> Approximate thoughts and feelings, words that have taken the
>   place of thoughts and feelings,
> There spring the perfect order of speech, and the beauty of
>   incantation.[35]

Davie thought it a scandal that lines recognizing the evil of verbal
imprecisions and approximations should end by recommending the
beauty of incantation. He hated talk of verbal magic or Pure Poetry.
So he was appalled to find Eliot appearing to take Poe's poetry seriously and letting it away with a cult of pure sound.

On the question of the auditory imagination, I never tried to clarify my position with Davie. Many of the poems I most cared for were
products of that imagination, and were intimate with verbal magic,
the caress of syllables, the echoes and recesses of words. Now that it's
too late, I'll try to put together a few considerations that might have
modified his impatience. I could have quoted this passage from Eliot's
"Note sur Mallarmé et Poe":

> Chez Poe et Mallarmé la philosophie est en partie remplacée par
> un élément d'*incantation*. Dans "Ulalume" par exemple, et dans
> "Un Coup de Dés," cette incantation, qui insiste sur la puissance
> primitive du Mot (Fatum), est manifeste. En ce sens le vers de
> Mallarmé, qui s'applique si bien à lui-même, constitue une bril-
> lante critique de Poe: *donner un sens plus pur aux mots de la tribu.*
> L'effort pour restituer la puissance du Mot, qui inspire la syntaxe
> de l'un et de l'autre et leur fait écarter le sonore pur ou le pur
> mélodieux (qu'ils pourraient, tous les deux, s'ils le voulaient, si
> bien exploiter), cet effort, qui empêche le lecteur *d'avaler d'un
> coup* leur phrase ou leur vers, est une des qualités qui rapprochent
> le mieux les deux poètes. Il y a aussi la fermeté de leur pas
> lorsqu'ils passent du monde tangible au monde des fantômes.[36]

But I'm not sure that Davie would have been open to persuasion on the primitive power of the Word, even with the addition of the parenthetical Fatum. Eliot evidently had in mind the Word in an entirely secular sense, not the Word of God as it was to be invoked three years later in "Ash-Wednesday." What else can that be but verbal magic, the resources of charms and runes? The firmness of step with which Poe and Mallarmé moved from the tangible world to the world of phantoms is a strange claim, unless Eliot has in view the abeyance of will, a poet's trust—short of confidence or certitude—in the power of language rather than the power of the self. Or a poet's conviction that language is the most reliable source of authority, because the most impersonal. When he became an Anglican, Eliot construed the Word in its religious sense, and resorted to it as prayer, ritual and liturgical observance, all the more vital for its traditional and sacramental repetition. But he did not abandon his sense of the power of the Word even in its secular manifestations. Presumably he felt no contradiction between the Word in both its secular and its religious senses.

VII

I should have discussed "Ash-Wednesday" with another friend I greatly admired and admire, Frank Kermode, but I was distracted by his commentary on Yeats in *Romantic Image*. It seemed to me that his description of the dancer in Yeats's plays and poems was too narrowly symbolist, predicated entirely on Jane Avril and Loie Fuller. In the dance-plays, I wanted to think of Martha Graham and to acknowledge the earthiness of Yeats's dancer rather than the ethereality, the Liberty silks and chiffons. But I should have paid more attention to the last pages of *Romantic Image,* where Kermode says that he could have put Eliot rather than Yeats at the center of the book—

and some points might have been more forcibly made by a discussion of the disposition of symbols in a work like "Ash-Wednesday": if the whole work is an image, how is it, to paraphrase Mrs. Langer, "articulated"? But Eliot's relationship with discourse is less easy than that of Yeats. The problem is the same, and it is magnificently solved: it is the problem of giving symbolic value to the "sense," of identifying dancer and dance. But "Ash-Wednesday" is, so to say, verbless, making no propositions and openly defying the intellect (though, not being illiterate, we all try to explicate what is by definition inexplicable). It is an arrangement of images, or an articulated image, requiring to be looked at "spatially." At the linguistic level Mr. Eliot has that precision of strange outline that all Symbolists require; nothing is more memorable in his verse than the immediate sense of exactness communicated, the impression of great resources of language delicately employed, and infinite flexibility of rhythm. And all this conveys the vitality of the Image, the movement in stillness and the life in death, without Yeats's concessions to the reader less privileged. Mallarmé would doubtless have been better pleased.[37]

This is finely stated, but Kermode's attempt to associate "Ash-Wednesday" with "the Image" should be resisted. It is true that the poem is, "so to say, verbless," and that it postpones main verbs by brooding on conjunctions, prepositions, and participles—"because" and "although," "between," "if," "against," "about," "bearing," "restoring," "wavering," "flying," and more. But it is not true that the poem is one image, or that the Lady is yet another version of Kermode's romantic Image, sister to Keats's Moneta, "bright-blanch'd / By an immortal sickness which kills not." The origins of the Romantic Image are in Pater's Mona Lisa, *Marius the Epicurean,* and "Emerald Uthwart," Symons's "Ballet, Pantomime and Poetic

Drama," Rossetti's Lilith, and the Salomes of Maeterlinck, Flaubert, Moreau, Wilde, and Yeats. But the Lady in "Ash-Wednesday," withdrawn to contemplation as she is, is not, like Rossetti's Lilith, "subtly of herself contemplative." She "honours the Virgin in meditation." It would be vulgar to say of her, as Kermode justly says of Lilith, that "it is the Image, unimpassioned, wise in its whole body, that attracts unbounded passion."[38] Between the Lady and the Virgin, and surrounding them, there are Christianity, the Church, the sacraments, and the laity, faithful and sinful: we are not merely observing "the Image," occult, self-possessed, "some Herodiade," as Yeats wrote in one of his symbolist moments, "dancing seemingly alone in her narrow moving luminous circle."[39]

[8]

"Marina"

Marina" is one of Eliot's most incandescent poems and one of his most elusive. We can't readily account for its power or say how the words are brought together. Kenner's comments on it fairly state the problem:

> Some parts of "Marina" can be treated as sentences and some parts cannot; nor can "Marina" as a whole be treated as though it were a long statement, even a statement of which parts are missing. Its organization is not syntactic at all. One probably wants to call it "musical," based on associations and recurrences, among them the Shakespearean associations aroused by the title. It is as far as Eliot ever went in that particular direction, but the direction is implicit in most of his work, and confirmed as well by work of Valéry's: the poem faced toward a domain of waking dream, so certain of its diction that we concede it a coherence it need not find means of specifying. It has no paraphrasable structure at all, and yet seems to affirm its elusive substance as authoritatively as Mozart.[1]

I'll quote the poem later and take it slowly.

A poem that takes as its title the name of a character in Shakespeare's *Pericles* and begins with an unattributed epigraph in Seneca's Latin—"Quis hic locus, quae regio, quae mundi plaga?"—is apparently not for the uninstructed or for that illiterate reader whom Eliot sometimes hoped to address. It is for initiates. This is not to say that "Marina" would be lost on an illiterate reader. Such a person might enjoy an experience beyond the reach of literates or aslant from it. But it is vain to imagine that any of us could erase what we know— however little we know—for the sake of becoming enablingly unlettered. I have loved the poem for many literate years.

"The theme is paternity; with a criss-cross between the text and the quotation," Eliot told E. McKnight Kauffer in July 1930.[2] Kauffer provided the illustration for "Marina" when it was first published, so presumably he wanted Eliot to be more explicit than he normally was about his work. In a postscript to a letter of May 9, 1930, to Sir Michael Sadler, on the occasion of presenting the draft of "Marina" to the Bodleian Library, Eliot developed the reference: "I intend a criss-cross between Pericles finding alive, and Hercules finding dead—the two extremes of the recognition scene—but I thought that if I labelled the quotation it might lead readers astray rather than direct them. It is only an accident that I know Seneca better than I know Euripides."[3] The epigraph is a line from *Hercules Furens*. Driven made by Juno, Hercules kills his wife and children. He falls into a swoon and when he begins to come to his senses he looks about in bewilderment and says, "Quis hic locus, quae regio, quae mundi plaga?"

We deduce from the title and other internal evidence that the implied speaker is Pericles and that the poem corresponds to the great recognition scene, Act 5, Scene 1, in which Marina is presented to him. Pericles can't trust his eyes and must convince himself that she is indeed his daughter, born at sea, long lost, and given up as having been murdered by those in whose charge she had been left. He has not seen her for many years; she is now a young woman. "But are you flesh and blood?" he asks her, and "Have you a working pulse?" A few moments later, with drowning and restoration still in mind, he says to Helicanus:

> O Helicanus, strike me, honour'd sir;
> Give me a gash, put me to present pain;
> Lest this great sea of joys rushing upon me
> O'erbear the shores of my mortality,
> And drown me with their sweetness . . .

Hearing or reading these questions, we recall the most indelible recognition scene in Shakespeare, Act 4, Scene 7 of *King Lear,* when Cordelia says to her distracted father, "Sir, do you know me?" and Lear answers, "You are a spirit, I know: when did you die?" In both cases the father undoubtingly perceives a spirit but he has to persuade himself—or be persuaded—that the spirit is also flesh, blood, and working pulse, an "embodiment without argument," as Charles Tomlinson writes in one of the poems of *The Return.* Eliot admired the recognition scene of *Pericles* and described it as featuring "the speech of creatures who are more than human, or rather, seen in a light more than that of day."[4]

The second thought—"or rather"—doesn't erase the first one. In "Marina," as in Shakespeare's last plays, we hardly know how to describe the personages even though they come to us with names and histories. If we begin with them as persons, we have to acknowledge the sense in which they are "more than human." Prospero is a person, a sequestered prince, alive in the time and place he has left, just as much as in the island on which he lives. But he is more than a person in the powers he commands, his relation to the natural world, Ariel and the other spirits. For the past two thousand years, Prospero and his like have been versions of Christ, even when they resemble Christ in no other respect than their being at once human and more than hu-

man. That is one way of putting it, if we start with Prospero and Pericles as men. But it is also possible to start with them as spirits, lesser
gods, and see them now as incarnate. The analogy with Christ still
holds. God becomes man, Word becomes flesh. In the first version we
start with body, time, and place, and we see these suffused with radiance. We hardly know what we make of the radiance, it is as miracu-
lous as Christ's changing water into wine. We see history become
myth. In the second version we start with myth, power, and miracle,
and we wait for it to become personal, historical, bodily. "What men
or gods are these?" Keats's witness to the figures on the Grecian urn
asks. It would make a difference if he said "What gods or men are
these?"

Eliot adopted the second version and waited for myth to become
personal and historical. He was guided in this direction by G. Wilson
Knight's "Myth and Miracle" (1929) and *The Wheel of Fire* (1930).
Eliot admired the several essays and books in which Knight, interpreting Shakespeare's last plays, elucidated what Eliot called "the pattern
below the level of 'plot' and 'character.' "[5] The greatest poetry, like
the greatest prose, has a quality of doubleness: "The poet is talking to
you on two planes at once."[6] Eliot often recurred to this doubleness. In
one of the Clark lectures he adverts to it as a quality of Chapman's
plays:

> Here and there the actors in his drama appear as if following an-
> other train of thought, listening to other voices, feeling with other
> senses; and acting out another scene than that visible upon the
> stage. . . . In *The Revenge of Bussy D'Ambois,* for example, there
> runs the curious theme of reconciliation, quite inconsistent with
> the motives and intentions of the personages, but never ludicrous,
> because it seems to belong to another plane of reality from which
> these persons are exiles. Even in the splendid final outburst of the
> dying hero of the previous play—

> Fly, where the Evening from th'Iberean vales,
> Takes on her swarthy shoulders *Heccate*
> Crown'd with a Grove of Oakes: flie where men feele
> The burning axletree: and those that suffer
> Beneath the chariot of the Snowy Beare:
> And tell them all that *D'Ambois* now is hasting
> To the eternall dwellers . . .

—it seems as if he, or Chapman through him, is conversing with an immaterial audience.[7]

Eliot's several references to this double vision in Chapman and Dostoevsky alert us to a similar emphasis in "Marina." We may approach it as a nuance of genre. "Marina," like *Pericles,* is a romance. Following Hawthorne's account of romance but exceeding it in subtlety, Henry James wrote in the preface to *The American:* "The only *general* attribute of projected romance that I can see, the only one that fits all its cases, is the fact of the kind of experience with which it deals—experience liberated, so to speak; experience disengaged, disembroiled, disencumbered, exempt from the conditions that we usually know to attach to it and, if we wish so to put the matter, drag upon it, and operating in a medium which relieves it, in a particular interest, of the inconvenience of a *related,* a measurable state, a state subject to all our vulgar communities."[8] "The real," James says, "represents to my perception the things we cannot possibly *not* know, sooner or later, in one way or another." The romantic stands "for the things that, with all the facilities in the world, all the wealth and all the courage and all the wit and all the adventure, we never *can* directly know; the things that can reach us only through the beautiful circuit and subterfuge of our thought and our desire."[9]

But we still have to say how, in "Marina," exemption from the inconvenience of conditions is achieved, and the difference such exemptions make. Generically, "Marina" is a romance, and like *Pericles* it reaches its supreme articulation as a recognition scene. In his essay on John Ford, Eliot says: "In Shakespeare's plays, this is primarily the recognition of a long-lost daughter, secondarily of a wife; and we can hardly read the later plays attentively without admitting that the father-and-daughter theme was one of very deep symbolic value to him in his last productive years: Perdita, Marina and Miranda share some beauty of which his earlier heroines do not possess the secret."[10] Formally, "Marina" is a dramatic monologue, but the relation between Eliot's speaker and his context is not, as it mostly is in dramatic monologues, circumstantial and contingent. In Browning, Fra Lippo Lippi lives contiguously to the "fig-skins, melon parings, rinds and shucks" to which he refers: he coincides with his conditions and inserts himself strenuously among them. We find him where we find them, in their vulgar communities. But in "Marina" we are aware of seeing the speaker's life in a light more or other than that of day, and we wonder where the light comes from. It may be directed upon the speaker from another perspective than his. The word "grace" implies a gift, even if it is not thought of as divine, a supernatural gift bestowed by God upon the soul for its salvation. Or the light may be the speaker's own, a feature of his conviction that the meaning of his life must be sought elsewhere than in its circumstances. Either way, it is characteristic of Eliot's early poems that the speakers, the personae, are related to their conditions but do not coincide with them. In some degree they stand apart from their circumstances, and it is the main purpose of Eliot's language to make them hover between their existence and an essence the poet seems to want for them. Eliot is not a novelist, or inclined to a realist disposition: there is always a shadow surrounding his figures that holds them apart or adrift from their circumstances. We never see them as individuals. We intuit them rather as presences indistinguishable from their words, figures hovering in the circuit and subterfuge of their thoughts, fears, and desires. In "Marina," Pericles's mind is in that respect abstract, but not abstracted. Wallace Stevens says of his "Notes Towards a Supreme Fiction" that the fictive abstract does not exist but that it is "as immanent in the mind of the poet as the idea of God is immanent in the mind of the theologian."[11] But there is no reason to think of abstraction as a sign of the speaker's disgust with the ordinary world, although that is what we are often told. Worringer claims that the impulse to abstraction arises from a "great inner unrest inspired in man by the phenomena of the outside world," and that in this unrest "life as such is felt to be a disturbance of the aesthetic enjoyment."[12] But it could be argued just as persuasively that the impulse arises from a conviction that the ordinary world, rich as it is in every other respect, cannot provide a valid perspective on itself and its processes. To achieve such a perspective the speaker must stand aside from his ordinary life and try to see it in another light than that of day. The capacity of abstraction is such a light, and Stevens makes a large humanist claim for it when he refers to "an abstraction blooded, as a man by thought."[13] Eliot's speaker tries to see his life not as he lives it moment by moment but as he conscientiously examines it. The determination to examine it is what Leavis ascribed to the Eliot of "Ash-Wednesday" and other poems in its vicinity, "a searching of experience, a spiritual discipline, a technique for sincerity—for giving 'sincerity' a meaning." The mark of such an effort is Eliot's "discipline of continence" in approaching familiar terms and concepts.[14]

II

The epigraph from Seneca reads, in the Elizabethan translation that Eliot liked well enough to write about it: "What place is this? what region? or of the world what coast?"[15] But the translation makes the line more interrogative than it is in Latin, where without a verb it has rather the force of an exclamation. It becomes a question only in the next line, "Ubi sum?" In "Marina" the two lines from Seneca become one longer sequence: it retains an echo or an aura of exclamation even when it becomes a question with the verb "return."

What seas what shores what grey rocks and what islands
What water lapping the bow
And scent of pine and the woodthrush singing through the fog
What images return
O my daughter.[16]

These words "suffice to compel the recognition they precede," as Eliot writes in "Little Gidding" of other formidable words. They could be read as a question to which Marina might be supposed willing to give an answer; but not necessarily. Or they might be spoken in a tone of wonder, hardly distinguishable from rapture, upon which no answer should intrude. The rhymes of syntax—"What seas . . . What water . . . What images"—hold in place the middle line, which is different in character. "And scent of pine and the woodthrush singing through the fog" extends the note of rapture not into a phalanx of particulars that might stay in one's mind when the line has been displaced by the next one, but into sensory events that remain, in the most intimate and internal respects, events of language. Relations among the words, as so often in Eliot, take precedence over the references the words also make. It is as if the words began as phonemes and went on to assent to the experience of acquiring meaning and reference. Marking the stretch of alliteration from "scent" to "singing," and the assonance of "pine" and both syllables of "singing," we register the consanguinities of sound that also make the line express the sound of sense.

In the next lines the old, dead life from which the new, hoped-for

life is to be differentiated is ascribed to Pericles's former selves—
"Those" who have lived the living death of four of the deadly sins
must be manifestations of himself according to different emphases of
interrogation and rebuke. They are not, I think, other people. Pericles must be seen walking within the gloom of his own shadow and
calling it Death. Otherwise he might justly be told to mind his own
business and attend with due humility to the state of his soul. The
lines, in their studied formality, are a ritual, an undoctrinal correlative to the Christian sacrament of penance:

> Those who sharpen the tooth of the dog, meaning
> Death
> Those who glitter with the glory of the humming-bird, meaning
> Death
> Those who sit in the sty of contentment, meaning
> Death
> Those who suffer the ecstasy of the animals, meaning
> Death
>
> Are become unsubstantial, reduced by a wind,
> A breath of pine, and the woodsong fog
> By this grace dissolved in place

Has the repudiation of world and sin been achieved too easily here?
Leavis claimed "that the mundane actuality, the world of inescapable
death, is elsewhere in the poems of the phase less easily dismissed." I
assume he had "Animula" in mind, where

> The heavy burden of the growing soul
> Perplexes and offends more, day by day;
> Week by week, offends and perplexes more
> With the imperatives of "is and seems"
> And may and may not, desire and control.

The pain of living and the drug of dreams
Curl up the small soul in the window seat
Behind the *Encyclopaedia Britannica*.[17]

The reduction of mundane life to unreality in Eliot's other poems of this period, Leavis thought, "is a different affair, having nothing of enchantment about it, and the unreality is not absence."[18] But the burden of the lines from "Marina" is not chiefly the "world of inescapable death"; it is escapable sin. We are given four of the deadly ones— Anger, Pride, Sloth, and Lust, in that unusual order.[19] Some readers have been scandalized by the four-times-insisted-on Death, but they have no good reason. Eliot's recourse to the tone of the Morality Play in that passage is made in a long sentence, sustained across the white space between the subjects—the repeated "Those"—and their verb. It is a mark of his poetic genius that the energy of the sentence lifts it, before it ends, to the earned sublimity of "grace." For a comparable act of faith we have to go to George Herbert's "Easter-Wings":

> With thee
> O let me rise
> As larks, harmoniously,
> And sing this day thy victories:
> Then shall the fall further the flight in me.

Here the internal rhyme of "shall" and "fall" propels the alliterative movement of "fall" and "further" into the "flight" of Easter-wings, soul, and Resurrection. In "Marina" the liturgical procession of Death is the ground of the later beseeching, the gift of grace with its hope—short of a promise—of redemption.

The next lines give the recognition scene, and it is appropriately close to the one in *Pericles:* the face to be recognized is conjured from the rhyme of "grace" and "place":

What is this face, less clear and clearer
The pulse in the arm, less strong and stronger—
Given or lent? more distant than stars and nearer than the eye

Leavis takes this passage together with the next two lines, though the indenting in any editions I have seen would keep them separate, at whatever cost to the grammar:

Whispers and small laughter between leaves and hurrying feet
Under sleep, where all the waters meet.

The face, as Leavis notes, "doesn't belong to the ordinary experience of life in time, and the effect of a higher reality is reinforced by the associations of the last two lines—associations that, with their potent suggestion, characteristic of some memories of childhood, recur so much in Eliot's later work."[20] The series of questions, hovering between less clear and clearer, less strong and stronger, given or lent, more distant and nearer, assents to the rhythm of alternating perception and an incipiently strengthening conviction. Ricks has written of the Ariel poems as "between-poems," and of "Marina" as the one in which "the energies of animosity are at once acknowledged to be substantial and believed to be so transcendable that they can 'become unsubstantial.' "[21] Not merely, as he notes, "insubstantial." Graham Martin has emphasized "the way the prepositions of place promise a kind of concreteness, a location for the laughter, which the nouns at once withdraw."[22] But no such promise has quite been made; none broken or withdrawn. We are responding again to a strange quality of Eliot's poetic language, its observance of other duties than that of denotation. Quoting a passage from "Burnt Norton"—

dignified, invisible,
Moving without pressure, over the dead leaves,
In the autumn heat, through the vibrant air,

—A. D. Moody says that "there can be no simple flow of feeling in such double vision, where what is most real is not real to sense, and where what is actually seen would contradict it."[23] Eliot's language makes the visible hard to see, and it compels us to divine in its phrasings something that can be felt as presence or pressure but not delivered in evidence. In "Marina" the words "between" and "under" offer to specify relations between entities which are themselves dissociated: it would be alien to the spirit of the lines to ask whose whispers, precisely, whose laughter, whose feet, or whose sleep. The pointedness of the qualifying clause, "where all the waters meet," makes it sound more indicative than it is: that place is not to be found on a map. These and other phrases in "Marina" do not refer to objects real or even notional. The main quality of the words is palpability, not transparency of reference. Verisimilitude is not sought. So the words and phrases are best received as marking the rhythm of rise and fall, assertion and concession. Nothing as steady as affirmation is entailed; everything is suggestive, tentative. What the words mean is what, being words in English, they can't help meaning.

It is surprising that the indenting of the lines that follow runs together two phases of a spiritual movement we might have regarded as separate:

Bowsprit cracked with ice and paint cracked with heat.
I made this, I have forgotten
And remember.
The rigging weak and the canvas rotten
Between one June and another September.
Made this unknowing, half conscious, unknown, my own.
The garboard strake leaks, the seams need caulking.
This form, this face, this life
Living to live in a world of time beyond me; let me

> Resign my life for this life, my speech for that unspoken,
> The awakened, lips parted, the hope, the new ships.

Here Pericles, like another Phoenician sailor Phlebas, passes the stages of his life and youth, rising and falling, entering not Phlebas's "whirlpool" but a deeper acknowledgment of his responsibility. As in other poems, Eliot translates the terms of moral responsibility into the language of consciousness—"Made this unknowing, half conscious, unknown, my own." So much a syllable can do, enabling crucial changes of purpose and direction while evading further specification. In that line the to-and-fro of consciousness links the first two subjective conditions acoustically with the second pair ascribed to the object, the ship according to Eliot's allegory of ship and shipbuilder. In the end the feeling reaches the committed stability of "unknown, my own," corresponding to "the hope, the new ships." Pericles's "let me / Resign my life for this life" is an offer he is not obliged to act upon. Such a sacrifice is a minor version of Christ's self-sacrifice on behalf of humanity, but Pericles does not need to give up his life so that Marina may come into her own. In Shakespeare's play she sufficiently comes into her life by regaining her mother Thaisa and her father: there is also her husband-to-be, Lysimachus. Pericles does not have to die to secure these blessings for his daughter. It is enough that Eliot's Pericles is willing to die, if need be, or that he feels the propriety of an old man dying and a beloved daughter moving into the new life of marriage. The motive is common to Eliot's sense of memory in "Little Gidding":

> This is the use of memory:
> For liberation—not less of love but expanding
> Of love beyond desire, and so liberation
> From the future as well as the past.[24]

Some readers have wondered whether Marina is to find the new life in this world or the next. In an early review of the poem Empson spoke of "the balance maintained between otherworldliness and human-ism." The essence of the poem, he said, "is the vision of an order, a spiritual state, which (the speaker) can conceive and cannot enter, but it is not made clear whether he conceives an order in this world to be known by a later generation (like Moses on Pisgah) or the life in heaven which is to be obtained after death (like Dante)." "One might at first think the second only was meant, but Marina, after all, was a real daughter; is now at sea, like himself, rather than already in the Promised Land; and is to live 'in a world of time beyond me,' which can scarcely be a description of Heaven. At any rate, the humanist meaning is used at every point as a symbol of the otherworldly one; this seems the main point to insist on in a brief notice because it is the main cause of the richness of the total effect. In either case the theme is the peril and brevity of such vision."[25]

Otherworldliness and humanism are not the right terms; they propose the wrong question. No one who believes in the Incarnation could accept Empson's version of the choice. Time, by the birth of Christ, became redeemable: that is the ground of a Christian's belief. In these Ariel poems Eliot is using the common words for time and place, landscapes and seascapes, journeys and returns, words for playing-cards and kings and queens, and testing them to see how far they can also suggest states of beatitude and the obstacles to such states. He is seeing these words, too, in a light greater than that of day-light and ordinary denotation. Dante is his example in deriving from the finite world such intimations of Heaven and blessedness as his poetry needs. The last three lines of the poem resume the first five, and conclude it as an exclamation rather than a question. But even more pointedly than "between" and "under," the last preposition of place, "towards my timbers," has the directive force of a verb, as if in anticipation of the woodthrush "calling through the fog":

> What seas what shores what granite islands towards my timbers
> And woodthrush calling through the fog
> My daughter.

III

I want now to consider "Marina" in the context of a debate that has arisen from time to time on the question of ends and closures. The debate might have started—but didn't—when James wrote the preface to *Roderick Hudson*: "Really, universally, relations stop nowhere, and the exquisite problem of the artist is eternally but to draw, by a geometry of his own, the circle within which they shall happily *appear* to do so."[26] Such appearances are closures. They raise a critical issue, not because a work of literature has to end somewhere but because the concept of a satisfactory ending is not innocent, it touches on ideological questions about the way a life should be in relation to the different way it is. Stevens's "The Course of a Particular" ends with a phrase—"until, at last, the cry concerns no one at all."[27]—which implies that the poem has ended by itself because there is nothing more to be said. The end seems to be in the nature of the case, so it is an end, not a closure. But that is a distinction without much difference: a writer who proffered the end as teleological would merely be using that as a further rhetorical ploy.

But the question of endings has also given rise to contention. In "Le Texte clos" and other essays Kristeva has argued that "all ideological activity appears in the form of utterances compositionally *completed*."[28]

"Marina" seems to proclaim its closure: its end is an epitome of its beginning, the movement is circular. An impression of closure is also strengthened by the fact that the poem is a reverie linking the three sentient acts which Augustine outlines in Book XI of the *Confessions.* "The present of past things is the memory; the present of present things is direct perception; and the present of future things is expectation."[29] Nothing in "Marina" falls outside the scope of these three: the poem moves freely but not arbitrarily among them, as among the categories of past, present, and future. If we regard the line from Seneca as setting the key signature for what follows or as providing the motif of bewilderment leading to recognition, then the poem moves from the present tense to the past to the future and back to the present. In any of these versions the finishedness of the poem seems clear.

But in another sense the poem is not at all closed. At every point it is porous to ambiguity. Just as "grace" may be supernatural or natural, a gift or a contingency, so "Those who sharpen the tooth of the dog, meaning / Death" may refer—I concede—to one sinful self or one's many selves, or to sinful humanity as such, or to sinners other than the speaker. I have a preference among those choices, but any one of them is sustainable. The phrase "meaning / Death" may describe what "Those" sinners intend to do to others, or it may denote what they constitute, in the scheme of deadly sin, by virtue of their actions. "Less clear and clearer . . . less strong and stronger . . . given or lent . . . more distant than stars and nearer than the eye" may mean that the impression of "less" arises from Pericles's sensory power and the impression of "more" attends his growing faith. But it may not: it may refer to the wavering, coming-and-going nature of his sensory capacity. Empson has further possibilities in view:

There may be some doubt as to whether *less clear and clearer* is said of the *face* (than what, in that case: than itself, so that the vision

wavers and seems unreal; than the *grace,* so that it is only a metaphor of the unseen glory and yet somehow strengthens it; or than
the sensual persons, the normal world, so that it is affirmed to be
more real than they, though a vision) or of the *pulse in the arm,*
which is at once more and less *clear* and *strong* than the *face*; in this
case it is the vision of the *face* which causes an exhilaration, a sense
of renewed youth, which is more certain than the reality of the
vision, though dependent on its reality, and though certain is yet a
sort of mirage in that it is not he who is made young and strong,
it is the daughter with whom he is in such sympathy as to share
her youth, in the discovery of her by which she seems as it were to
be reborn.[30]

"Small laughter" may mean gentle, like the "small rain" in "Westron
Wind," or barely audible, or the laughter of children among the
leaves. "Between one June and another September" may indicate that
Pericles built the ship between June and the September of the following year, or the September of a still later year. Or it may mean that the
rigging became weak and the canvas rotten in some indefinite interval. The last words—"My daughter"—may be what Pericles thinks
the woodthrush is calling or they may be what he says to Marina,
having no need to say more. My sense of the poem is that its content,
its story, is Eliot's conversion to Christianity, his waking up to find
himself a Christian and wondering what to make of it all. The poem is
his Recognition Scene as a Christian: he fulfilled his poetic temperament by making the scene remote and ghostly even to himself.

Stevens and Eliot

There is a passage in *The Phenomenology of Mind* that I think I understand. Hegel has been administering cold but not equally cold comfort to believers and *philosophes*. His official theme is *Aufklärung*, Enlightenment, and for many pages he has been personifying Enlightenment and belief and scolding each in turn: they do not know themselves, they cannot recognize their mutual bearing. Having set them apart and brought them together again, he makes the contrast between them one within Enlightenment itself:

> Since belief is without content and cannot continue in this barren condition, or since, in getting beyond finitude, which is the sole content, it finds merely the empty void, it is a sheer longing: its truth is an empty beyond, for which there is no longer any appropriate content to be found, for everything is appropriated and applied in other ways. Belief . . . has in fact become the same as enlightenment—the conscious attitude of relating a finite that inherently exists to an unknown and unknowable Absolute without predicates; the difference is merely that the one is enlightenment satisfied, while belief is

enlightenment unsatisfied. It will yet be seen whether enlightenment can continue in its state of satisfaction; that longing of the
troubled, beshadowed spirit, mourning over the loss of its spiritual
world, lies in the background.[1]

I should not have thought it possible for Enlightenment to continue
long in its state of satisfaction, but I have heard Richard Bernstein and
two or three equally sensitive scholars declare that they are indeed
content. It seems strange, after genocide in Russia, Poland, Germany, Austria, Cambodia, Rwanda, Kosovo, and other countries,
technologically accomplished slaughter in Hiroshima and Nagasaki,
the gas chambers in Auschwitz. I thought the Enlightenment promised that such acts would cease. I am not blaming our modern philosophes for these horrors, but I remain bewildered by their insistence on the adequacy of Enlightenment thinking. Not that the human
record of belief is clean.

Hegel's account of Enlightenment and belief is invidious to both
parties, though on balance an adept of Enlightenment would feel
justified rather than disgraced. Believers are bound to take it hard to
be pushed into Enlightenment in the end and allowed to retain mainly
the dignity of their dissatisfaction. Perhaps the distinction is merely
an opportunism, but I am convinced that there are men and women
of goodwill who would accept it. I assume that such people, adepts of
a satisfied Enlightenment, would explain themselves somewhat in
these terms: I am an individual. I have the use of my faculties and
notably of my reasoning capacity. I take full responsibility for the
exercise of my mind and for whatever I do in that light. No external
authority, church or state, has my allegiance unless I choose to give it.
If I exhibit benevolence toward other people, it is because I choose to
act in that way. I do not kill other people; I decide, day by day, not to
kill them. I conduct my life as a "permanent creation of myself in my

autonomy"—the phrase I find in Foucault's "What Is Enlighten-ment?"[2] If other people act on different reasons or no reason that I can see, so much the worse.

It hardly matters whether I have characterized these adepts justly or caricatured them; it is enough that I point to a certain motive, indeed a prejudice, and mark its provenance in American life. It is an active force whenever Americans feel that life is their oyster, that at any moment they can make a fresh start, hit the road. Franklinism is another name for it, but the name is inaccurate; Franklin had a wider culture and a more complex sense of life than he is regularly given credit for. The motive I am describing comes into political life when Americans cannot understand why other people evidently do not want to live like Americans. The ideology of America as Redeemer Nation depends on this prejudice and on the still-deeper prejudice by which reality is taken to be the scientific account of it, or the positiv-ist's version of it.

Exemplars of unsatisfied Enlightenment are more interesting peo-ple. Hegel calls them believers, but only because they are not fully at home in Enlightenment. They probably believe just as much as any-one else, but their beliefs are likely to be theologically unexacting; no church is low enough for them. Sometimes they take pride in their atheism, but they are not, in practice, immune to credences just as unaccountable as any theism. As for pragmatism, which thinks itself superior to beliefs because independent of them, Eliot pointed out that the pragmatist believes his own doctrine in a sense that is not pragmatic but absolute. The error of pragmatism is "to treat certain other concepts, like 'usefulness' or 'success,' as if they had the abso-luteness denied to truth."[3] There is no reason to credit professed unbelievers when they insist that they are unbelievers: they merely act on beliefs they don't feel obliged to articulate. Those who belong to what Hegel calls the unsatisfied Enlightenment believe just as much as the pope does, but they take pleasure in claiming that they, unlike him, have chosen the objects of their faith. The claim is bogus. The main difference between the pope and Wallace Stevens is that the pope does not claim to have invented, or deduced from his private desires, the articles of his belief. This is what Stevens claims, and he is self-deceived, since most of what he claims to have invented he has inherited from a certain philosophic tradition.

The satisfied inheritors of the Enlightenment claim that their reasoning power gives them unmediated access to truth and that they may therefore dispense with all the official mediations—traditions and myths, especially those myths that speak of an accredited origin from which meaning is derived. The unsatisfied ones try to walk in the presumed light of reason, find themselves disappointed, and deal with the disappointment as best they can; usually by retaining the terminology of Enlightenment and making it, if they can, more flexible, more responsive. This device, when practiced in Europe, is called romanticism; when practiced in America, it is called transcendentalism, and Emerson and Thoreau are regarded as its saints. Devotees no longer speak of reason—Stevens mocked that capacity as "Reason's click-clack"—but of vision or imagination.

Stanley Cavell, who represents Enlightenment unsatisfied in a style that mourns the loss of its spiritual world, tries to redeem his enlightened vocabulary by speaking not of knowledge but of acknowledgment. He has made disappointment his theme. In *In Quest of the Ordinary* he speaks of romanticism as "working out a crisis of knowledge, a crisis I have taken to be (interpretable as) a response at once to the threat of skepticism and to a disappointment with philosophy's answer to this threat, particularly as embodied in the achievement of Kant's philosophy—a disappointment most particularly with the way Kant balances the claims of knowledge of the world to be what you may call subjective and objective, or, say, the claims of knowledge to be dependent on or independent of the specific endowments—sensuous and intellectual—of the human being." This in turn, Cavell says, "perhaps means a disappointment in the idea of taking the success of science, or what makes science possible, as an answer to the threat of skepticism, rather than a further expression of it."[4]

I have been referring to European romanticism and American transcendentalism as attempts to go beyond the Enlightenment or to take the harm out of it by exceeding its characteristic terms. For the moment, I have been taking Hegel at one or two of his words and construing a certain story as if it were still one of the stories of the Enlightenment. But I do not set this procedure against the other way of interpreting the same experience, which is to take it as evidence of the "secularization of inherited theological ideas and ways of thinking" in England, France, Germany, and therefore the United States in the middle of the nineteenth century. The phrase just quoted comes from M. H. Abrams's *Natural Supernaturalism: Tradition and Revolution in Romantic Literature* (1971), where the case I imply is made.[5] Either we construe the case of transcendentalism (to hold with that) as one of unsatisfied Enlightenment and a device to cope with the disappointment Cavell describes, or we see it as a "translation downward" of fundamental terms in theology and religion. It makes a difference. In the first version, disappointment is likely to be incorrigible, since the extension of the terms of Enlightenment is bound to appear opportunistic. Cavell is not convincing when he speaks of acknowledgment as a further mode of knowledge and not a departure from it. In the second case, there is likely to be a conviction of bad faith if the terms of faith are smartly secularized. In practice—by which I mean in the diverse practices of Wordsworth, Coleridge, and Emerson for the most part—there is honest recognition that much has been sacrificed to obtain the easier certitudes.

In commoner practice, the question comes to this: Is Christianity compatible with Enlightenment thinking? If it is not, so much the worse for Christianity. If it is, or might be, is it still Christianity?

II

The issues between Eliot and Stevens—not that they ever debated them—concern reason, faith, and authority. I want to approach them by reading a book that raises these issues in ways hardly to be looked for in poetry. Josiah Royce's *The Problem of Christianity* (1913) at least puts the main question clearly: What is the essence of Christianity, the particular understanding or vision of the world, such that a "modern man" may believe it and live according to its light? Royce emphasizes that he is not concerned, as William James was, with the particular religious experiences of individuals. "My main topic," he says, "is a form of social religious experience, namely, that form which, in ideal, the Apostle Paul viewed as the experience of the Church."[6] Some readers may feel that Royce is giving short shrift to Jesus, as the one who founded an institution far more important than himself. Royce is concerned with Christianity, in its historical manifestation, only at the moment in which it becomes, mainly through Paul, a spiritual and social community. The basis of this community is not its shared "imitation of Christ," but the multiple acts of interpretation that constitute its social existence. The gist of Royce's argument is that a community is founded on the will to interpret.

By emphasizing this will in C. S. Peirce's terms, Royce assures himself that when he comes to believe something, what he believes will be compatible with the procedures not only of reason but of natural science and logic. As a Darwinian, Royce accepted notions of evolution and progress with a degree of buoyancy now hard to credit: he found it easy, apparently, to believe that the human race has been the beneficiary of education to the point at which he can project a fictitious entity called "modern man" and endow him with exemplary capacities: "For by the 'modern man' most of us mean a being whose views are supposed to be in some sense not only the historical result, but a significant summary, of what the ages have taught mankind. The term 'modern man' condenses into a word the hypothesis, the postulate, that the human race has been subject to some more or less coherent process of education. The modern man is supposed to teach what this 'education of the human race' has taught to him. The ages have their lesson. The modern man knows something of this lesson."[7] Readers of Stevens will recognize some features of Royce's "modern man" in the "major man" of Stevens's *Notes Toward a Supreme Fiction,* his greatest poem.

It is not surprising that Royce, making so little of the life, death, and resurrection of Christ, concludes:

> Let your Christology be the practical acknowledgment of the Spirit of the Universal and Beloved Community. This is the sufficient and practical faith. Love this faith, use this faith, teach this faith, preach this faith, in whatever words, through whatever symbols, by means of whatever forms of creeds, in accordance with whatever practices best you find to enable you with a sincere intent and a whole heart to symbolize and to realize the presence of the Spirit in the Community. All else about your religion is the accident of your special race or nation or form of worship or training or accidental personal opinion, or devout private mystical experience—illuminating but capricious. The core, the center of the faith, is not the person of the individual founder, and it is not any other individual man. Nor is this core to be found in the sayings of the founder, nor yet in the traditions of Christology. The core of the faith is the Spirit, the Beloved Community, the work of grace, the atoning deed, and the saving power of the loyal life. There is

nothing else under heaven whereby men have been saved or can be saved. To say this is to found no new faith, but to send you to the heart of all true faith.[8]

I quote this passage mainly to indicate what a short step it would take to reach the churchless Church, the beliefless Belief of Robert Bellah, who took the title, and much else, of his famous book from a line of Stevens's poem "Flyer's Fall": "dimension in which / We believe without belief, beyond belief."[9]

III

I'll refer briefly to a few poems by Stevens, starting with "Sunday Morning," his most celebrated poem and the one in which he first addressed, explicitly if not justly, the experience of wanting to believe. Stevens said that "Sunday Morning" is "not essentially a woman's meditation on religion and the meaning of life. It is anybody's meditation. . . . The poem is simply an expression of paganism, although, of course, I did not think that I was expressing paganism when I wrote it."[10] In the poem, a woman's thoughts on a Sunday morning, when she might well have gone to church, resolve themselves from time to time into words and are scolded by the narrative voice for wanting more than paganism. Despite the secular comforts of life, she thinks of Christ, "the dark / Encroachment of that old catastrophe," and is immediately rebuked for having such thoughts and for giving the bounty of her consciousness to the dead. The narrative voice is disingenuous in saying that the woman should be just as well satisfied by the thought of pungent fruit and the beauty of the earth as by thought of heaven. These, Stevens says, are the "measures destined for her soul." Perhaps they are, but it is graceless to demand that she be fulfilled in them. The third stanza seems to allow for more. It refers

to Jove and his descent to love, an allegory that gives human life at
least partial access to divinity:

> Jove in the clouds had his inhuman birth.
> No mother suckled him, no sweet land gave
> Large-mannered motions to his mythy mind.
> He moved among us, as a muttering king,
> Magnificent, would move among his hinds,
> Until our blood, commingling, virginal,
> With heaven, brought such requital to desire
> The very hinds discerned it, in a star.
> Shall our blood fail? Or shall it come to be
> The blood of paradise? And shall the earth
> Seem all of paradise that we shall know?
> The sky will be much friendlier then than now,
> A part of labor and a part of pain,
> And next in glory to enduring love,
> Not this dividing and indifferent blue.[11]

Stevens refers to Jove again, in "Two or Three Ideas," where somewhat puzzlingly he speaks of the gods not "in their religious aspects
but as creations of the imagination." Puzzling because generally Stevens thinks of the gods as creations of the imagination and as nothing
else:

> When we think of Jove, while we take him for granted as the
> symbol of omnipotence, the ruler of mankind, we do not fear
> him. . . . To speak of the origin and end of gods is not a light
> matter. It is to speak of the origin and end of eras of human belief.
> And while it is easy to look back on those that have disappeared as
> if they were the playthings of cosmic make-believe, and on those
> that made petitions to them and honored them and received their

benefits as legendary innocents, we are bound, nevertheless, to concede that the gods were personae of a peremptory elevation and glory. It would be wrong to look back to them as if they had existed in some indigence of the spirit.[12]

So in "Sunday Morning" mention of Jove is enough to make Stevens feel some misgiving, not about his humanism but about his identification of it with a taste for coffee and oranges.

In the fourth stanza, for the first time, the woman is allowed to be heard:

> She says, "I am content when wakened birds,
> Before they fly, test the reality
> Of misty fields, by their sweet questionings;
> But when the birds are gone, and their warm fields
> Return no more, where, then, is paradise?"

The reply to this is, in effect, that no paradise according to any of the accredited mythologies—Christian, Greek, Roman, Arabic, or any other—"has endured / As April's green endures." The woman is not convinced: "She says, 'But in contentment I still feel / The need of some imperishable bliss.' " The answer, this time, is that "Death is the mother of beauty." The inevitability of death intensifies one's experiences and makes up for their transience, an admonition that Stevens's poem entrusts to a Keatsian rhetoric of heartbreaking authority. Imperishable bliss would soon become tedious because it would lack the character we crave, that of change. However we imagine paradise, it would be a mere repetition of the same.

In the seventh stanza Stevens seems to reach for the peremptory glory that he ascribed to the cult of Jove and the ancient gods, but he now projects it toward some future occasion of worship—with a difference. The worshippers are to chant their devotion to the sun,

"Not as a god, but as a god might be." The difference seems to be that the worshipped force is an object not of belief but of pure imagination. The energy of the ritual will come from one's identification with the natural world, the winds, the trees, the lakes. In the last stanza, the woman does not speak in her own voice, but she hears a voice:

> She hears, upon that water without sound,
> A voice that cries, "The tomb in Palestine
> Is not the porch of spirits lingering.
> It is the grave of Jesus, where he lay."

Stevens's answer to this message is that our only life is the life we know, the planet on which we live, an "old chaos of the sun":

> We live in an old chaos of the sun,
> Or old dependency of day and night,
> Or island solitude, unsponsored, free,
> Of that wide water, inescapable.
> Deer walk upon our mountains, and the quail
> Whistle about us their spontaneous cries;
> Sweet berries ripen in the wilderness;
> And, in the isolation of the sky,
> At evening, casual flocks of pigeons make
> Ambiguous undulations as they sink,
> Downward to darkness, on extended wings.

This, too, gorgeous as it is, merely brushes the woman's misgivings aside; there is to be no talk of Jesus, resurrection, or immortality.

In "Two or Three Ideas," Stevens says that "in an age of disbelief, or, what is the same thing, in a time that is largely humanistic, in one sense or another, it is for the poet to supply the satisfactions of belief, in his measure and his style."[13] He does not mean that he wants poets to recover the old beliefs. Poets are to appease one's desire to believe by working out the unlimited possibilities of the "increasingly human self," which is in any case all there is. It is as if Stevens retained the project of Enlightenment but proposed to pursue it by recourse not to reason but to imagination. He retains the hierarchical terms of Christianity but "translates them down," turning God into a human being, according to the formula of "Final Soliloquy of the Interior Paramour": "We say God and the imagination are one." Other equations or substitutions follow. Christ becomes a person, merely, like any other. The church becomes the fellowship of one's mind with other minds, or with a few notable minds, as in Royce and certain poets and philosophers. Prayer becomes not an elevation of the soul to God in praise, but verbal brooding on nearly any theme that occurs; hence Stevens's favorite form, variations on a theme having to do with reality and the imagination. Where Christianity speaks of truth or revelation, Stevens speaks of fictions, structures devised by acts of individual imagination. The ideal form of such fictions is what Stevens calls a Supreme Fiction; it is his version of theology. Instead of the Christian sacraments, Steven works out the possibilities of a few leading ideas, not because they are true but because they are poetic, beautiful, or sublime. In that sense Stevens may be called a post-Christian poet—not because Christianity has died, which is evidently not the case, but because the structure of Stevens's desires is that of Christianity, the validity of which he no longer accepts.

It would be a serious error of judgment, and certainly of tact, to try to turn Stevens into a philosopher. He liked reading philosophy and used it for five-finger exercises. He was a poet, and the poetic character of his poems and essays is not the same as the character, whatever that may be, of the ideas he mulled over. Beyond an uncertain point, it is misleading even to advert to these ideas; they are no more than raw material with which he worked and to which he gave the sustained attention of an amateur. It is clear, nonetheless, that a certain paradigm is useful to a reader of Stevens's poems, and may be at worst a working hypothesis. It may be better than that, if only because Stevens's poems offer evidence of it at every point.

The paradigm goes like this: we live in a place that we have not made; therefore it is not our own. The sky is an indifferent blue. Our only capacity is consciousness: we think ourselves into the distinctive form of being which we call human being. But it may be possible to continue with those acts of consciousness to the point at which we seem to have transformed the world into ourselves. At that point we would be in no respect inferior to the gods, or to the Christian God in whom we no longer believe. Poetry is the form of a consciousness turned toward that project and, ideally, capable of carrying it forward if not carrying it out. If it could be done, the poet would be "major man."

Before I quote from *Notes Toward a Supreme Fiction* the passage in which this paradigm is most explicit, I want to refer to a comment on Hegel that Royce includes in *The Problem of Christianity*. It is by R. H. Mackintosh:

Christianity receives (according to Hegel) absolute rank, but at the cost of its tie with history. For only the world-process as a whole, and no single point or person in it, can be the true manifestation of the Absolute. . . . Thus, when Hegel has waved his wand, and uttered his dialectical and all-decisive formula, a change comes over the spirit of the believer's dream; everything appears to be as Christian as before, yet instinctively we are aware that nothing specifically Christian is left. When once the Gospel has been severed from a historic person, and identified with a complex of metaphysical ideas, what it ought to be called is scarcely worth discussion; that it is no longer Christianity, is clear. . . . The proposed identification of the Christian faith with the ontological theory that

God and man are one—God the essence of man, man the actuality of God—is an utterly hopeless enterprise, which the scientific historian cannot take seriously.[14]

This enterprise is close to Stevens's, although Stevens undertook it not on behalf of Christianity but to claim for humanity the attributes of God. The project is an extreme version of idealism—quite different in its extremity from Eliot's—according to which consciousness is deemed to account for the whole of one's experience. Here is the passage from *Notes Toward a Supreme Fiction*:

From this the poem springs: that we live in a place
That is not our own and, much more, not ourselves
And hard it is in spite of blazoned days.

We are the mimics. Clouds are pedagogues.
The air is not a mirror but bare board,
Coulisse bright-dark, tragic chiaroscuro

And comic color of the rose, in which
Abysmal instruments make sound like pips
Of the sweeping meanings that we add to them.[15]

This passage reveals Stevens in only one of his moods, even if it is one of the most suggestive; it is not a culmination. It marks his project, but chiefly the difficulties it has to face. Stevens seems to have accepted, as Royce did, Peirce's system of Firstness, Secondness, and Thirdness, where Firstness is the conception of being or existing independent of anything else; Secondness is the conception of being relative to, or in reaction against, something else; and Thirdness is the conception of mediation, whereby a first and second are brought into relation.[16] According to Stevens's parable, Adam and Eve were the first humanists, because—like Descartes—they conceived the world in their own terms and practiced their reason in doing so. They made a second earth by construing the first in terms favorable to themselves. They founded the Enlightenment. In the meantime, things have become more difficult; it is hard to see the air as mirror of oneself. There is too much evidence that the constituents of reality are opaque. In *The Necessary Angel* Stevens endorses an argument he found in an essay by the philosopher H. D. Lewis: "Mr. Lewis says that poetry has to do with the matter that is foreign and alien. It is never familiar to us in the way which Plato wished the conquests of the mind to be familiar. On the contrary, its function, the need which it meets and which has to be met in some way in every age that is not to become decadent or barbarous, is precisely this contact with reality as it impinges upon us from outside, the sense that we can touch and feel a solid reality which does not wholly dissolve itself into the conceptions of our own minds. It is the individual and particular that does this."[17] This passage expresses Stevens's scruple not about his project but about the empty ease with which it might seem to be achieved. If, as in Peirce's account of idealism, the idealist is one who deems the psychical law alone as primordial and the physical law as derived and special, it is always a question how the deriving is done, and what is the status of the particulars derived. That we add our own sweeping meanings is not to be disputed, unless the claim is made in extravagant terms.

But it is a strange if not extravagant feature of Stevens's project that, having reduced God to human status, the poet should not be content with the reduction. He sets about trying to recover the loss and to add it, however implausibly, to humanity's account. In a letter of January 12, 1943, to Hi Simons, who had enquired about a later passage in *Notes Toward a Supreme Fiction,* Stevens wrote: "The trouble with humanism is that man as God remains man, but there is an extension of man, the leaner being, in fiction, a possibly more than human human, a composite human. The act of recognizing him is the act of this leaner being moving in on us."[18] This notion of a composite human, a more than human human, is a conceit good enough to cut a dash in the poem but, outside the poem, good for nothing but mystification. Perhaps Stevens is merely imagining a fabulous being, as predecessors imagined the Minotaur and other hybrid creatures, to express the inexpressible, or even as sages from Longinus to Boileau, Edmund Burke, and Kant posited the Sublime as a category of inner disturbance for which nothing reasonable but something formidable nonetheless could be said. Stevens's attempt to ascribe such experiences not even to a genius but to a composite figure is bold: it seems to require us to believe in such a thing.

IV

When we consider Eliot's writings in relation to knowledge and belief, we come on far more ambiguous, if not more complex, evidence than we had anticipated. It is clear from the documents Jeffrey Perl has elucidated in *Skepticism and Modern Enmity* that Eliot did not regard philosophy as an adjunct or set of prolegomena to belief. He was never much taken with the project of the Enlightenment or with the ambition of coming to truth by philosophic reasoning. In a letter of January 6, 1915, to Norbert Wiener, he said that philosophy was "chiefly literary criticism and conversation about life": "The only reason why relativism does not do away with philosophy altogether, after all, is that there is no such thing to abolish! There is art, and there is science. And there are works of art, and perhaps of science, which would never have occurred had not many people been under the impression that there was philosophy."[19] At Harvard, Eliot entertained an interest in many philosophic traditions, with a particular affection for Buddhist writings. He regarded the history of metaphysics, in any Western sense, as mostly a record of vanity. Much as he admired Aristotle, he thought that he had set metaphysics on an erroneous track, in quest of "being unconditioned": 'It is only the persistent faith in a difference between thought and reality which prevents Aristotle from explicitly handling metaphysics as the investigation into the ultimate meaning of thought as expressed in the forms of language. He conducts himself as if he were analysing things and not ideas."[20] Not that the damage could be undone. Eliot worked up enough interest in metaphysics to complete his dissertation on Bradley, and he remained at least mildly interested in Bradleyan idealism as a philosophy at one with a distinguished prose style. But the manuscripts that Perl has studied—mostly Eliot's essays for Royce's seminar at Harvard—show that, so far as Eliot took a position at all, it was that of skepticism or conventionalism. The merit of skepticism or conventionalism is that it regards truth as the coherence of all the available terms within a limited field of discourse. In his work on Bradley, Eliot attacked epistemology for its assumption "that there is one consistent world . . . and that it is our business to find it." In a paper on Kant and agnosticism, he wrote: "Knowledge is only knowledge when 'taken internally.' If you contemplate knower and known from the outside, what you find is *not* simply knower and known, but a peculiar complex of existents, and knowledge fades into ontology. Hence to know we must begin with *faith.*"[21] Eliot did not believe that the royal way to faith was by starting with knowledge. As in other experiences of life, one starts with a vague or acute feeling of discontent, and tries to ease the distress by whatever means. Pascal was one whose conduct in this regard Eliot found edifying. It is not enough to say of Eliot's Christianity that the dogma of the Incarnation and the deeply apprehended sense of original sin were crucial. No single element in Christianity was more crucial than any other; "you must either take the whole of revealed religion or none of it."[22] The consideration that made the project of the Enlightenment appear shoddy to him was his distrust in unaided reason, which he derided as the inner voice so cherished by John Middleton Murry. "The possessors of the inner voice," Eliot said, "ride ten in a compartment to a football match at Swansea, listening to the inner voice, which breathes the eternal message of vanity, fear, and lust."[23] More urbanely, Eliot regretted that the Protestant bishops at the Lambeth Conference in 1930 placed so much reliance "upon the Individual Conscience": "Certainly, anyone who is wholly sincere and pure in heart may seek for guidance from the Holy Spirit; but who of us is always wholly sincere, especially where the most imperative of instincts may be strong enough to simulate to perfection the voice of the Holy Spirit?"[24] The enemy was always what he called secularism, an inability or a refusal to understand "the primacy of the supernatural over the natural life."[25]

Many passages in Eliot's poetry rebuke the Enlightenment project. In some of them, the rebuke is implicit; in others, explicit, as in "The Dry Salvages," where such optimistic notions as those of development and evolution are regarded as mere stratagems for disowning the past. That poem should be set beside a section in "East Coker" in which Eliot pours cold water on any assumptions, popular or not, about knowledge and experience:

> There is, it seems to us,
> At best, only a limited value
> In the knowledge derived from experience.
> The knowledge imposes a pattern, and falsifies,
> For the pattern is new in every moment
> And every moment is a new and shocking
> Valuation of all we have been. We are only
>   undeceived
> Of that which, deceiving, could no longer harm.[26]

In a full consideration of this passage, it would be well to place it beside the earlier poem "Animula" and the later passage in "Little Gidding" in which a familiar compound ghost makes stringent comment on the wisdom of experience.

V

With the example of Eliot before us, it would be absurd to stay with Hegel's account of the Enlightenment, or to think that the concept of Enlightenment can house both Enlightenment and belief. Belief, as we use the word in describing Eliot's poetry from "Ash-Wednesday" to "Little Gidding," can't be contained within any feasible account of the Enlightenment as a system of values. Not that opposition to Enlightenment is exerted only by Christians—many who oppose the Enlightenment agree on nothing else. Think of Eliot's Christian poems, and then of Blake's *Four Zoas,* Lawrence's *Women in Love,* Michael Polanyi's *Knowing and Being,* Michael Oakeshott's *On Human Conduct,* Marjorie Grene's *Knower and Known,* Leavis's *Nor Shall My Sword,* the last with its references to "our technologico-Benthamite world" and the "blind enlightened menace." We are not, all of us, men and women of the Enlightenment; there is no consensus.

So far are we from enjoying a consensus on being men and women of the Enlightenment that each of us is free to reconsider the program that goes by that name. It may be that the whole project that includes eighteenth-century Enlightenment and nineteenth-century romanticism and transcendentalism has come to an end. Habermas has argued, in *The Philosophical Discourse of Modernity* (1987), that "the paradigm of the philosophy of consciousness is exhausted."[27] He has reached this conviction after a remarkably just analysis of Kant, Hegel, Schiller, Nietzsche, the Frankfurt school, Husserl, Heidegger, Derrida, Bataille, and Foucault. I do not see how his account of the philosophy of consciousness can be much faulted. Consciousness obviously includes the "reason" of the Enlightenment and claims to go beyond it, so it is the subject-based character of philosophy that comes under Habermas's scrutiny. I am not sure about his own proposal, that philosophy should become politics and seek "mutual understanding between subjects capable of speech and action."[28] As Mahatma Gandhi is said to have responded when asked what he thought of Western civilization, "It would be nice." Habermas assumes that the language in which the communications he favors would take place is translucent, equally available to all its speakers, given ordinary goodwill. But Lyotard is right in saying that language is like a highly complex archipelago, involving regimes of discourse so different—descriptive, prescriptive, evaluative, and so forth—that they are opaque to the program Habermas has in view.

Even if philosophers were to abandon the philosophy of consciousness, as Habermas recommends, the validity of individual consciousness and introspection would not be disgraced. Acts of consciousness would still count as experiences: only the claims made for them would be reduced. Stevens's poems would not be invalidated. We would read them as if they turned particular acts of consciousness into experiences that might be shared; which is the way we read them now. The only difference Habermas's program would make to my reading of Stevens is that I would not assume, as I have tended to, that a subject-based poetry (the lyric poem) is bound to have the privilege I have been giving to a subject-based philosophy. Habermas is not as forthcoming about this as I would like him to be. His descriptions of the communication he recommends are bound to have their main resonance in social and political action, but this would be a Pyrrhic victory if it required the devaluation of inwardness. There is no need to posit a philosophy of inwardness, to begin with, and to find some means of moving from subject to object and therefore to a decent

politics. It is enough if my subjectivity is allowed for in a correspondingly generous politics and linguistics. Levinas is entirely right to say,
in *Totality and Infinity,* that "the inner life is the unique *way* for the real
to exist as a plurality," and again that interiority constitutes an order
in which "what is no longer possible historically remains always possible."[29] It would be wicked to remove that possibility or to try to
make people feel ashamed of themselves for resorting to it. The
soliloquy is an entirely respectable form of expression; it does not
entail a refusal of communicative practice.

It is in Levinas rather than in Habermas that one finds the necessarily radical change of heart. If one accepts Habermas's argument, as
on the whole I do, about the exhaustion of the metaphysics of being
and knowledge, ontology and epistemology, then Levinas's *Totality
and Infinity* and *Otherwise Than Being* are the books to read. Levinas
proposes not only to set aside the fixation on ontology and epistemology, on being, the same, the one, totality, and the claims of power
they enforce, but to ground philosophy itself on the primordial imperative of ethics. "Ethics precedes ontology," he maintains.[30] The
great meditation, in *Totality and Infinity,* on the "face" and the recognition its coming into view entails is the point from which to start.

VI

So far as I know, Eliot did not write anything about Stevens. He may
have written jacket copy for the Faber and Faber edition of Stevens's
Collected Poems, but I doubt it. Stevens's comments on Eliot were
frigid, not surly, as William Carlos Williams's were, but designed to
fend off any possible attraction. A month after "The Waste Land" was
published in *The Criterion,* Stevens sent sour grapes to Alice Corbin
Henderson: "Eliot's poem is, of course, the rage. As poetry it is
surely negligible. What it may be in other respects is a large subject

on which one could talk for a month. If it is the supreme cry of despair it is Eliot's and not his generation's. Personally, I think it's a bore."[31] On October 15, 1940, Stevens told Henry Church that he regarded Eliot as "a negative rather than a positive force." "Eliot and I are dead opposites," he told William Van O'Connor. And he claimed, writing to Richard Eberhart, that "I am not conscious of being influenced by anybody and have purposely held off from reading highly mannered people like Eliot and Pound so that I should not absorb anything, even unconsciously."[32] This is a curious remark, since his own poems and essays are far more mannered than Eliot's or Pound's. In fact he absorbed a good deal from *Prufrock and Other Observations,* as "Le Monocle de Mon Oncle" shows. But he kept out of Eliot's poetic way in later years.

Not completely, however. It is commonly agreed that the "X" in Stevens's "The Creations of Sound" and the third section of "Extracts from Addresses to the Academy of Fine Ideas" is Eliot. There are other passages, notably in "Esthétique du mal," which may conceivably glance at Eliot, but the glance is too brief to be commented on. In "The Creations of Sound" Stevens gets Eliot entirely wrong:

> If the poetry of X was music,
> So that it came to him of its own,
> Without understanding, out of the wall
>
> Or in the ceiling, in sounds not chosen,
> Or chosen quickly, in a freedom
> That was their element, we should not know
>
> That X is an obstruction, a man
> Too exactly himself, and that there are words
> Better without an author, without a poet,
>
> Or having a separate author, a different poet . . .

In fact, the poetry of X is music, and Stevens's first six lines, which offer to say what X's poetry is not, say with notable accuracy what it is. The next lines misunderstand X's poetry with equal adroitness. Stevens is recommending a theory of inspiration, according to which the poet is a willing instrument, an Aeolian harp, through which the creative spirit blows. But he seems to think that this theory refutes Eliot. In truth, it confirms his poetry, except that Eliot calls the creative spirit variously language or tradition or orthodoxy. Eliot is in no respect "a man / Too exactly himself," he does not coincide with himself, desperately dispersed as he is among intolerable feelings and visions. In the next lines Stevens becomes more specific and more erroneous:

> Tell X that speech is not dirty silence
> Clarified. It is silence made still dirtier.
> It is more than an imitation for the ear.
>
> He lacks this venerable complication.
> His poems are not of the second part of life.
> They do not make the visible a little hard
>
> To see nor, reverberating, eke out the mind
> On peculiar horns, themselves eked out
> By the spontaneous particulars of sound.
>
> We do not say ourselves like that in poems.
> We say ourselves in syllables that rise
> From the floor, rising in speech we do not speak.[33]

Eliot never thought that speech was "dirty silence / Clarified." When he wrote, in "Burnt Norton," that "Words, after speech, reach / Into the silence," he meant silence as the place of form, pattern, and prayer. When the familiar compound ghost of "Little Gidding" says—

> Since our concern was speech, and speech impelled us
>   To purify the dialect of the tribe . . .

he says what any responsible poet, not only Eliot and Mallarmé, would say. As for Eliot's poems not making the visible a little hard to see, that is precisely what they do. I assume that when Stevens says that "his poems are not of the second part of life" he means that the first part is the one in which of necessity we see what is there, without yet transfiguring it as an Idealist would. That is work of the second part: Idealism, subjectivity. In that part the visible, the given, is transformed to make it appear one's own or, better still, oneself. But in Eliot's poems the visible is made very hard to see: it is never defined, cut out from its context, as if it embodied value and sense in that sole state. There is always a shadow, for thought and desire, between mind and the thing seen. And the horns reverberate in those poems more memorably than in any other modern poetry, except for a few of Yeats's poems. What can Stevens be thinking of, to read Eliot so badly? Why was he so afraid of Eliot's poetry?

In the third section of "Extracts" he is more concerned with Eliot in relation to the question of religious belief:

> The lean cats of the arches of the churches,
> That's the old world. In the new, all men are priests.
>
> They preach and they are preaching in a land
> To be described. They are preaching in a time
> To be described. Evangelists of what?

A good question. Stevens is so Emersonian in this passage that he doesn't hear the thud with which his "all men are priests" falls. All men are priests. Is that all that Stevens's creed comes to, a self-deluding Humanism? When he tries to answer his own question, "Evangelists of what?" he has nothing to offer, as content of their

belief, but a secular translation of Christianity, the shell of belief with
the belief left out. Instead of the God of Christianity we get "a dark-
blue king"; instead of Mary, "a queen, / An intercessor by innate
rapport"; and for substance, nothing but "their bread and their remembered wine." In the next lines Stevens comes back to the arches:

> The lean cats of the arches of the churches
> Bask in the sun in which they feel transparent,
> As if designed by X, the per-noble master.
> They have a sense of their design and savor
> The sunlight. They bear brightly the little beyond
> Themselves, the slightly unjust drawing that is
> Their genius: the exquisite errors of time.[34]

There is a suggestion that these followers of Eliot feel transparent in
the sunlight of their God but shouldn't; as if Eliot's Christianity
weren't the profound doubting belief it is, contiguous to Augustine,
St. John of the Cross, and Pascal. Besides, Stevens is in no position to
deride anyone's feelings, his own being omnivorous. His poems assume that having a feeling is enough; there is no warrant for inter-
rogating it. "The little beyond / Themselves" parodies their spiritual
range in the vacancy across the line. It is a riposte to Eliot's "Tradition
and the Individual Talent": it implies that Eliot and his school are
limited to inscribing petty footnotes to Tradition as they apprehend
it. "The slightly unjust drawing," as if they hadn't the courage of the
bold, Nietzschean injustices. "The exquisite errors of time": small
veerings from the official text. To resort to such a travesty of Eliot,
Stevens must have feared for his Emersonian soul.

The Idea of a Christian Society

On June 29, 1927, T. S. Eliot was baptized into the Church of England by William Force Stead: the following day he was confirmed by the Bishop of Oxford. As the author of "The Waste Land" he was an irrefutable force in poetry, but he was not an abundant poet. He wrote few poems, and those with difficulty. For the next twenty years he was prolific only as an essayist, lecturer, and BBC broadcaster on behalf of Christianity. As editor of *The Criterion* he regularly intervened on the major political issues: religion, literature, fascism, communism, humanism, popular culture. But he concentrated his attention most vigorously on the possibility of a Christian society. He brought *The Criterion* to an end in January 1939 mainly, I think, because the events of September 1938—specifically, Chamberlain's appeasement of Hitler—had cast him into such dejection that he could not continue. In his last editorial for *The Criterion* he said that the "present state of public affairs" had induced in him a "depression of spirits so different from any other experience of fifty years as to be a new emotion."[1] He was appalled that Britain had shown itself, as it appeared in the months before the war, incapable of responding to Hitler's convictions with moral force at least equal and opposite to his. In *The Idea of a Christian Society,* Eliot wrote:

> I believe that there must be many persons who, like myself, were deeply shaken by the events of September 1938, in a way from which one does not recover; persons to whom that month brought a profounder realization of the general plight. It was not a disturbance of the understanding: the events themselves were not surprising. Nor, as became increasingly evident, was our distress due merely to disagreement with the policy and behaviour of the moment. The feeling which was new and unexpected was a feeling of humiliation, which seemed to demand an act of personal contrition, of humility, repentance and amendment; what had happened was something in which one was deeply implicated and responsible. . . . Was our society, which had always been so assured of its superiority and rectitude, so confident of its unexamined premises, assembled round anything more permanent than a congeries of banks, insurance companies and industries, and had it any beliefs more essential than a belief in compound interest and the maintenance of dividends?[2]

The events of September 1938 raised in a peculiarly intense form the question of a democratic culture and the necessity, as it appeared to Eliot, of creating a Christian society. He approached this question in fear and trembling and often in despair. The four talks he gave on the BBC in March and April 1932 were a first draft of *The Idea of a Christian Society,* a series of three lectures he delivered at Corpus Christi College, Cambridge, in March 1939.

On March 17, 1933, Eliot gave one of his Norton Lectures at Harvard under the title "The Modern Mind"; the text forms the seventh chapter of *The Use of Poetry and the Use of Criticism,* published in November 1933. Eliot took the occasion to look again at I. A. Richards's

Science and Poetry—a book he reviewed shortly after it appeared in
1926—and incidentally to dissociate himself from Richards's notion
that "The Waste Land" had effected a "complete severance between
poetry and all beliefs."[3] Toward the end of the lecture, having sufficiently disagreed with Richards on that matter, Eliot quoted two
sentences from Jacques Maritain. In the first, Maritain wrote that
"the unconcealed and palpable influence of the devil on an important
part of contemporary literature is one of the significant phenomena of
the history of our time."[4] Eliot commented that he did not expect
many of his readers to take Maritain's remark seriously but that those
who did would have very different criteria of criticism from those
who did not. In the second sentence, Maritain said that "by showing
us where moral truth and the genuine supernatural are situate, religion saves poetry from the absurdity of believing itself destined to
transform ethics and life: saves it from overweening arrogance."[5]
While preparing *The Use of Poetry and the Use of Criticism* for publication, Eliot added a footnote to Maritain's first quoted sentence, to the
effect that "with the influence of the devil on contemporary literature
I shall be concerned in more detail in another book."[6] The book
turned out to be *After Strange Gods,* the Page-Barbour Lectures he gave
some months later at the University of Virginia.

Eliot became dissatisfied with *After Strange Gods,* for reasons not
yet clear enough. He soon came to think that his soul was ill when he
gave the lectures, but he may also have decided that they did not live
up to the promise he had made for them. He did not allow the book
to be reprinted. But his note on Maritain's sentence makes it clear
that the theme of *After Strange Gods* was carefully chosen, the lectures were not delivered on the spur of an exacerbated moment. It is
clear, too, that Maritain, even more than Christopher Dawson, V. A.
Demant, and the other Christian writers whose assistance Eliot acknowledged, convinced him that if he intended to assert the primacy

of ethics, he would have to approach the task directly and explicitly; he could not rely upon poetry, even the poetry of "Ash-Wednesday" and the Ariel poems, to do the job for him. Eliot's note also shows that in the work of diagnosis, as in his several attempts as a social critic to straighten things out, he was willing to affront his readers rather than let down a good cause. I can't think of any Christian writer who would now promise or threaten to write a book about the influence of the devil on contemporary literature. Father William Lynch's *Christ and Apollo* offers the nearest comparison, at least in its intention, to Eliot's, but it is a far more tactful and lenient book. In the meantime the concept of evil has been diluted so that it now means only misfortune, hardship, the unsatisfactoriness of things, sheer necessity. The most blatant acts are regularly explained away by pointing to one's early environment, one's parents, the conditions in the streets. Charles Manson can be explicated. *American Psycho* can be received for sociology.

As I have indicated, Eliot's concern for public issues did not begin as late as 1932. In his early literary criticism he was always alert to the social bearing of literature and of the literary positions he took. By the time of his conversion in 1927 he had lost interest in the velleities of formal philosophy and turned to the more urgent issues of politics and religion. From 1927 to 1948 the possibility of creating a Christian society was a preoccupation so momentous that, by comparison, even the terrible events of September 1938 and the war that followed might be deemed diversions from a much greater question. In the poem "A Note on War Poetry," he wrote:

> War is not a life: it is a situation,
> One which may neither be ignored nor accepted,
> A problem to be met with ambush and stratagem,
> Enveloped or scattered.[7]

Throughout those dreadful years, Eliot's question remained the same: What would constitute a life, as distinct from a situation, however appalling? How could the Christian vision of such a life be elucidated and advanced? In the years following his conversion, he addressed that question in poems, plays, essays, and lectures. But the question had special urgency for him, it appears, from 1932 to 1948. The BBC talks on Christianity and Communism, followed by *The Use of Poetry and the Use of Criticism* (1933), *After Strange Gods* (1934); various essays and broadcast talks, including "Church, Community, and State" in February 1937, and a chapter in a book called *Revelation,* edited by John Baillie and Hugh Martin in 1937, make clear the degree of the preoccupation. During the war Eliot wrote several essays in the same cause, notably "Towards a Christian Britain," published in *The Listener* on April 10, 1941. This discursive phase of his work culminated in *Notes Towards the Definition of Culture* (1948). After 1948 he seems to have felt that he had done what he could, except for whatever he might yet do indirectly through his plays.

The book I have merely mentioned is *The Idea of a Christian Society,* a revised and extended version of the lectures given at Corpus Christi College in March 1939. It is a difficult book to like, mainly because Eliot is so persistently dismayed by the social forces he has to engage. He assumed that he was speaking to people who regarded themselves as Christians; he apparently hoped that he could persuade his audience and readers to become better Christians by requiring them to think, and to practice their thinking along certain theological lines. He argued that ostensibly political problems were really religious ones and that they could be understood only by examining the ends they prescribed for themselves. The immediate context of the lectures was Eliot's sense of the intolerable position of those who try to lead a Christian life in a non-Christian world. "We have today," he said, "a culture which is mainly negative, but which, so far as it is positive, is still Christian."[8] Eliot made persistent and serious play with the terms "negative" and "positive," short of defining them. A positive value, I assume, is one by which I am prepared to live, at whatever cost. Something is negative to Eliot if in practice it is neither one thing nor another but a mere pretense of being something definite. He maintained that Liberalism was negative because it exhibited merely a tendency to go away from some value rather than a determination to seek a particular end. Similarly, but not identically, the concept of democracy, according to Eliot, "does not contain enough positive content to stand alone against the forces that you dislike—it can easily be transformed by them." A thoroughgoing secularism would be possible, but Eliot maintained that it would be found objectionable in its consequences, "even to those who attach no positive importance to the survival of Christianity for its own sake."[9] These forces or sentiments—liberalism, democracy, secularism—are, Eliot implies, nothing in themselves: they have no intrinsic character but are merely the dilution of other values as a consequence of moral inertia. It is not surprising that they provide a setting for the sentimentalities that Eliot derided in *After Strange Gods*. One of these, brought forcibly to Eliot's attention by John Middleton Murry's writings, entailed recourse to the Inner Light, which Eliot regarded as "the most untrustworthy and deceitful guide that ever offered itself to wandering humanity." Another of these "negative" sentiments involved capitulation to the cult of personality, regardless of the quality of that attribute in a particular case—in Thomas Hardy's, for instance.

Eliot insisted that these forces are merely negative, and he was ready to suggest what would count as positive. But he was reluctant to put forward specific proposals. "What we are seeking is not a programme for a party, but a way of life for a people."[10] He committed himself to the "primacy of ethics" and thought that it had the best chance of establishing itself in a certain social setting. In *Notes Towards the Definition of Culture* he maintained that "the primary channel of transmission of culture is the family." Ideally, a family would persist, extending itself over several generations in the same place in which its members were born:

> Now the family is an institution of which nearly everybody speaks well: but it is advisable to remember that this is a term that may vary in extension. In the present age it means little more than the living members. Even of living members, it is a rare exception when an advertisement depicts a large family or three generations: the usual family on the hoardings consists of two parents and one or two young children. What is held up for admiration is not devotion to a family, but personal affection between the members of it; and the smaller the family, the more easily can this personal affection be sentimentalised. But when I speak of the family, I have in mind a bond which embraces a longer period of time than this: a piety towards the dead, however obscure, and a solicitude for the unborn, however remote.[11]

Some of Eliot's disgust with the anonymous and rootless factors in modern society is expressed by the reference, in "The Waste Land," to "those hooded hordes swarming / Over endless plains." A quotation from a rather hysterical passage in Hermann Hesse's *Blick ins Chaos* gave Eliot companionship in that disgust. Not that he believed that rural societies were necessarily happy. He once confessed that he would find it as difficult to live in a village as to give up smoking. Nonetheless, he thought that, for a Christian society, the best paradigm was the parish. He referred to "the idea, or ideal, of a community small enough to consist of a nexus of direct personal relationships, in which all iniquities and turpitudes will take the simple and easily appreciable form of wrong relations between one person and another."[12] Eliot valued a settled, homogeneous community—even though he chose to live in London; besides, he thought of London as a nexus of villages. He thought that such a community would be sustained by a sense of continuity operative through local change; a sense of tradition, which in his Christian years he chose to call orthodoxy; a community educated upon Christian principles and unified by observance of Christian doctrine and dogma.

We come back, necessarily, to certain awkward questions about Eliot's social philosophy. My view is that if we attend to the detail as well as to the broad outline of his social thought, even his most notorious utterances become understandable, if still contentious. Let me repeat: Eliot believed the best personal unit is the family and the best social unit the parish—a settled community having the same religious backkground. He preferred social unity and cohesion to divisiveness. It was inevitable, therefore, that he would see any self-differentiating element in that society as undesirable. The passage in *After Strange Gods* about "free-thinking Jews" is objectionable, but not for the reasons commonly given: it is objectionable because it is badly written, and, being badly written, it leaves in disorder the feelings from which it issued. The passage doesn't make clear whether Eliot's objection, given that the community he has in mind is a Christian one, is to the divisive presence in it of Jews as such, Orthodox or not; or to their being free thinking; or to their supposedly being both free thinking and Jews. The passage is a mess; the clearest sign of the mess is the insertion of an innocuous sentence between two sentences that cogently if argumentatively go together: "What is still more important is unity of religious background; and reasons of race and religion combine to make any large number of free-thinking Jews undesirable."[13] If Eliot had in view, as I am sure he had, a Christian society, the social attitude here does not seem to me pernicious. By free-thinking Jews I assume he means people who are Jews by historical or ancestral experience—their grandparents escaped from a pogrom in Warsaw—but who do not believe in their religion or practice it. An ambiguity that Eliot should have avoided is caused by the pairing of "race" with "Jews" and of "religion" with "free-thinking": some of the disapproval that Eliot feels about free thinking is bound to spill over upon the otherwise neutral term "Jews." J. M. Cameron has argued, convincingly I think, that in his reference to free-thinking Jews Eliot "is echoing the *Maurrasien* teaching on the role of the *métèque* in a society 'worm-eaten with Liberalism.' "[14] But in fact Eliot's social philosophy at this point is no more questionable than if he were to say, alive and writing now, that reasons of race and religion combine to make it undesirable that any large number of Palestinians should live in the predominantly Jewish state of Israel, or undesirable that a large number of Irish Catholic nationalists should live in the predominantly Protestant and loyalist Northern Ireland, or that a large number of Protestants and loyalists should live in the predominantly Catholic and nationalist Republic of Ireland, or that a large number of ethnic Albanians should live in Serbia. The resultant heterogeneity, it would be reasonable to say, is bad for everybody, including the dominant party.

Eliot goes on to say that "there must be a proper balance between urban and rural, industrial and agricultural development." Again, the sentiment is harmless, except that it has nothing to do with the matter in hand, and it conceals the bearing of the preceding sentence upon this one: "And a spirit of excessive tolerance is to be deprecated." A spirit of anything excessive is to be deprecated. The particular excess that Eliot had in mind was a matter of special concern to a writer who complained that what Christians in Britain mainly had to put up with was the condition of being tolerated: repressive tolerance, though the phrase was not then in use. Clearly, Eliot felt that it would not be good to have Christians put in the position of implying, to other people, that what they believed, or whether they believed anything, didn't matter. That would be bad for the Christians, injurious to their souls.

There are some unpublished letters that bear upon this episode.[15] In 1940, J. V. Healy wrote to Eliot to complain of apparent anti-Semitic tendencies in his writings. Eliot asked Healy to cite any relevant passages. Healy referred to the "free-thinking Jews." (The letters are not available for publication.) Eliot answered, in effect: yes, I supposed that you would point to that passage, but in fact I meant what I said. He then explained that by free-thinking Jews he meant Jews who no longer believed or practiced their religion and who had not attached themselves to any other one. A large number of free thinkers of any race would be regrettable: free-thinking Jews were only a special case. Eliot went on to say something interesting in view of his own Unitarian upbringing: that Jews who gave up their religion tended to lapse into a colorless kind of Unitarianism. Europeans or Americans who gave up their religion tended to retain many of the moral habits of Christianity or at least to live in communities in which those habits survived. The Jew who has abandoned his religion is therefore far more deracinated than the corresponding lapsed Christian. Deracination is the problem and the danger; it leads to irresponsibility. It is quite possible, of course—Eliot acknowledged to Healy—that this distinction would lose its meaning if all Christians should give up their faith.

In reply, Healy said he was not at all satisfied; the passage in dispute still seemed to him pernicious. If Eliot meant what he now said he meant, why pick on Jews as presenting a case in point? Why not pick on free-thinking Irish people, who would certainly fight back? Eliot at that point was weary of the correspondence, and he replied that the tone of *After Strange Gods* was so violent as now to be deprecated, but that he still held to the sentence in question. The correspondence ended on that note.

There is also a curious textual change in *Notes Towards the Definition of Culture*. A sentence in the 1948 edition reads:

> In certain historical conditions, a fierce exclusiveness may be a necessary condition for the preservation of a culture: the Old Testament bears witness to this.

Eliot added a footnote at that point:

> Since the diaspora, and the scattering of Jews amongst peoples holding the Christian Faith, it may have been unfortunate both for these peoples and for the Jews themselves, that the culture-contact between them has had to be within those neutral zones of culture in which religion could be ignored: and the effect may have been to strengthen the illusion that there can be culture without religion.

In the 1962 edition, Eliot revised the first part of the footnote to read:

> It seems to me that there should be close culture-contact between devout and practising Christians and devout and practising Jews. Much culture-contact in the past has been within those neutral zones of culture in which religion can be ignored, and between Jews and Gentiles both more or less emancipated from their religious traditions.

I

Eliot's procedure in his social and religious writings was not to oppose one set of sentiments with another. It was more typical of him to deal with each situation by bringing to bear upon it a higher perspective—religious, invariably—and a more demanding system of values. When he writes of the value of memory, for instance, in "Little Gidding," he doesn't locate it on its own ground but in a worthier state beyond any common understanding of its value: in that state it offers "liberation from the future as well as the past."[16] It is a strange account of memory, a faculty we normally think of as enriching us in the moments in which we exercise it, or in the moments in which we recall something involuntarily that seems extraordinarily telling. Few of us would think of memory as a device to liberate us from desire or as a way of replacing one relation to the beloved thing with another. In his social criticism Eliot tended to fasten upon some public or conventional sentiment, diagnose it as neither one thing nor another, and then force the consideration of it into a category in which a deliberate choice must be made. By deeming some such sentiment to be merely negative, he could show that it was not what it pretended to be but was rather the obfuscation of a genuine value not commonly recognized as such. He rarely looked back, once he had disposed of the allegedly negative sentiment. Nor did he expend much sympathy trying to understand why someone might in good faith adhere to that sentiment. He preferred to force the matter to a choice, according to the most exacting criteria of definition. The clearest instance of this procedure is in his essay on Baudelaire, where he insists that "so far as we are human, what we do must be either evil or good; so far as we do evil or good, we are human; and it is better, in a paradoxical way, to do evil than to do nothing: at least, we exist." (I don't appreciate the paradox: its appeal to existence is spurious.)

Much of the argument of *The Idea of a Christian Society* is derived, too explicitly, from a metaphor. "We are living at present in a kind of doldrums," Eliot says—he is speaking in March 1939—"between opposing winds of doctrine, in a period in which one political philosophy"—

he means liberalism—"has lost its cogency for behaviour, though it is still the only one in which public speech can be framed."[17] If the wind of liberalism has waned, as Eliot thinks, then the only escape from the doldrums is turning a negative into a positive condition, and the only way to do that is by presenting the real choice as one between Christianity and paganism. "The fundamental objection to fascist doctrine," Eliot says, "the one which we conceal from ourselves because it might condemn ourselves as well, is that it is pagan."[18] So the entire rhetorical force of *The Idea of a Christian Society,* as of the books and essays surrounding it, is directed toward the conversion of political terms into religious terms, as if to say that the ostensibly real political terms are in fact obfuscations or self-delusions; the real issue, in every case of a consideration of values, is a question of religious belief and practice.

Eliot's rhetorical device is implicit in the title of *The Idea of a Christian Society.* His model, as he acknowledges, is Coleridge's *On the Constitution of Church and State According to the Idea of Each* (published in December 1829). Coleridge's occasion was the controversy in England and Ireland before the passage, on April 13, 1829, of the Catholic Relief Bill, colloquially known as Catholic Emancipation. His book was one of his several attempts to define the principles that should be recognized in the consideration of church and state according to the idea of each. "By an *idea,*" he said, "I mean (in this instance) that conception of a thing which is not abstracted from any particular state, form, or mode, in which the thing may happen to exist at this or at that time; nor yet generalized from any number or succession of such forms or modes; but which is given by the knowledge of *its ultimate aim.*"[19] Coleridge's definition, in turn, entailed a distinction between a concept and an idea. A conception, he says, "*consists* in a conscious act of the understanding, bringing any given object or impression into the same class with any number of other objects, or impressions, by means of some character or characters common to them all."[20] The conceptualizing act is one of classification, the recognition of a type or genre, based on a perception of the attributes common to its members. An idea is independent of whatever attributes happen to be present in a given situation; it respects only the end, the ultimate or defining purpose of a thing. Newman's idea of a university is not constrained by the character of any university that exists or has ever existed. As Coleridge puts it: "That which, contemplated *objectively* (i.e. as existing *externally* to the mind), we call a LAW; the same contemplated *subjectively* (i.e. as existing in a subject or mind), is an idea."[21] In the same spirit, and in a direct relation to Coleridge, Eliot does not analyze any society that exists and thinks of itself as Christian. He asks, rather: what is the end, the ultimate aim, of a Christian society, whether or not this end is discernible in any existing society or any past society? What would a Christian society be, if it were to come into being? And what changes in a Christian's social attitudes would be required to bring it about?

The type of intellectual activity that Eliot engages in—I am referring to *The Idea of a Christian Society* and the other writings in its vicinity—we may call, as he did, mythical; it is a procedure by which the mind adverts to contingent events but refuses to be intimidated by the local conventions on which they operate; it calls upon a higher system of values by which the immediate event or situation may be judged. Eliot admired the working of the mythical imagination in Yeats and Joyce, but his chief example of it comes from *The Republic,* Book 9, where in answer to Glaucon's remark "I understand you mean the city the establishment of which we have described, the city whose home is in idea only; for I do not believe that there is such a city on earth," Socrates says, "Perhaps it is laid up as a pattern in heaven, which he who desires may behold and, beholding, may set his own house in order."[22] Eliot thought so well of that passage that he

put it into the first version of "The Waste Land"—Pound deleted it—
and he translated it into secular terms in his essay on Kipling, where
his theme is Kipling's vision of the British Empire: "He had always
been far from uncritical of the defects and wrongs of the British Empire, but held a firm belief in what it should and might be. In his later
phase England and a particular corner of England became the centre
of his vision. He is more concerned with the problem of the sound-
ness of the *core* of empire: this core is something older, more natural
and more permanent. But at the same time his vision takes a larger
view, and he sees the Roman Empire and the place of England in it.
The vision is almost that of an idea of empire laid up in heaven."[23] The
distinction between the actual empire and the idea of an empire—*urbs
aeterna*—is much the same as Kant's distinction, in the *Critique of Pure
Reason,* between a concept, which has its source in understanding,
and an idea, which is independent of experience and has its source in
reason. In Kant, as Deleuze has explained, reason forms transcendental ideas that go beyond the possibility of experience: they are ideal
limits where the concepts of the understanding converge.[24] These
ideas are not fictions; they have an objective value. The purpose of
Eliot's book is to persuade his readers, Christians at least in some
sense, to contemplate a certain idea, a possible pattern, a social idea
of unity, and to move their wills in accordance with it. He is trying to
transform the reader, on every occasion of a dispute on the level of
understanding, by appeal to the higher if more abstract terminology
of reason. This gesture, on Eliot's part, marks the fundamental character of his imagination, in his poetry even more than in his plays and
essays. The idea of a pattern laid up in heaven is always at hand, in the
later poems as in the social criticism, wherever Eliot speaks of a
pattern as distinct from whatever *sensibilia* or concepts apparently
hold the ground of a dispute. "Unless you can find a pattern in which

all problems of life can have their place, we are only likely to go on complicating chaos," he says in *The Idea of a Christian Society*.

There is no merit in being dainty about the risks incurred by Eliot's imagination, so far as it was—if I am right—essentially mythical. He was capable of seeing objects that presented themselves to him, though he was not a novelist. Just as clearly as Joyce in *Ulysses*, Eliot saw what went on in the streets, though he didn't give it the same exemplary value that Joyce did. He saw, too, as Joyce did, the different things that went on in a person's mind. Eliot could imagine, though with evident difficulty, what occurred in a mind other than his own. But there is always a risk, if your respect for a pattern laid up in heaven compels the spirit in which you recognize what goes on in the street, that you will get into the habit of thinking the events in the street unimportant. If the pattern has priority, the immediate events are likely to appear merely contingent. In practice, this cast of mind enabled Eliot to remain detached in the presence of many events that other people worried about and acted on. It also enabled him, even when he cared about the events in his own way and for his own reasons, to hold himself aloof from the particular considerations of them that engrossed the attention of other people. He cared about the Spanish Civil War, but not in the same way that other people in England cared about it. Many people were distressed by the apparent success of fascism. Eliot, too, was distressed about it, but—as I have remarked—for his own reason: not because it was an Italian regime for Italians and otherwise humbug, but because it was a form of paganism.

The Idea of a Christian Society has had a bad press, and if it continued to be read it would probably get a worse one, but it has been condemned for the wrong reasons and left, therefore, mainly unread. Some readers—Blackmur is a case in point—simply declared themselves unbelievers, assumed that Christianity could no longer be believed, and made no serious attempt to imagine what Eliot was doing. In *The Expense of Greatness* Blackmur reviewed Eliot's book on the assumption, premature and unexamined (since there are millions of practicing Christians extant), that "a Christian state, a Christian education, a Christian philosophy, are as outmoded as the Christian astronomy which accompanied them when they flourished."[25] The point is a poor one, since the church has had no real difficulty surviving the passage of Ptolemaic astronomy. A Christian state is, theoretically, just as conceivable as a Jewish one or an Islamic one; a Christian education is still feasible, and a Christian philosophy is demonstrably available in more contemporary philosophers than one has time to read—Rahner, Gadamer, Taylor, MacIntyre, Balthasar. Blackmur dealt with Eliot's book as if the idea it offered could be judged solely on its probable results, the character it would acquire by being embodied in corresponding institutions. I can't see how Blackmur thought himself in a strong position to guess what form these institutions would take; since he couldn't imagine the possibility that the idea might ever be realized, it was vain of him to pronounce that the realization would be hapless. As an unbeliever, Blackmur could not imagine that some other readers, Christians perhaps, would find the contemplation of Eliot's idea of a Christian society a chastening or otherwise edifying experience. "Mr. Eliot's idea of a Christian society—his idea of what is aimed at—cannot be realized in this world: . . . The urban, suburban, industrialised, lower-middle-class society—neutral or pagan—which Mr. Eliot describes, has other ears to the ground: it listens to itself, all other voices failing."[26] So much the worse, I would say.

If Eliot's idea of a Christian society is not to be judged on Blackmur's terms, on what terms may it be judged? Deleuze's book on Kant is again a help, especially to someone like me who is not a philosopher. If we take seriously the notion of an idea in Eliot's terms (or Coleridge's, or Kant's) and if, as Deleuze says, "an end is a representation which determines the will," then the success or failure of Eliot's idea depends on the degree to which it engages and persuades the will of a reader toward that end. Further, and still from Deleuze, "in the ends of reason, it is reason which takes itself as its own end." Reason, that is, as distinct from understanding. A reader's conviction of this, in dealing with Eliot's book, would depend upon the degree to which he or she is convinced that the idea is independent of experience and that it corresponds to the faculty of desire in the reader. One does not question a vision. Further still, and recurring to the notion of Eliot's higher perspective, the success or failure of the book is the degree to which the expression of its idea enables the reader to judge other things, the degree to which readers are impelled to feel that the idea is the perspective in which they will now judge various local issues. The idea is the light, not the things seen in it; it enables us to see those things "under its particular auspices." Finally, and still having recourse to Deleuze: "The categories are applicable to all objects of possible experience; in order to find a middle term which makes possible the attribution of an *a priori* concept to *all* objects, reason can no longer look to another concept (even an *a priori* one) but must form *Ideas* which go beyond the possibility of experience. This is, in a sense, how reason is induced, in its own speculative interest, to form transcendental Ideas. These represent the *totality of conditions* under which a category of relation may be attributed to objects of possible experience; they therefore represent something *unconditioned*."[27] In *The Idea of a Christian Society* the unconditioned character of the idea corresponds to its being "a pattern laid up in heaven." Its freedom includes freedom from the zeal with which we give an idea only the destiny of applying it in accordance with our partiality.

My remarks on the philosophical issues are the jottings of an amateur. But I take heart from a recent conversation with Robert Nozick, in which he suggested a possible line of argument. The content of an ideal, he said—I can't quote him exactly or hold him responsible for my version—is not exhausted by the way or ways in which we manage to work it; it also includes its realization by better people. The idea of communism, or liberalism, or capitalism may fail for several reasons, one of which may be the fact that, in given conditions, the people who try to put it into practice are not equipped to do so. When we try to pursue a philosophical ideal, Nozick remarked, we associate our lives with how the ideal would have worked out in other and better worlds or with how it might still work out in a better world. I interpret Nozick as saying that an idea, in Eliot's or Coleridge's or Plato's terms, might if nothing else enrich the reverberation of our lives. Or, especially in *The Idea of a Christian Society,* it might enforce upon us the scruple of attending to a daunting system of values. Aldous Huxley asked, in a famous essay, what it would be like to read Wordsworth in the tropics. Well, it would depend upon the imaginative reach of the reader. An incompetent reader of Wordsworth would merely apply intimations of the Lake District to her immediate context, hoping for an edifying fit. A better reader would imagine the forms and shapes of being, other than her own, elicited by Wordsworth's poems, and would not be deflected from this imagining even in the tropics. I don't claim that this would be as easy in the tropics as in a temperate Windermere of the reader's choice, but the implied form of attention in each case is the same.

I feel some misgiving about this commentary on *The Idea of a Christian Society.* The poetry is the thing, isn't it? But the poetry, especially *Four Quartets,* is implicated in social and religious thought. Eliot has been under attack for many years, ever since he converted to Christianity. It is now not only permissible but almost obligatory, in intellectual circles, to attack Christianity and to deride any Christian's faith—and the attack is regularly made by people who claim to be appalled by anti-Semitism. To hate Christianity is not deemed to reflect badly upon the hater. Nobody holds it against Empson that he published, with reiterated insistence, denunciations of Christianity. I was rebuked recently by Jonathan Culler for finding Empson's hatred of Christianity the most tedious part of his mind. Quoting that phrase in *Framing the Signs,* Culler added, "as Catholic Denis Donoghue smugly calls it." The implication that only by being a Catholic could anyone find Empson's hatred of Christianity tedious, speaks clearly of a particular prejudice on Culler's part. I appreciate the fact that, since the Holocaust, Jews must be treated with particular tenderness. In American politics, Israel is treated as a special case; the sensibilities of its citizens are cherished beyond the consideration given to other people. But the convention by which exceptional tenderness is maintained toward those sensibilities should be questioned. Israel has shown that in war and peace it conducts itself in much the same spirit as any other worldly nation and is just as ready as its opponents to play rough and dirty.

The bearing of these remarks on Eliot and *The Idea of a Christian Society* should be clear. That he is accused of anti-Semitism seems to me an injustice. Harold Bloom refers, in *Shakespeare: The Invention of the Human,* to the "incessantly anti-Semitic T. S. Eliot."[28] The charge is as specious as if I accused Eliot, citing his reference to "Apeneck Sweeney," of being prejudiced against the Irish. Anthony Julius's *T. S. Eliot, Anti-Semitism, and Literary Form* (1995) is an essay in the imputation of guilt by association. It holds Eliot personally and morally responsible for every anti-Semitic prejudice in Europe in the twentieth century. Julius does not understand that one of the common attributes of Eliot's generation—which later generations have lost—was the maintenance of friendships, person to person, despite what we would regard as lethal ideological differences between them.

Think of Eliot's friendships with Pound, Wyndham Lewis, Richards, Babbitt, and Paul Elmer More; and of the disagreements they accommodated. It would require long and careful exposition to give a just account of Eliot's dealings with Maurras, Lawrence, and Yeats, an exposition that would include nuances of appreciation, liking and disliking, repudiation of one aspect, respect for another. Specifically, Eliot admired Maurras and regarded him as a strong writer, but he deplored the violence of his political interventions, and he had an extremely complex sense of Maurras's relation to *Action Française*. It seems to me that such complexities, like mixed friendships, have not survived: divisions have become sharper, friendship has become a narrower and more exclusive sentiment. The reason may be that intellectual relations in Europe were contorted by the combined impact of the Dreyfus case and the Algerian War: thereafter, mixed friendships, such as that between Eliot and Pound, became rare achievements. To compare large with small: Donald Davie brought his friendship with me to an end because of one sentence in a long review I published of his second book on Pound: "The relation between Davie's mind and its contents has always been experimental." Davie interpreted it as saying: "Davie has never been able to think."

Can we straighten out the problem of *After Strange Gods, The Idea of a Christian Society,* and *Notes Towards the Definition of Culture?* Eliot's writings in the service of Christianity are mainly of interest to Christians. The fact that his poetry from "Ash-Wednesday" to "Little Gidding" is animated by a commitment to Christianity may be a problem for Leavis, Empson, and some other readers; they must deal with it as best they can. It should not be impossible for readers to imagine having certain convictions that they don't otherwise feel. The chief justification for reading literature is that it trains the reader in the exercise of that imagination.

But I continue to feel some misgiving. Eliot's writings on social, political, and religious themes—I refer to his prose, not the poetry—have been the cause of so much comment, much of it beside any reasonable point, that I sometimes wish he had never written a line on such matters. Suppose he had written only the poems and handed them over to his readers without saying a word of defense or justification. Could we not have intuited from the poems a vision, a pattern, all the better for not being explicit? It is regrettable that Eliot allowed himself to be led—by Maritain, on several occasions—into explicitness far beyond need. That the social commentary has damaged his reputation, I do not doubt: it is what many readers fasten upon, as if it were the main thing. Eliot was a formidable social analyst. The fact that English political life has moved in a direction in most respects contrary to the one he advocated is not a decisive point.

So why should we be reading *The Idea of a Christian Society* now and thinking of its themes in our own context? Communism has collapsed in Russia, defeated by television, the market, and global Americanization. Even with the example of China before us, the main conflict is no longer between Christianity and Communism: it is between those who think that the ultimate questions are religious and those who think that religious questions have been set aside by the combined force of politics, sociology, psychology, and economics. Many of Eliot's minor arguments no longer seem persuasive: his argument for retaining the Established Church of England, for instance, is feeble. Neither the Church of England nor the monarchy gains much by the constitutional link that joins them. J. M. Cameron and other Roman Catholics think it a question "whether, on any theory of the Church, there is available today any solution better than that of the neutral society on the American model."[29]

The continuing interest of *The Idea of a Christian Society,* as of *Notes Towards the Definition of Culture,* is consistent with our attributing a far higher value to Eliot's poems. The prose for Christianity is valuable not merely as work of edification; though indeed it is edifying to find Eliot willing to annoy his readers and to demand that they question their certainties. That is not a small thing. But the much larger consideration is that, as Cameron puts it, Eliot "has kept steadily before us man's dependence upon and hunger for the Absolute; and his capacity for the Eternal."[30] These are difficult terms to use; they appear to have significance mostly algebraic. Perhaps we should retain them subject to translation into a cooler language. It is Eliot's great distinction as a writer for the idea of a Christian society that he insisted upon examining local forces and conditions within the highest perspective and the most demanding articulations.

Reading *Four Quartets*

W e have four poems, each in five parts; clearly an elaborate structure, indicating that the character of the work is likely to be disclosed not in any culminating moment but in the organization of the whole, the relations among the parts, the correspondence of one part to its counterpart in the other poems. After "Burnt Norton" the later poems will exhibit not a development in the plot as beginning presses toward middle and middle toward end, but at every moment a new beginning, another raid on the inarticulate, as the poems indicate not positions reached but the reaching of positions, the struggle toward an object not promised, not in the contract. While the poems have a high proportion of abstract terms, suggesting that the experience has been brought to an unusually high degree of generalization, the poet will take the harm out of these certitudes by going back over them and discarding those now deemed inadequate. The work will not be "dramatic," it will not drive itself toward the fulfillment of a form as in a play. And yet while the leading analogies are musical (like those obtaining between air, earth, water, and fire) rather than logical (as in the parts of a syllogism or a detective story) the poems will be as dogmatic, in their way, as *The Dunciad* and *Night Thoughts*. The dogmas will be declared by making their substitutes seem illusory or incomplete. For this purpose the poet will use the camouflage of different voices; he will not, like the author of *Night Thoughts,* make everything depend upon the fiat of a single voice. The strategy of *Four Quartets* is to set up several voices, each charged with the evacuation of one area, until nothing is left but "prayer, observance, discipline, thought and action." At that point, the reader is ready to "know the place for the first time."

The Structure of the Quartets

Part I of each poem renders a mode of being in which we impose upon our experience our own meaning and think that it is decisive; but it is sometimes illusory and, at best, partial. In "Burnt Norton" it is the deception of the thrush, the rose-garden of experience. In "East Coker" it is the "daunsinge"-scene, handsome, archaic; Sir Thomas Elyot's couples are led off with half-gentle irony, blessings on their heads. In "The Dry Salvages" the anxious women try to reckon the sea in their own terms, "calculating the future," forgetting that "the sea is all about us," a reality encompassing us for which we are not responsible, incorrigibly real because—like the Word—it is not our invention. In "Little Gidding" the pilgrimage is only "a shell, a husk of meaning" because we, the pilgrims, have chosen our object and (worse still) made the choice in accordance with our own mere "sense and notion."

I'll glance at one of these parts, but I'll be looking at it more closely in the next chaper. "Burnt Norton" begins with four statements about Time, each spoken by a different voice. First, Time as a continuous chain of events. Second, Time as eternally present and therefore unredeemable because it excludes history, process, and the flux. Third, Time as a continuum of events that might have been different. Last, these possibilities are pointed toward a divine purpose not ours and therefore "the ground of our beseeching." "Burnt Norton" was written as a separate poem, several years before its companions, but each of its opening statements about Time becomes the ground of meditation for its corresponding poem in the sequence. This would go some distance to meet one of the persistent problems of the *Quartets,* the tone of "The Dry Salvages," the idea being that the poem has to work out the implications of

> What might have been is an abstraction
> Remaining a perpetual possibility
> Only in a world of speculation

—hence the feeling of words issuing from a merely speculative universe of discourse. (But this problem can wait.)

The next lines in "Burnt Norton" translate "what might have been" into footfalls which echo in the memory

> Down the passage which we did not take
> Towards the door we never opened
> Into the rose-garden

—a purely linguistic event featuring the unfulfilled possibilities strewn across our past lives, offering themselves only as a fantasy sound-box in which "my words echo." To disturb the fictive past is futile, but it will be disturbed, because we have filled the garden with our own echoes, and nothing is sweeter than self-deception. The rose-garden is my fantasy-refuge, the realms of experience which I declare my private property. So I arrange the scene to disclose myself, the roses are my guests, the dry pool is filled with water out of sunlight for my benefit because a vital harmony between myself and Nature is my great Romantic illusion. But I exaggerate my control over reality:

> Then a cloud passed, and the pool was empty.
> Go, said the bird, for the leaves were full of children,
> Hidden excitedly, containing laughter.
> Go, go, go, said the bird: human kind
> Cannot bear very much reality

—even the reality of laughing children. In the third part of "East Coker" "the laughter in the garden" is invoked again as part of our fantasy, but there it is defined immediately as "echoed ecstasy," not something that must be abandoned or evacuated but "requiring, pointing to the agony / Of death and birth." Here in "Burnt Norton" when we have connived with the deception of the thrush, we get as much as we deserve if the thrush chases us from the garden; if the illusion is broken we have only ourselves to blame. Part I ends with the several variants of Time gathered together now and "pointing" toward one end, "which is always present." In Part V when the hidden laughter of children in the foliage is pointed in this way, the time is redeemed.

Part 2 of each poem is a statement of the true condition, set off against the preoccupations that prevent its recognition. In "Burnt Norton" it is given as the dance of consciousness, concentration, the still point, *Erhebung;* against the diverse impediments of garlic, sapphires, the practical desire, the "enchainment of past and future." In "East Coker" it is the true wisdom of humility, set off against the vortex, "the autumnal serenity / And the wisdom of age," the goodwill of mere Tradition, "the knowledge derived from experience," and the fear of old men. In "The Dry Salvages" it is "the meaning,"

the Annunciation; menaced by the "currents of action" which cover
our past lives. In "Little Gidding" it is the refining fire of the dancer;
obscured by the vanities of spiritless culture, last year's words, "the
gifts reserved for age."

In "East Coker" this second part is particularly vivid. The true
condition is given, as in "Little Gidding," only at the end of this part,
when the ground has been cleared and the necessary discriminations
imposed. The motto for this process is given in the opening lines of
the third part of "Little Gidding":

> There are three conditions which often look alike
> Yet differ completely, flourish in the same hedgerow:

In a secular or neutral context no discrimination is possible; only the
vision of spirit can reveal the differences—the difference, to take one
example, between the darkness inhabited by "distinguished civil servants, chairmen of many committees," in "East Coker," and that
other darkness which is the "darkness of God." So the second part of
"East Coker" begins with an experimental jeremiad, an answer to the
"reconciliation" passage in the corresponding part of "Burnt Norton." Instead of the still point there is the vortex, which extends to
the whole world the fate of three victims in "Gerontion":

> De Bailhache, Fresca, Mrs. Cammel, whirled
> Beyond the circuit of the shuddering Bear
> In fractured atoms.

That was a way of putting it; but the poet now begins again, rejecting
the jeremiad, or rather translating it into more urbane terms. Not
that the poetry matters: if it must be evacuated along with the rest,
well and good; a fresh start is more important. The first obstacle is
the dead weight of an unemployed past; this must be cleared away,

especially if it comes with the self-righteous panoply of words like "calm" and "serenity." If Tradition is merely an antique drum, we must get rid of it: the past is dead, by definition, unless it is alive. Eliot holds the vaunted terms close to the light of a genuinely live tradition; under this scrutiny the serenity is only a "deliberate hebitude," the wisdom "only the knowledge of dead secrets." The editorial plural of "it seems to us" is the voice of antiseptic discrimination; its object is "the knowledge derived from experience," a platitude from whose warmth we must be ejected. The ejecting force is the concept of Tradition as "a new and shocking / Valuation," every moment, of all that we have been. The tone becomes more astringent as the editorial we focuses in a single rebuking voice:

> Do not let me hear
> Of the wisdom of old men

and the wisdom is given as a self-congratulating fiction, a mere mockery. In "Ash-Wednesday" the speaker prays to be delivered from this hall of distorting mirrors: "Suffer us not to mock ourselves with falsehood," meaning our private intelligences. In the second part of "Little Gidding" Eliot makes yet another attempt, using Yeats's *Purgatory* and the Ghost of Hamlet, merging the wisdom of old men with the gifts reserved for the senile humanist. In "East Coker" the answer is: "Humility is endless."

Part 3 of each poem is a statement of our time-ridden condition, and a proper admonition to "wait" without choosing our object. In "Burnt Norton" it is the tube-station "flicker" of apathy and distraction, followed by the warning "Descend lower." The descent, if we agree to it, is guided by Heraclitus and St. John of the Cross, and it features the voiding of all claims to property, sense, fancy, and even—the last surrender—spirit. The key word is evacuation. But the lines that form the starting point for the corresponding part of "East Coker" are

This is the one way, and the other
Is the same, not in movement
But abstention from movement; while the world moves
In appetency, on its metalled ways
Of time past and time future.

In Part 3 of "East Coker" this "scene" is extended. Some of the travelers are named, notably those who travel by limousine:

Industrial lords and petty contractors, all go into the dark,
And dark the Sun and Moon, and the Almanach de Gotha
And the Stock Exchange Gazette, the Directory of Directors.

But if we gloat upon the discomfiture of the rich, "we all go with them, into the silent funeral." Silent because anonymous; since we have obliterated our own identities, "there is no one to bury." The proper admonition is: "Be still"; wait, without choosing even the objects of our faith, hope, or charity. Then this admonition, in turn, is intensified in the last lines of this part and will eventually become Celia's story in *The Cocktail Party:* "You must go by a way wherein there is no ecstasy." The last line should probably be read as: "And where you *are* is where *you* are not." In "Little Gidding"—to defer the special problems of "The Dry Salvages"—Part 3 gives our time-ridden condition as indifference, desire, the enchainment of past and future; and the admonition, under Lady Juliana's auspices, is to purify the motive:

And all shall be well and
All manner of thing shall be well
By the purification of the motive
In the ground of our beseeching.

Lady Juliana's *Shewings* bears witness to the Logos common to all, now partially revealed through her but independently of her will: their truth does not depend upon her. She does not suggest that the visions were important because they attended her. There is a reality not ourselves, not our property, not our "supreme fiction." This is the transition between Parts 2 and 3 of "The Dry Salvages." When a discursive voice says, "I sometimes wonder if that is what Krishna meant," the fresh start, the new version of our time-ridden condition, is the facile notion of Time itself as a spatial category in which the self occupies a gratifyingly secure present tense, looks "back" to a fixed past and "forward" to a future rich in anticipated pleasures. The anxious worried women of Part 2 were at least in a more dignified position,

> Between midnight and dawn, when the past is all deception,
> The future futureless . . .

F. H. Bradley had already undermined the cozy assumptions of the travelers in chapter 4 of *Appearance and Reality*. Eliot's admonition is given in two voices, the nocturnal voice which snubs the travelers, "you who think that you are voyaging," and the voice of Krishna, persuading Arjuna to go with purified motive into battle. The first voice comes from a reader of Bradley:

> You are not those who saw the harbour
> Receding, or those who will disembark

and virtually challenges the travelers to declare their "personal identity" and prove it. But the travelers can still be saved, if they heed Krishna. The quoted lines are taken from Canto VIII of the *Bhagavad-Gita,* with a glance at Canto II. The relevant sentences are these:

> He who at his last hour, when he casts off the body, goes hence remembering Me, goes assuredly into My being. Whatsoever being a man at his end in leaving the body remembers, to the same he always goes, O son of Kunti, inspired to being therein. There-

fore at all times remember Me, and fight; if thy mind and understanding are devoted to Me, thou wilt assuredly come to Me. . . .
In Works be thine office; in their fruits must it never be.[1]

Eliot's version is:

> At the moment which is not of action or inaction
> You can receive this: 'on whatever sphere of being
> The mind of a man may be intent
> At the time of death'—that is the one action
> (And the time of death is every moment)
> Which shall fructify in the lives of others:
> And do not think of the fruit of action.
> Fare forward.

That is as close as we are likely to come to the dogmatic center of this
dogmatic poem. The moment which is not of action or inaction is
presumably the moment of incarnate thought, concentration without
elimination, in our own lives hardly more frequent than Wordsworthian "spots of time," since human kind cannot bear very much
reality. Krishna's message concerns the moment of death as his pupil goes into battle, but Eliot's Heraclitean parenthesis gives it a
strangely Christian latitude; if we die every moment and if at every
moment we are intent upon the highest sphere of being, then—the
Dantean promise runs—this "intention" will fructify in the lives of
others. This is another version of the promise made in Part 2, after
the equation of "the meaning" with "the one Annunciation"; that the
past experience revived in the meaning "is not the experience of one
life only / But of many generations." It is also, looking back to "East
Coker," the "lifetime burning in every moment." If we add, from
"Ash-Wednesday," "Redeem the time," and from "Burnt Norton,"
"only through time time is conquered," we have a node of Christian

emphasis, depending upon the Incarnation, which is as close as the *Quartets* at any one moment will come to "the meaning."

Part 4 of each poem is a lyric of purgation; not persuasion toward the act but the act itself. In "Burnt Norton" when we have renounced the pretentions of action and the black cloud has carried away the sun, we are at the "ABC of being"—Stevens's phrase—and in a fit state to ask the appropriately modest questions. "Will the clematis / Stray down, bend to us" is one of four questions, each a preparation for prayer. Clematis, the Virgin's bower of blue, Mary's color, and the fingers of yew point the questions toward death and the Christian hope of immortality. But the last lines are provisional: the harmony between the kingfisher's wing and nature's light is less than a final comfort; these are merely "notes toward" prayer. In "East Coker" the lyric of purgation hovers over Adam's curse, original sin. The tone is strangely crude; indeed, this is one of the weaker parts of the poem. The analogies of health and disease, surgeons, patients, and hospitals are marginally appropriate, but far too dependent upon our reading "the wounded surgeon" as Christ, "the dying nurse" as the church, the hospital as the earth, "the ruined millionaire" as God the Father, the briars as the thorns of Christ. When we have effected these translations little remains but the satisfaction of having done so. The corresponding part of "The Dry Salvages," is much finer, a prayer continuous with that of Part 5 of "Ash-Wednesday." Then the last version, in "Little Gidding," is the Pentecostal Fire, the Descent of the Holy Ghost. The German bomber, the "dark dove" of Part 3, is now transformed:

> The dove descending breaks the air
> With flame of incandescent terror

and if the old dove was deadly the new one is far from being domesticated. Heraclitus's account of the Death of the Elements is relevant,

but the entire lyric is an extended version of the lines in the corresponding part of "East Coker":

> If to be warmed, then I must freeze
> And quake in frigid purgatorial fires
> Of which the flame is roses, and the smoke is briars.

—with a glance at Adam's curse and "the one discharge from sin
and error." The first lyric, in "Burnt Norton," was all question; the
second, in "East Coker," a sermon of rude reminders; the third,
the prayer of "The Dry Salvages." And now the question can be
answered:

> Who then devised the torment? Love.
> Love is the unfamiliar Name
> Behind the hands that wove
> The intolerable shirt of flame
> Which human power cannot remove.
>> We only live, only suspire
>> Consumed by either fire or fire.

In the third part of "Ash-Wednesday" the devil of the stairs wore the
"deceitful face of hope and despair." In "East Coker" the faith and the
hope and the love were all "in the waiting." And now the tenable hope
is specified in "the choice of pyre or pyre," taking up where Part I left
off, "pentecostal fire / In the dark time of the year." The collocation
of Fire and Love, as the poet remarked of the ascetic conjunction of
the Fire Sermon's "Burning burning burning burning" and St. Augustine's "O Lord Thou pluckest me out," in "The Waste Land," "is
not an accident."

Part 5 of each poem is a meditation on the redemption of Time. In
Night Thoughts, Young asks, innocently enough, "Redeem we time?"
In "Ash-Wednesday" the voice intones:

                              Redeem
    The time.   Redeem
    The unread vision in the higher dream
    While jewelled unicorns draw by the gilded hearse.

Part 5 of "Burnt Norton" is the first attempt, a tentative and frus-
trated figuring of time redeemed in Love. It begins with a Chinese jar
that "still / Moves perpetually in its stillness," but this is merely a
slight specification of the "daylight" of Part 3,

    Investing form with lucid stillness
    Turning shadow into transient beauty
    With slow rotation suggesting permanence.

But clearly the Chinese jar won't do; nor will the stillness of the
violin. Then the syntax lurches in dazed considerations of beginning
and end. The words strain and crack because they are not the Word,
they are one man's fancies, his "private intelligence," his disconsolate
chimeras, the "merely" human voices which, in "The Love Song of
J. Alfred Prufrock," "wake us, and we drown." Or perhaps the "dae-
monic, chthonic powers" of "The Dry Salvages." The last lines give
up the attempt to offer comparisons from a familiar medium and
confront the problem directly, beginning with Aristotle's God as the
Unmoved Mover, Dryden's Universal He, "Unmade, unmov'd; yet
making, moving All." Eliot's version is

    Love is itself unmoving,
      Only the cause and end of movement,
    Timeless, and undesiring
    Except in the aspect of time
    Caught in the form of limitation
    Between un-being and being

—which I interpret as the Incarnation, a later version of a choric passage in the seventh Part of *The Rock:*

> A moment not out of time, but in time, in what we call history:
>   transecting, bisecting the world of time, a moment in time
>   but not like a moment of time,
> A moment in time but time was made through that moment:
>   for without the meaning there is no time, and that moment
>   of time gave the meaning.

"Un-being" is what *The Rock* calls "negative being": "being" is the still point. "Burnt Norton" ends:

> Sudden in a shaft of sunlight
> Even while the dust moves
> There rises the hidden laughter
> Of children in the foliage
> Quick now, here, now, always—
> Ridiculous the waste sad time
> Stretching before and after.

This sounds definitive, especially when it is set off against the "waste sad time." But each of its terms has already been circumscribed. God as the Timeless is immanent in the temporal, yes, here as in the *Paradiso.* He descended into history and thereby "made time." But we have already seen that the rose-garden is each man's fantasy-refuge, not absurd or trivial but incomplete, like the children's laughter. And the proof is in the shaft of sunlight which will flash again across the corresponding part of "The Dry Salvages," focusing on an experience declared incomplete. Two conditions are described in this part, and they are distinguished as firmly as in *The Cocktail Party*; that of the saint, Celia, and that of the rest of us, Edward and Lavinia at the end of the play, "a good life" but not sanctity or the refining fire. Critics who were angered by this separation in the play did not remark that the same plot is inaugurated in Part 5 of "The Dry Salvages." This part begins with an account of "men's curiosity" which searches past and future / And clings to that dimension." But then there is sanctity:

> But to apprehend
> The point of intersection of the timeless
> With time, is an occupation for the saint—
> No occupation either, but something given
> And taken, in a lifetime's death in love,
> Ardour and selflessness and self-surrender.

Celia, clearly. But most of us are Edwards or Lavinias, and for us

> there is only the unattended
> Moment, the moment in and out of time,
> The distraction fit, lost in a shaft of sunlight,
> The wild thyme unseen, or the winter lightning
> Or the waterfall, or music heard so deeply
> That it is not heard at all, but you are the music
> While the music lasts

—the unheard music in the shrubbery of "Burnt Norton." In that poem the words crack and strain before the birth of Celia. When she goes on the "way of illumination" in Part 5 of "The Dry Salvages," the rest of us do what we can in the middle style:

> And right action is freedom
> From past and future also.
> For most of us, this is the aim
> Never here to be realised;
> We are only undefeated
> Because we have gone on trying;

—a counsel from which we extract whatever juice we can, perhaps more and perhaps less than Edward when he remarked:

> But Sir Henry has been saying,
> I think, that every moment is a fresh beginning;
> And Julia, that life is only keeping on;
> And somehow, the two ideas seem to fit together.

In Part 5 of "East Coker" the meditation on Time is carried further than in "Burnt Norton," beginning with a rather damp consideration of life "in the middle way," where, "For us, there is only the trying." Eliot seems now to repudiate the rose-garden,

> Not the intense moment
> Isolated, with no before or after

in his rush to define the great mode as

> a lifetime burning in every moment
> And not the lifetime of one man only
> But of old stones that cannot be deciphered

—which is an interim version of "a lifetime's death in love," prefigured in "East Coker" as

> Love is most nearly itself
> When here and now cease to matter.

The last lines seem to imply that we can even yet make ourselves Celias:

> We must be still and still moving
> Into another intensity
> For a further union, a deeper communion
> Through the dark cold and the empty desolation,

> The wave cry, the wind cry, the vast waters
> Of the petrel and the porpoise

—an impressive account of Kinkanja, and a reminder that even the "way of illumination" leads through the temporal; as Reilly declared that the saint in the desert, with spiritual evil always at his shoulder, also suffered from "hunger, damp, exposure / Bowel trouble, and the fear of lions."

The distinction between the saint and the rest of us occupied the last moments of "The Dry Salvages" because it bore down hard on the redemption of time, and the same distinction was to be worked out even more problematically in the plays; but in Part 5 of "Little Gidding" the distinction is set aside in a vision of time redeemed. The hint is picked up from "East Coker": "Old men ought to be explorers." Our words are not the Logos, but if we resist our self-engrossing fancies and try to apprehend "the meaning"—and this is what the exploration amounts to—instead of imposing our own, then "every phrase and every sentence is an end and a beginning." The temporal is the locus of value because it is the only locus we have and value must exist; in the temporal we may still try to apprehend the meaning of the Incarnation; it is our condition—at its best, a condition of complete simplicity, costing "not less than everything." So the poet gathers up, still in time, all the broken images, the hints and guesses, Dante's scattered leaves ("Nel suo profondo vidi che s'interna, / legato con amore in un volume, / cio che per l'universo si squaderna") and folds them into "one simple flame," the light of Eternal Love.[2]

A Special Problem: "The Dry Salvages"

The critical reception of *Four Quartets* has taken a curious turn. I'll describe it briefly, especially where it bears on "The Dry Salvages."

The new reading began with Kenner's essay "Eliot's Moral Dialectic" (1949) and was pushed to a formidable extreme some years later by Donald Davie.[3] Kenner argued that the structural principle of *Four Quartets* is adumbrated in "Burnt Norton"; two terms, opposed, falsely reconciled, then truly reconciled. Light and darkness, opposed, are falsely reconciled in the tube-station "flicker," then truly and paradoxically reconciled in the Dark Night of the Soul. In "Little Gidding" attachment and detachment, opposed, falsely reconciled in indifference, are truly reconciled in love. In *The Invisible Poet* Kenner does not urge us to acknowledge this pattern in each of the four poems. Instead, he suggests that the structural principle of "Burnt Norton" applies also to the organization of the *Quartets* as a whole. The "recurrent illumination" of "Burnt Norton" and the "pervasive sombreness" of "East Coker" are to be taken as opposing conditions, "alternative ways in which the mind responsible for their existence deceives itself"; they are then falsely reconciled in the "conciliating formulae" of "The Dry Salvages" and truly reconciled in the taut revelations, the "refining fire" of "Little Gidding." This implies that everything leading up to the last part of "Little Gidding," from the first words of "Burnt Norton," is, more or less, parody; the disclosure of moral positions which Eliot—the suggestion runs—has never inhabited or from which he has detached himself. As if the poem were a long "Gerontion." This is hard to take. I can't believe that when the voice of Part 2 of "East Coker" says

> The only wisdom we can hope to acquire
> Is the wisdom of humility: humility is endless

we are to interpret this as yet another moment in which the mind responsible for its existence is deceiving itself.

A moderate version of Kenner's argument holds that "The Dry Salvages" becomes the "flicker" stage in the plot of *Four Quartets:* this follows Davie's suggestion that "The Dry Salvages" is deliberate parody. And yet, even this modest version; is it credible? Who is parodying what?

> And on the deck of the drumming liner
> Watching the furrow that widens behind you,
> You shall not think 'the past is finished'
> Or 'the future is before us.'

This does not sound like "The Hollow Men," but it is not parody, it is a praeceptorial voice making our clichés uninhabitable, just as, later, a similar voice performs this service in

> Men's curiosity searches past and future
> And clings to that dimension.

There is more in "The Dry Salvages" than conciliating formulae.

But this may be the hint we need. Kenner might have made his structural pattern cover "The Dry Salvages" by taking action and passion as the opposing terms, falsely reconciled in the mere motion of Part 2, the "currents," and truly reconciled in the "right action" of Part 5 which is "freedom / From past and future also." This would have acknowledged that the poem is all transit, comings and goings, with the attendant temptation of choosing our direction and the near certainty of getting lost. But let that be. There is a great deal in "The Dry Salvages" that requires explanation or apology. My own impression is that after the dark admonitions of "East Coker" Eliot, for a fresh start, sought a new tone, something much more conversational. The new voice should be more discursive, to begin with; becoming sharper as the decorum changes and the consideration of "what might have been" becomes more arduous. I think he wanted the voice to begin like Lord Claverton and end like Harry Monchonsey. The passage beginning

You cannot face it steadily, but this thing is sure,
That time is no healer: the patient is no longer here.

When the train starts, and the passengers are settled
To fruit, periodicals and business letters

is taken up again after many years for *The Elder Statesman:*

It's just like sitting in an empty waiting room
In a railway station on a branch line,
After the last train . . .

—and the voice that speaks of human questioning as mere curiosity is
like Harry Monchonsey's, engaged in the demolition of family inquests:

What you call the normal
Is merely the unreal and the unimportant.

So there can hardly be any question of parody. If "The Dry Salvages"
is mostly bad it is bad because it fails to be good, not because Eliot
meant it to sound "bad" in a sophisticated way.

The Lord Claverton voice begins, "I do not know much about
gods" and speculates about the river as a "strong brown god." Eliot
took rivers and gods seriously, especially when he thought of the
Mississippi at St. Louis and when he read Mark Twain and Whitman.
But here the river is everything in ourselves which we elect to ignore,
all the intractable forces within the self which we disregard because
they do not lend themselves to our cliché-purposes—conveying com-
merce, building bridges, dwelling in cities, and worshipping ma-
chines. Dazzled by the cliché-fancies of our invention, we ignore the
river, but it proceeds, however deviously, to a place alien to our
purposes. And yet it was always with us:

His rhythm was present in the nursery bedroom,
In the rank ailanthus of the April dooryard.

Whitman has led Eliot astray. The syntax is as flabby as Davie says it is. If Eliot wanted to suggest a spectral presence in the April dooryard, he would have done better with something like this passage from "The Waste Land":

> Who is the third who walks always beside you?
> When I count, there are only you and I together
> But when I look ahead up the white road
> There is always another one walking beside you
> Gliding wrapt in a brown mantle, hooded

or the later version of this style in *The Cocktail Party*. "The river is within us, the sea is all about us"; the sea being an omnivorous impersonal reality alien to man and therefore suicidally attractive as a refuge from his consciousness. It has many voices and it measures "time not our time," but we deceive ourselves like the anxious women and try to take the sea's measure, using our own counters.

But the real embarrassments of "The Dry Salvages" begin in Part 2. I think Eliot wanted to make his anxious women of Part 1 into a choric voice, like the Women of Canterbury in *Murder in the Cathedral*, expressing the usual laments in their own terms; and then to bring in a Monchonsey voice to evacuate the whole area of plangent cliché and point to one meaning. The hint is clear enough in

> The backward look behind the assurance
> Of recorded history, the backward half-look
> Over the shoulder, towards the primitive terror

and in the fact that the notorious rhymes of Part 2 are inaugurated in the last lines of Part 1 with "The future futureless." The first stanza of Part 2 is beautiful. But Eliot's determination to add five stanzas and to make each line-end rhyme with its counterpart in the other stanzas was disastrous. There is nothing as difficult in the choruses of *The Rock*

or *Murder in the Cathedral*. The whole passage is so contorted, so alien
to the character of the English language, that while reading it I wonder whether F. W. Bateson wasn't right, after all, in saying that the
American T. S. Eliot never wrote English as a native speaker. The
poet may have been impressed by the air of worldwide plangency that
Coleridge evoked from "measureless" in "Kubla Khan," or by Hopkins's efforts with "motionable" in "The Wreck of the Deutschland,"
but for an artist whose vocational concern was speech there is no
excusing the coinage of "oceanless," "erosionless," and "devotionless." The OED gives a certain pale authority for "emotionless," but
when Eliot writes

> the trailing
> Consequence of further days and hours,
> While emotion takes to itself the emotionless
> Years of living among the breakage
> Of what was believed in as the most reliable—
> And therefore the fittest for renunciation . . .

I do not know what he means by emotion taking to itself the emotionless years. Does he mean that our undisciplined squads of emotion,
instead of leaving the symbolic sea of Part I well alone ("emotionless"
meaning, if anything, emotionally null) are constantly trying to take
possession of it; and the more successful the emotions in these ex-
ploits, the more impoverished our lives, the more—if we are to
"live"—we shall have to renounce? The next stanza is an early version
of the "gifts reserved for age" in "Little Gidding." "The unattached
devotion which might pass for devotionless" can hardly mean much
more than "the capacity for devotion that continues even when it
lacks an object"; but I don't know why it should try to "pass for"
devotionless. After the apocalyptic chorus Eliot returns to the Claverton voice, "It seems, as one becomes older," to modulate into the

Monchonsey voice which will clear the way for the meaning. The anxious chorus feared that the whole human scramble was ridiculous, rather like the fears of the Aunts and Uncles in their trance-moments in *The Family Reunion*. But the stern voice now says that the meaning redeems time and because it is the Rock, is itself:

> in the sombre season
> Or the sudden fury, is what it always was.

We need not go through the poem: most of its blemishes have been noted. The defects of "The Dry Salvages" are real and serious; where they occur, they are the result of Eliot's failure to conduct a piece of music which he scored for an unmanageable number of voices. It would be easier in the plays, where he can take whatever time he needs to establish his figures, such as they are. In the other quartets and especially in "Little Gidding" the voices are fewer, clearly distinguishable, and under impeccable control.

[12]

"Burnt Norton"

For even when hours and days go by in silence and the phone
Never rings, and widely spaced drops of water
Fall from the eaves, nothing is any longer a secret
And one can live alone rejoicing in this:
That the years of war are far off in the past or the future,
That memory contains everything. And you see slipping down a
 hallway
The past self you decided not to have anything to do with any
 more
And it is a more comfortable you, dishonest perhaps,
But alive.
                              —John Ashbery, from "A Wave"

The first readers of "Burnt Norton" did not know that they were
rehearsing a quartet or that it might be useful to think of certain
works by Bartók and by Beethoven. Or that the poem was the first of
a sequence rather than what it appeared to be, the last poem of *Collected Poems, 1909–1935*. Residents of Gloucestershire might have
known that Burnt Norton was an old manor house, no longer occupied, two miles from Chipping Campden, and that the house had a

neglected garden and pools now dry. Many readers thought that Eliot's career as a poet was finished and that he had committed himself to literary, social, political, and religious criticism. "Burnt Norton" had an air of finality about it: the end of a book of poems collected, not selected.

Readers who knew Greek probably assumed that Eliot, a poet much given to epigraphs, had left two fragments from Heraclitus untranslated because no translation into English could encompass the diverse meanings of the Greek *logos*. Readers who did not know Greek probably assumed that Eliot's English would give the gist of the Greek matter in due time. A few readers may have translated the Greek somewhat in these terms: (1) Although the Word is common to all, most people live as if each had a private intelligence of his own, and (2) The way up and the way down are one and the same. A rebuke, followed by an opacity, directed those readers into a poem that begins with its own opacity, four sentences about time.

In 1936, readers could not know that those statements in the first fourteen lines of the poem were originally written for the Second Priest in *Murder in the Cathedral,* to follow Thomas's speech after the departure of the Second Tempter. The passage was cut before the first performance, but Eliot liked it well enough to use it as the opening meditation of a poem he took more seriously than anything else in *Collected Poems, 1909–1935.* No reader in 1936 knew that Burnt Norton was a special place for Eliot, that one day probably in early September 1934 he had wandered about the garden in the company of Emily Hale, a woman he had met and fallen in love with in February 1913 and might have married if he had not, two years later, married Vivienne Haigh-Wood. In May 1933, Eliot started a legal process of separation, but in every spiritual sense he was still married. The emotions he felt in the company of Emily Hale in 1934 may have included regret for years largely wasted and remorse for things ill done, but there was no question of seeking divorce and starting a new life with Emily Hale or any other woman.

The only advantage we have over the first readers of "Burton Norton" is our sense of the significance of the poem's coming between *Murder in the Cathedral* and *The Family Reunion,* two plays in which many feelings barely disclosed in "Burnt Norton" are more explicitly expressed: notably self-disgust, a conviction of the meaninglessness of any life closed against divine grace, a sense that the important consideration is not our feelings but the pattern we may make of them. The plays feature the same imagery as "Burnt Norton": enchanted garden, sudden illuminations, gates opened or closed, clouds concealing the the sun, children in foliage, the still point of a turning world; these, and motifs of loss, revulsion, temptation, inner and outer compulsion, and in the end achieved patience, assent to the will of God.

The first readers of "Burnt Norton" knew as much as they needed to know about Eliot's beliefs, or at least about the beliefs that inhabit the poem: they were clearly stated in Eliot's introduction to the *Pensées* of Pascal: "The great mystics, like St. John of the Cross, are primarily for readers with a special determination of purpose; the devotional writers, such as St. François de Sales, are primarily for those who already feel consciously desirous of the love of God; the great theologians are for those interested in theology. But I can think of no Christian writer, not Newman even, more to be commended than Pascal to those who doubt, but who have the mind to conceive, and the sensibility to feel, the disorder, the futility, the meaninglessness, the mystery of life and suffering, and who can only find peace through a satisfaction of the whole being." That passage, available since 1931, gives as much of Eliot's belief, and of his insistence on it, as a reader of "Burnt Norton" needs to know. Not that even as much as this is necessary, because something approaching it can be deduced from the poem. The merit of knowing the nature of Eliot's belief and its particular vocabularies—sufficiently indicated by reference to Augustine, St. John of the Cross, Donne, Andrewes, Hooker, George Herbert, Pascal, and the English medieval mystics—is that we know what not to expect, the concessions and felicities in the absence of which Leavis and other readers of "Burnt Norton" have been affronted to the point of rejecting the main thrust of the poem. There is no need to feel affronted: the poetry does not depend upon a doctrine professed but upon a doctrine felt. To read "Burnt Norton" it is necessary only to conceive a form of feeling, different from one's own if it has to be, and to imagine what the form means to a mind that holds it or is possessed by it.

The four statements about time with which the poem begins can't have won many readers; they sound like a bewildered seminar. Their value consists not in what they say about time but in starting a form of discourse in which the nature of the speaker is the least germane consideration. These sentences are propelled not by a speaker in charge of them but by solemn, impersonal agitations maintained as if without human intervention. Progress from one phase to the next is made chiefly by repetitions of the emphasized words—"time," "past," "present," "future"—and the discrimination of conditions in their vicinity: what might have been, what has been. Not that the sentences are trivial. The first one—"Time present and time past / Are both perhaps present in time future, / And time future contained in time past"—implies determinism, since every aspect of time is already inscribed in a future we can't know. The second—"If all time is eternally present / All time is unredeemable"—moves the determinism to the present continuous tense but doesn't otherwise improve the situation: "unredeemable" because not open to change. In *The Family Reunion,* Harry tries to tell Charles and Gerald how he feels:

> I am the old house
> With the noxious smell and the sorrow before morning,
> In which all past is present, all degradation
> Is unredeemable.

Later, he says to Dr. Warburton:

> Your ordinary murderer
> Regards himself as an innocent victim.
> To himself he is still what he used to be
> Or what he would be. He cannot realise
> That everything is irrevocable.
> The past unredeemable.

The poem's third statement— "What might have been is an abstraction / Remaining a perpetual possibility / Only in a world of speculation"—posits a world like Stephen Dedalus's in *Ulysses,* where Stephen diverts himself with Aristotelian notions of potentiality and actuality: "Or was that only possible which came to pass?" In the fourth sentence, not a moment too soon, determinism seems to be set aside— "What might have been and what has been / Point to one end, which is always present"—a release effected by letting several possibilities, including hopeful ones, hover upon the hospitably ambiguous "end." We read this "end" as purpose, the ultimate aim, as well as the conclusion. Nothing in the sentence makes forgiveness impossible, or the reception of divine grace, or the reconstitution of one's life in another pattern.

The direction of this passage, its abstracting style, maintains a distanced relation to events. No impression of immediacy, of an irresistibly punctual convergence of deed and word, experience and the words for it, is allowed to enforce itself. Events will intrude, but only at the remove of memory. Even then, they are events that didn't happen but might have happened. So while the governing style seems to change from abstract to concrete, from generalizing to narrative, the change is only ostensible, at the double remove of "memory" and "echo."

In Eliot's poetry, birds, not people, urge one to seize the day, and often the listener lives to regret the urging. Or in the presence of birds one is willing to risk immediacies of sense, as in "Cape Ann": "O quick quick quick, quick hear the song-sparrow." Now in "Burnt Norton": "Quick, said the bird, find them, find them, / Round the corner"—and even then, if a human intelligence is present, it warns of the "deception of the thrush."

Many sources or analogues have been suggested for Eliot's rose-garden: *Alice in Wonderland,* Kipling's "They," Elizabeth Barrett Browning's "The Lost Bower," Frances Hodgson Burnett's *The Secret Garden,* and a recollection of Eliot's own "New Hampshire" with its "Children's voices in the orchard." All that is required (and nearly any *Kinderscenen* would intimate it) is a sudden, momentary sense of the sublime, of unity sufficient to put one beside oneself or beyond oneself, an otherwise impossible conviction of unity among the constituents of the occasion; human, natural, botanic, meteorological—the complete consort implying perfection of being, its brevity of no damaging account:

> Into our first world.
> There they were, dignified, invisible,
> Moving without pressure, over the dead leaves,
> In the autumn heat, through the vibrant air,
> And the bird called, in response to
> The unheard music hidden in the shrubbery,
> And the unseen eyebeam crossed, for the roses
> Had the look of flowers that are looked at.

The movement of the verse is such as to discourage our asking who "they" were—perhaps the quiet-voiced elders who emerge more clearly in the second part of "East Coker." Here they are figures in a ballet of childhood, called upon to be nothing more than present. The main direction of the passage gives another instance of the disjunction between existence and essence, between the actual and the real, between temporal enchainment and time redeemable. The bird's song is in response to unheard music. As in Keats's distinction between heard melodies and those unheard, unheard music is absolute, the essence of sound as distinct from its sensible existence. The essence of sound, as Kenneth Burke has remarked, would be soundless, by definition removed from the experience of sound, just as the unseen eyebeam testifies to the essence of seeing rather than to mere seeing. That the bird, rather than the children or the elders, should respond to it is entirely appropriate—they have fewer distractions—just as the roses seem to be looked at. The status of these looks and responses is notional, only to be stabilized—and even then not in mere existence—by memory.

It is appropriate, too, that the bird should convey the admonition— "human kind / cannot bear very much reality"—which Thomas has given to the terrified Chorus in *Murder in the Cathedral*. We can't bear very much reality unless and until we see it fulfilled as the figure of God's purpose:

Peace, and be at peace with your thoughts and visions.
These things had to come to you and you to accept them.
This is your share of the eternal burden,
The perpetual glory. This is one moment,
But know that another
Shall pierce you with a sudden painful joy
When the figure of God's purpose is made complete.

You shall forget these things, toiling in the household,
You shall remember them, droning by the fire,
When age and forgetfulness sweeten memory
Only like a dream that has often been told
And often been changed in the telling. They will seem unreal.
Human kind cannot bear very much reality.

In "Burnt Norton" the sublime moment—"And the lotus rose, quietly, quietly, / The surface glittered out of heart of light"—is one in which existence and essence seem to be one and the same. That is what the experience of the sublime comes to, an epiphany, an intuition of divine grace, given lest we despair. In "Burnt Norton," as in *The Family Reunion,* a black cloud occludes the sun almost before we have apprehended its dazzle and the heart of light from which it issues. In one sense, the brevity of the experience doesn't matter; it is an epitome, a sample of the ultimate experience, beatitude, the Heaven of God's presence. In another, nothing matters more, because the disjunction between existence and essence makes existence appalling unless we live it in the demanding light of eternity.

It would be absurd to repeat the canard that Eliot hated life and longed only to be rid of it. The poet who wrote, here in "Burnt Norton," "Dry the pool, dry concrete, brown edged, / And the pool was filled with water out of sunlight," felt the ravishments of sense just as keenly as those poets who advertise their possession of such opulence. Asceticism did not come to Eliot more naturally or more easily than to anyone else who practices it. We may wonder why he felt impelled to live among such imageries, but the speculation is null: that was the form his spiritual genius took. I believe that Eliot was a man of emotional and spiritual dread, living on the edge of the rational imagination, compelled by imageries of pain—think of his infatuation with the martyrdom of St. Sebastian—and irregularly but irresistibly coming upon the other sublimity, of exaltation and joy.

In the second part of "Burnt Norton" we see the poetic as well as the spiritual form of Eliot's genius. When he read Symons's *Symbolist Movement in Literature,* he saw that the modern French form of Symbolism effected yet another disjunction between existence and essence. The motives were secular, chiefly a refusal of the conventions, the positivist syntax, of everyday life. But the otherwise diverse procedures of Baudelaire, Mallarmé, Corbière, and Laforgue could serve a religious end by repudiating current axioms of stability. The notion that reality could be verified merely by describing its constituents was just as trivial as the commonplace assumptions of evolution and progress.

The first lines of this second part of the poem indicate Eliot's kinship for the time being with Mallarmé: "Garlic and sapphires in the mud / Clot the bedded axle-tree." A manuscript of "Lines for an Old Man" has "Thunder and sapphires" with the thunder scored out and replaced by "Garlic," a change in the direction of Mallarmé's "M'introduire dans ton histoire"—"Tonnerre et rubis aux moyeux." There is also a recollection of Mallarmé's "Le Tombeau de Charles Baudelaire": "Sépulcrale d'égout bavant boue et rubis." How garlic got into the line I have no idea, but it causes among the words "the shock of their inequality" even more than Mallarmé's "thunder" does. The axle-tree stayed in Eliot's mind from an early reading of Chapman's *Bussy D'Ambois:* "fly where men feel the cunning axle-tree." In a typed draft of "Burnt Norton" and in the American *Complete Poems and Plays, 1909–1950,* the last line of "The trilling wire in the blood / Sings below inveterate scars / Appeasing long forgotten wars" appears as "And reconciles forgotten wars," a poorer line if only because the repeated "reconciles / reconciled" nudges an apparently drowsy reader. But in either version we are in the poetic world of Poe, Baudelaire, and Mallarmé, sufficiently glossed by Eliot's "Note sur

Mallarmé et Poe" in its reference to "un élément d'incantation."
With "Ulalume" and "Un Coup de Dès" in view, Eliot refers to
"cette incantation, qui insiste sur la puissance primitive du Mot
(Fatum)."[1] The first meaning of *fatum* is a divine utterance, the expressed will of a god, as in Cicero's *fata Sibyllina*. Eliot is claiming for
"la puissance primitive du Mot" in poetry what he has claimed for
logos in theology, by way of the epigraph from Heraclitus: the force
we can't put into our words but may find already there. Such force is
primitive and for that reason irrefutable, as Eliot recognized more
fully than any other modern poet. Given a choice, he would have
voted for the visual imagination—Dante, lucidity, transparence—
rather than the auditory imagination—primitive power, working below consciousness or prior to it. But he did not have a choice. Highly
conscious as he was, he knew that his talent was imperious: his susceptibility to divination exposed him to impulses far below consciousness. When he knew himself best, he acknowledged without fuss
states of being for which there is no rational accounting. I don't think
he sought mystical epiphanies or prayed for such privileges, but he
revered the tradition—if it is a tradition—of Christian mysticism, and
read its records without irony. He dismissed Yeats's dealings with the
occult because they were willful, egotistical—they sought the wrong
kind of supernatural experience—but Lady Juliana's visions were unquestionable.

The opening passage of the second section of "Burnt Norton" is
a motion terminating in words available mostly, if not solely, to
divination:

> The dance along the artery
> The circulation of the lymph
> Are figured in the drift of stars
> Ascend to summer in the tree

We move above the moving tree
In light upon the figured leaf
And hear upon the sodden floor
Below, the boarhound and the boar
Pursue their pattern as before
But reconciled among the stars.

Blackmur found in these lines the effect of behavior rising into belief, and made much of the two reconciliations, one as something that happens in the blood under scars, the other as something that happens among the stars; made much, too, of the superior drift not only of stars but of the universal course of things. The drift is figured in the rhymed formality of the lines, and in the murmuring of a language that appeases itself in the reception of "stars" and "figured," the rhyme of "tree" with itself, the drift from "move" to "moving," and the rhyming melody of "floor," "boarhound," "boar," and "before." In this style of incantation, "Ascend to summer in the tree" is joined grammatically to "Are figured in the drift of stars," but it is mobile enough to anticipate the "We" of the line that follows. If the passage shows behavior rising into belief, the behavior is a force at work in life, and the belief is as if congenital, given by the gods. So it is useless to ask who is speaking these words: they issue from an impersonal source and are heard as if overheard from afar.

A phrase repeated from "Coriolan," "At the still point of the turning world," alters the rhythm of "Burnt Norton" at this point, but not the belief. What follows clears or cures the ground by removing the commonplace possibilities of description. The pattern (neither this nor that) becomes the structural figure of the third section of the poem. As in the remaining *Quartets,* when a personal voice is heard, it is heard confessing its inability to say exactly what it means or to make enough sense to satisfy the desires it has recognized: "I can only say, *there* we have been: but I cannot say where. / And I cannot say, how long, for that is to place it in time."

The first consequence of these inabilities, in the next passage, is that the language deploys nine lines and sixty-three words without completing a sentence; intoned phrases explicate one another without sending their vibrations in one direction rather than another. The whole passage sounds as if it were spoken by Thomas à Becket, explaining yet again why humankind cannot bear very much reality:

> Yet the enchainment of past and future
> Woven in the weakness of the changing body,
> Protects mankind from heaven and damnation
> Which flesh cannot endure.

Heaven and damnation are both belief, the one above the moving tree and among the stars, the other beneath the inveterate scars. Each involves a scale of values terrifyingly different from those which are gratified by the convergence of our interests upon the daily events that appease them. Because Baudelaire recognized as much, he knew, according to Eliot, that what really matters is Sin and Redemption, and therefore "he walked secure in this high vocation, that he was capable of a damnation denied to the politicians and the newspaper editors of Paris."

The second movement of the poem ends with a resumption of its first style—brooding on time—and with a crucial appeal to the higher perspective of memory. The merit of memory is not otherwise self-evident. Why we remember one episode rather than another is, of course, interesting, and Eliot often wondered about it, as in *The Use of Poetry and the Use of Criticism,* but the memory he invokes in "Burnt Norton" is valuable mainly because it is another disjunction between the actual and the real; between the immediacy of an event and the saving grace of distance in which we consider its meaning:

Time past and time future
Allow but a little consciousness.
To be conscious is not to be in time
But only in time can the moment in the rose-garden,
The moment in the arbour where the rain beat,
The moment in the draughty church at smokefall
Be remembered; involved with past and future.
Only through time time is conquered.

Smokefall got itself into the Supplement to the OED ("after 'night-fall' ") with an explanation by Helen Gardner: "the moment when the wind drops and smoke that had ascended descends." In *The Family Reunion*, Eliot indulged himself in snobbery by separating Harry so far from the company at Wishwood—"You are all people / To whom nothing has happened." But in "Burnt Norton" no distinction is imposed between those who are conscious and those who are not: memory is available to anyone who doesn't capitulate to every whim of the moment. At least the "strained time-ridden faces" aren't named, though only a brave reader would claim to be exempt from the condition. "Conquered" is a gruff word—"Only through time time is conquered"—when there has been so much talk, in Eliot's early poems and in his essay on Dante, about the redemption of time. It is conquered, presumably, because in the perspective of memory an event can't be peremptory, as it was when it occurred.

It is not necessary to say much about the third section of the poem. Kenner's version of the pattern in process is convincing: opposite values, falsely reconciled, and at last truly reconciled. I might add: truly reconciled not by any Hegelian synthesis but by giving a more demanding sense to one of the values. As here: light and darkness are the opposing values, falsely reconciled in the "flicker" of the third movement, the London Underground episode, then truly reconciled by recourse to the Dark Night of the Soul in St. John of the Cross. The motif of the second movement (neither this nor that) is repeated: neither daylight nor darkness; neither plenitude nor vacancy. But the vacated space is now filled with the flicker of distraction. St. John's distinction between the "night of sense" (available to ordinary penitents) and the "night of soul" (only to adepts of sanctity)—"This is the one way, and the other / Is the same, not in movement / But abstention from movement"—seems to have suggested itself to Eliot by his remarking the two ways (the stairs and the lift) of getting to the train at Gloucester Road.

The fundamental motive of "Burnt Norton" is to void the claim of spontaneity; to represent as vulgar any immediate response to an event; to imply a form a life in which the meaning of an event comes long after its occurrence and in a light which is not that of punctuality. According to the rhetoric of Eliot's Christian poetry, the only event in which meaning coincides with the act is the Incarnation.

In the fourth movement of "Burnt Norton" a brief lyric transacts events of the past—"Time and the bell have buried the day." And the present continuous—"The black cloud carries the sun away"— lingers upon an entirely hypothetical future:

> Will the sunflower turn to us, will the clematis
> Stray down, bend to us; tendril and spray
> Clutch and cling?
> Chill
> Fingers of yew be curled
> Down on us?

It then reverts to a present indicative steadied by the repeated "still": "After the kingfisher's wing / Has answered light to light, and is silent, the light is still / At the still point of the turning world." Again the effect of the four questions—about sunflower, clematis, tendril and spray, and yew—is to keep the phrases hovering indeterminately above the ground of our yearning. The whole passage, one of Eliot's consummate achievements, is at once impersonal, as if the words were uttering themselves in a ritual to make sense of man's presence in the natural world, and irresistibly personal in the turns and trillings of the phrases. The sunflower turns to the sun, but we do not feel obliged to ask who is the "us" to whom it may also turn. An extraordinarily personal presence inhabits the phrases, but in such a way, and with such unaggressive emphasis, as to remain within the weavings of word and word; the rhyming "turn to us," "bend to us," and "curled / Down on us"; the imperative "Chill" occupying a whole line of verse without our knowing, at first reading, whether it is a noun (like the beginnings of its companion questions: sunflower, clematis, tendril and spray) or the adjective it turns out to be. The word stays in the air of our minds till it finds its rhyme, three lines later, in "still," another word we can't construe—adjective or adverb?—till the last line makes it clear. Hopkins's kingfishers ("As kingfishers catch fire") made a parable of selving, the flame of face testifying to the type of individuality. Eliot's kingfisher speaks of answering light to light, of the silence into which words after speech reach, and the stillness poised upon the axle of the turning world.

The fifth and last movement of the poem is its most contentious part. Much depends on the value we give the first three lines: "Words move, music moves / Only in time; but that which is only living / Can only die." The sentence recapitulates the statement about being conscious and remembering; as if to say that while we have to live in time, we are not obliged to live according to its chronometer or in deference to its "metalled ways." The distinction between Chronos (Yeats: "the cracked tune that Chronos sings") and Kairos, the time of meaning and value, is to the point here. The silence into which words reach is, so far as it is attended to, their meaning, not their defeat:

Only by the form, the pattern,
Can words or music reach
The stillness, as a Chinese jar still
Moves perpetually in its stillness.
Not the stillness of the violin, while the note lasts,
Not that only, but the co-existence,
Or say that the end precedes the beginning,
And the end and the beginning were always there
Before the beginning and after the end.
And all is always now.

In *The Living Principle,* Leavis allowed himself to be scandalized, in his commentary on "Burnt Norton," by Eliot's insistence—at least it appeared to Leavis to be insistence—on "the unreality, the unlivingness, of life in time."[2] But Eliot is not insisting, he could not have believed such unreality, such unlivingness, while in communion with a church founded on the redemption of time by the Incarnation. How Eliot judged those forms of temporal life that were content to be, in every limiting sense, merely temporal and to obey the call of punctuality and immediacy, is a different matter: on that, the evidence he has left is clear. In "Burnt Norton," the words that induced Leavis to protest are those that seem to entail a claim, on Eliot's part, to know what "the meaning" is: such words as "form," "pattern," and "the dance." But form, pattern, and dance are merely analogues, ways of putting not "eternal reality" but the poet's striving to apprehend it. They don't denote anything; they suggest the means by which an event may be brought to disclose its meaning; brought, by exerting upon it the pressure of a more demanding moral and spiritual perspective than any judgment immediately imposed. The value of these words consists in their inability to do more than suggest.

That the meaning is dynamic is clarified by the "Chinese jar" which "still / Moves perpetually in its stillness." Where Eliot fails is in his attempt to be more specific than that, distinguishing between a visible and an audible stillness, and trying to go beyond the distinction. "Not that only, but the co-existence": the co-existence of what? He finds it impossible to say just what he means, as the passage about the incapacity of words goes on to confess almost at once.

In the interval between *Murder in the Cathedral* and *The Family Reunion,* Eliot had temptation much on his mind—the temptation of Thomas à Becket, of Harry's father, of Christ in the desert, and more generally the temptation of silence to dissolve in chatter. The last lines of this movement are melodramatic:

> The Word in the desert
> Is most attacked by voices of temptation,
> The crying shadow in the funeral dance,
> The loud lament of the disconsolate chimera.

I can't find any cogent meaning in the last two lines: what the shadow is, or who or what the disconsolate chimera is. Eliot is rattling old bones.

The poem ends more quietly in another attempt to represent the pattern as dynamic:

> The detail of the pattern is movement,
> As in the figure of the ten stairs.
> Desire itself is movement
> Not in itself desirable;
> Love is itself unmoving,
> Only the cause and end of movement,
> Timeless, and undesiring
> Except in the aspect of time
> Caught in the form of limitation
> Between un-being and being.

Structurally, it is a return to the beginning: a discursive passage about time, love, and desire, a passage in which the English language, like Mallarmé's French, seems to be intoning itself without requiring either a speaker or a listener in attendance. As in the first movement, we are released from its monitions to the imagery of gardens, children, laughter. The figure of the ten stairs comes from St. John of the Cross and may be left unglossed; it sustains the Heraclitean motif of the way up and the way down. This is what "Burnt Norton" and the other *Quartets* are about: starting from the unquestionably rich ground of laughing children in the foliage, how to avoid losing or, worse still, humiliating the promise implicit in the sunshine and laughter. How to convert the low dream of desire into the high dream of love.

In the chapter on *Alice in Wonderland* in *Some Versions of Pastoral,* Empson remarks how a certain feeling about children developed in England after the eighteenth-century settlement had come to seem narrow and inescapable, a feeling "that no way of building up character, no intellectual system, can bring out all that is inherent in the human spirit, and therefore that there is more in the child than any man has been able to keep." This idea of the child, "that it is in the right relation to Nature, not dividing what should be unified, that its intuitive judgment contains what poetry and philosophy must spend their time labouring to recover, was accepted by Dodgson and a main part of his feeling."[3] "Burnt Norton" is full of this feeling, along with a doomed conviction that it can't be secured, and that the only thing possible is to recover one's memory of such unity, and start again from there under better, because more exacting, auspices.

The success of "Burnt Norton" is still in dispute. The reason is, I think, that none of the critical procedures developed and employed in the fifty years since the publication of the poem has been responsive to the kind of poetry we find in "Burnt Norton." Briefly: nobody has taken up where D. W. Harding's account of the poem left off. Most of the critical procedures that have been used in the analysis of poems have concentrated upon image, symbol, and structure. No critical method has arisen that proposes to show the poetic character and potentiality of discourse. It is still an effort to take the harm out of the word "discursive," as reviews of John Ashbery's poems sufficiently indicate.

Harding's 1936 review of "Burnt Norton" was the place to begin:

> Ordinarily our abstract ideas are over-comprehensive and include too wide a range of feeling to be of much use by themselves. If our words "regret" and "eternity" were exact bits of mosaic with which to build patterns, much of "Burnt Norton" would not have had to be written. . . . One could say, perhaps, that the poem takes the place of the ideas of "regret" and "eternity." Where in ordinary speech we should have to use those words, and hope by conversational trial-and-error to obviate the grosser misunderstandings, this poem is a newly created concept, equally abstract but vastly more exact and rich in meaning. It makes no statement. It is no more "about" anything than an abstract term like "love" is about anything: it is a linguistic creation. And the creation of a new concept, with all the assimilation and communication of experience that that involves, is perhaps the greatest of linguistic achievements.[4]

Harding goes on to indicate, too briefly perhaps, how Eliot's methods in "Burnt Norton" differ from ordinary attempts "to state the meaning by taking existing abstract ideas and piecing them together in the ordinary way." It might have been expected, especially after the publication of Stevens's *Notes Toward a Supreme Fiction,* that a critical method sensitive to poetry as a work in the creation of new concepts might have been developed. It has not happened. Readers are still encouraged to believe that a poem is an action (or a structure) of words chiefly concerned with the development of the resources of imagery and symbolism within the fiction of dramatic monologue. The discrimination of concepts (not this precisely . . . or even that) is regarded as fit matter for an essay, but not for a poem. We don't know what to do with such passages as the first lines of "Burnt Norton." The problem differs from that of "argufying in poetry"— Empson's program—because such argufying is content to take concepts as they come, and to engage in conversation with them. That is a different matter.

The Communication of the Dead

Eliot's conversion to the Anglican communion has been the object of such intemperate comment that a protest is in order. It is apparently necessary to say that Eliot's right to become a Christian is as clear as anyone else's right not to. I don't understand why his Christian belief attracts more aggressive attention than any other writer's agnosticism. If it could be shown that Eliot's conversion resulted in the impoverishment of his poetry, that would be a different matter, though a small one, but it hasn't been shown. I agree with Geoffrey Hill that "The Waste Land" is Eliot's greatest poem, but not that the poetry of his Christian years shows a falling off. A list of Eliot's most achieved poems that did not find places for "Marina," "Ash-Wednesday," and three of the four Quartets—I could live without "The Dry Salvages"—would be an eccentric show. But it is reasonable to ask not what Eliot believed and practiced but what tradition or traditions in Christianity he avowed, since there is a certain latitude in that faith.

When he rejected the Unitarianism in which he was brought up, Eliot moved toward the most stringent theology he could find. "It is rather trying to be supposed to have settled oneself in an easy chair when one has just begun a long journey on foot," he told Paul Elmer More.[1] On Shrove Tuesday 1928 in another letter to More, he referred to von Hügel's description of those who lack a religious instinct and said that he found them "to be unconscious of any void—the void that I find in the middle of all human happiness and all human relations, and which there is only one thing to fill." "I am one whom this sense of void tends to drive toward asceticism or sensuality, and only Christianity helps to reconcile me to life, which is otherwise disgusting."[2] In a letter of July 29, 1926, to his brother Henry, Eliot said that "Unitarianism is a bad preparation for brass tacks like birth, copulation and death, hell, heaven and insanity: they all fall within the classification of Bad Form."[3] I wince at some of those phrases. How can Eliot know whether a person who seems to lack a religious instinct is unconscious of any void? But there is no doubt that he regarded issues of belief, grace, damnation, and redemption as crucial: by comparison, poetry was a matter of indifference.

Two traditions in Christianity engaged Eliot. One was Augustinian: it involved theological exactitudes extending from Augustine to Pascal. The other was the mystical tradition—which Eliot understood mainly from Evelyn Underhill's book on mysticism—as embodied in the English medieval mystics and especially Juliana of Norwich. He found enough scholasticism, Aristotle, and Aquinas in the *Divine Comedy* and the *Vita Nuova* to reconcile every theological tradition he valued. He told More that "Ash-Wednesday" was "a first attempt at a sketchy application of the philosophy of the *Vita Nuova* to modern life."[4] Those affiliations might with equal force have led Eliot into the Roman Catholic rather than the Anglican Church. He regarded himself as combining "a Catholic cast of mind, a Calvinistic heritage, and a Puritanical temperament."[5] But he submitted to Canterbury rather than to Rome because he wanted to pay tribute to the England of the early seventeenth century from which his ancestors had set out to

make a new life in America. He revered the church of Lancelot Andrewes, Donne, Herbert, and Nicholas Ferrar. Besides, he did not
regard the differences between Canterbury and Rome as at all comparable to those that distinguished Christianity from paganism or
secularism.

For Eliot, as for any Christian, the founding event of the Christian
story is the Incarnation, the birth of Christ as Son of God. The chief
purpose of human life, seen in the light of the Incarnation, is "to
glorify God and enjoy Him for ever."[6] In that pilgrimage, the crucial
force is faith, which takes precedence even over morals: religion "is
not, and can never survive as, simply a code of morals." Two years
after his conversion Eliot told More: "To me religion has brought at
least the perception of something above morals, and therefore extremely terrifying; it has brought me not happiness but a sense of
something above happiness and therefore more terrifying than ordinary pain and misery; the very dark night and the desert. To me, the
phrase 'to be damned for the glory of God' is sense and not paradox; I
had far rather walk, as I do, in daily terror of eternity, than feel that
this was only a children's game in which all the contestants would get
equally worthless prizes in the end."[7] Eliot considered morals a consequence of one's faith, not a cause of it. Faith is never as secure as a
believer would wish it to be, but doubt and uncertainty "are merely a
variety of belief."[8] Genuine blasphemy, as in Baudelaire, depends
upon the belief it affronts. Like any other Christian, but with unusually reiterated emphasis, Eliot believed in original sin, and he
insisted—as did T. E. Hulme, a writer he excessively admired—that
without a conviction of that categorical guilt, human life becomes
trivial or brutal. In *After Strange Gods* he claimed that the diabolic
element in modern literature was related to the loss of the idea of
original sin: with that loss, and "with the disappearance of the idea of
intense moral struggle, the human beings presented to us both in

poetry and in prose fiction today . . . tend to become less and less real." It is "in moments of moral and spiritual sanctions," Eliot says, "rather than in those 'bewildering minutes' in which we are all very much alike, that men and women came nearest to being real."⁹ The bewildering minutes—Tourneur's phrase from *The Revenger's Tragedy*—are those in which, through lust or other violence, we merely lose ourselves.

Eliot's most emphatic statements on sin are in his essays on Dante, Pascal, and Baudelaire. In the essay on Baudelaire he says that "in the middle nineteenth century, the age which (at its best) Goethe had prefigured, an age of bustle, programmes, platforms, scientific progress, humanitarianism and revolutions which improved nothing, an age of progressive degradation, Baudelaire perceived that what really matters is Sin and Redemption." To such a mind, the "recognition of the reality of Sin is a New Life; and the possibility of damnation is so immense a relief in a world of electoral reform, plebiscites, sex reform and dress reform, that damnation itself is an immediate form of salvation—of salvation from the ennui of modern life, because it at last gives some significance to living."¹⁰ Eliot insists on the letter of Christian doctrine that refers to Hell, Purgatory, and Heaven, and construes its spirit in Augustinian terms. Of the *Inferno,* he says, "the torment issues from the very nature of the damned themselves, expresses their essence; they writhe in the torment of their own perpetually perverted nature."¹¹ Eliot regarded Hell, Purgatory, and Heaven as states of being, eternal conditions that, even on earth and in time, we could at least imagine. One could begin in this life to suffer the eternity of Hell. In a letter to More, he said: "The man who disbelieves in any future life whatever is also a believer in Hell. For in this life one makes, now and then, important decisions; or at least allows circumstances to decide; and some of these decisions are such as have consequences for all the rest of our mortal life. Some people find themselves consequently in circumstances such that the whole of their mortal life *must* be a torment to them. And if there is no future life then Hell is, for such people, here and now."[12] Eliot took the idea of Purgatory with corresponding gravity. He was shocked that Yeats, writing *Purgatory,* did not recognize a purgatorial process. In the section of "Little Gidding" where Eliot refers to the refining fire by which the soul may be restored, he took the theology of Purgatory so seriously that he scolded his friend John Hayward for questioning the diction of the passage. In one of the drafts of that section, Eliot had the soul learning to swim in that fire, and when Hayward demurred over the swimming, Eliot reminded him that in Canto 26 of *Purgatorio* the people who talk to Dante "are represented as not wanting to waste time in conversation but wishing to dive back into the fire to accomplish their expiation."[13] Hayward should have remembered that Eliot put the relevant line into "The Waste Land"—"Poi s'ascose nel foco che gli affina"—and quoted it again in his main essay on Dante, remarking that "in purgatory the torment of flames is deliberately and consciously accepted by the penitent." The souls in Purgatory, Eliot said, suffer "because they *wish to suffer,* for purgation": "And observe that they suffer more actively and keenly, being souls preparing for blessedness, than Virgil suffers in eternal limbo. In their suffering is hope, in the anaesthesia of Virgil is hopelessness; that is the difference."[14] Blessedness, which Eliot usually called beatitude, is the soul's eternal gift, received from God, of His presence.

I risk indelicacy in suggesting that Eliot's reflections on Hell, Purgatory, Limbo, and Heaven come with particular force from a man who suffered and prayed that his suffering would turn out to have been purgatorial and not meaningless. It is clear that Eliot's early poems issue from an acutely personal context in which the predominant emotions are guilt, self-disgust, and revulsion. A religious faith that offered to make sense of guilt and suffering by extending the hope that these emotions could be turned to spiritual purpose would have special salience for him.

The awkward side of this is the question of human relations in such a world. Eliot's satiric gift was propelled by what he regarded as inescapable cause. He felt that much of human life was disgusting. In his Christian years he believed that his best practice, in addition to daily prayer, was to regard human relations as provisional and ancillary to some relation beyond them. In his essay on Baudelaire he presents that poet "reaching out towards something which cannot be had *in,* but which may be had partly *through,* personal relations." The force of this position in Eliot is as if to say: love God, then do as you wish. Or: act on the belief that what we do must be either good or evil; we live in the choice—so far as we make it—between salvation and damnation.

But since we are afflicted with original sin, and if the blessedness of Heaven cannot be enjoyed in this life, what is the status of personal relations? Eliot argues that we must be willing to postpone our demand upon happiness and enjoy it in the eternal company of God. In the essay on Dante he speaks of not expecting more from life than it can give, or more from human beings that they can offer, and of looking "to death for what life cannot give."[15] But sometimes in his poems, early and late, he allows the reader to feel that intimations of beatitude occur and that one's experience of them is not necessarily a delusion.

The question is complicated by the fact that in Eliot's poems an event and its significance rarely coincide: the fact and the myth are discontinuous. The meaning of an event becomes available only when it is recalled; when it rushes back into one's mind, by grace of memory; or when it is reconsidered in relation to something else, on another level of being, by an act of hope. But this order of precedence in the structure of Eliot's interests entailed grave moral risk. So far as biographical evidence is available, it suggests that Eliot located his spirituality far above his mere deeds, and set a pattern in place before there was any pressing need of it. I can't otherwise explain, and can't explain away, his apparently heartless treatment of some people who cared for him. I'm thinking of Emily Hale, Mary Trevelyan, and John Hayward, people whose lives, in one degree or another, Eliot appropriated; it was as if they had nothing better to do than to facilitate the pattern he prescribed for himself. In the end, it becomes difficult to exonerate Eliot from a charge of moral obtuseness; and the matter is not resolved by quoting his distinction between "the man who suffers" and "the mind which creates."

The necessary distinction is between Eliot's prose and his poetry. They served different motives. In his prose, as perhaps in his personal life, the myth takes precedence over the fact and imposes stringent criteria in determining the facts to be recognized. Bakhtin and other critics have argued, though not with Eliot especially in mind, that a myth exercises hegemony over language, just as language exercises pressure on the perception and conceptualization of reality. In Eliot's prose, the myth determines the principles to be applied, and in turn the facts to be recognized. Failures in this regard are then subjected to doctrines of sin and purgation. The fact that one does not always commit sin is ascribed to divine grace. But in the poetry, experiences that are authenticated by being remembered, by emerging irresistibly from Eliot's past life or from a buried life of images, are never disowned. The myth by which they will be tested is held at arm's length until the experiences are acknowledged. The pattern of this acknowledgment in the poetry is one of emergence: its most compelling paradigm is that of features forming themselves into a face. So, in reading the poems, the misgiving we feel about the polemical prose becomes far more honorably a matter of degree and emphasis as we act upon the elusive movements of tone that establish themselves with extraordinary delicacy.

II

On May 25, 1936, Eliot visited Little Gidding, site of an Anglican community of about forty members, which Nicholas Ferrar and his family established in 1625; it is between Huntingdon and Oundle in Huntingdonshire. The community was of some historic significance: it sheltered King Charles I after his defeat at Naseby, it was ransacked by Cromwellian soldiers in the winter of 1646, it was destroyed by fire, the chapel was rebuilt in the eighteenth century and added to in the nineteenth. Five years after his visit, Eliot started drafting a poem of that name, the last of the *Quartets,* this one having not earth, air, or water, but fire as its element, appropriately, since its setting was the London of the war, German bombing raids, and the Battle of Britain. It is clear from the manuscripts that the governing theme of the poem was the return of the dead, a summoning of spirits from the past. The past in question was English history, and it culminated in Eliot's own struggles as a poet in the English language. Beyond those considerations, there was the Christian theme, the communion of saints— according to the Catholic catechism, "the union that exists between the members of the true Church on earth with one another, with the saints in Heaven, and the suffering souls in Purgatory." Eliot's first scribbled notes for the poem include this program: "They vanish, the individuals, and our feeling for them sinks into the flame which refines. They emerge in another pattern & recreated & reconciled redeemed, having their meaning together not apart, in a union which is of beams from the central fire. . . . Invocation to the Holy Spirit."[16] In the final version, published on October 15, 1942, this note became the lines:

And what the dead had no speech for, when living,
They can tell you, being dead: the communication
Of the dead is tongued with fire beyond the language of the
   living.

Here we have another "beyond," a further perspective upon the com-
placencies of communication.

The most admired passage in the poem is an elaborate summoning
of the dead in the form of a familiar compound ghost. The immediate
source is Dante's encounter with his dead master Brunetto Latini in
Canto 15 of the *Inferno*. There are also continuities between Eliot's
early poems and this passage of "Little Gidding," notably the face of
the compound ghost "still forming" and the recognition the spoken
words precede. The passage is Eliot's most achieved scene of recognition. Gradually it emerges that the ghost is compounded of Yeats,
Mallarmé, Swift, and one or more of Eliot's earlier selves. The dead
master is encountered as if on a London street on the morning after
an air raid. The words the master speaks come from the dead; in that
perspective, there is no obstacle between life and death:

But, as the passage now presents no hindrance
To the spirit unappeased and peregrine
Between two worlds become much like each other. . . .

This spirit is still in the world, still in London, but with evidence of
death all around him is ready to go through the fires of Purgatory.
Dante met Brunetto Latini in Hell: the encounter in "Little Gidding"
is with Eliot's literary masters. So the first consequence of "peregrine" (foreigner, pilgrim) is to displace the meeting from Hell to
Purgatory and to interpret transition as the possibility of purgation
and eventually of beatitude. The first sign of that progress is that the
ghost finds "words I never thought to speak." The next is that what

Eliot shared with the ghost is the common pursuit of true judgment, another achievement of perspective, a compound act of aftersight and foresight. This perspective offers a revision of standard axioms about growing wise by growing old:

> Let me disclose the gifts reserved for age
>   To set a crown upon your lifetime's effort.
> First, the cold friction of expiring sense
> Without enchantment, offering no promise
>   But bitter tastelessness of shadow fruit
>   As body and soul begin to fall asunder.
> Second, the conscious impotence of rage
>   At human folly, and the laceration
>   Of laughter at what ceases to amuse.
> And last, the rending pain of re-enactment
>   Of all that you have done, and been; the shame
>   Of motives late revealed, and the awareness
> Of things ill done and done to others' harm
>   Which once you took for exercise of virtue.

This is Eliot's redaction of many lives and experiences besides his own. I hear in it much of the Anglican morality of the early seventeenth century. The rage at human folly is Swift's, "laceration" a Swiftian word that John Hayward suggested. The "re-enactment / Of all that you have done, and been" is Yeats's, in *A Vision, Purgatory,* and other later plays, and the poem "Vacillation." The "things ill done" that "once you took for exercise of virtue" strike close to home and speak, I imagine, of Eliot's sense of his own actions, or of some of them. There is also, later on, the sense of the mug's game of having spent one's life as a poet, wrestling with words and meanings. Stevens reported that "Ariel was glad he had written his poems."

Eliot was not so sure. His doubt on that score was expressed by alluding to several writers as partial myths of the life of literature.

Of the writers implied in "Little Gidding," Yeats is the one most emphatically summoned. This is strange. For much of Eliot's early life as a poet he did not take Yeats seriously; he was put off by the elder poet's dealings with magic and spooks, and he strongly criticized Yeats's attempt to make a religion for himself out of folklore, superstition, and table-rapping. Eliot regarded Yeats as a heretic, though not as dangerous as D. H. Lawrence in that respect. So he held back from appreciating him till April 1916, when he saw *At the Hawk's Well* in London. Thereafter, Eliot knew that Yeats was a major poet, and he read the middle poems in a more admiring light. But Yeats had to die before Eliot gave him full recognition as the greatest poet of his time, a tribute he paid in his memorial lecture in Dublin. Praising Yeats as "pre-eminently the poet of middle age," Eliot quoted "The Spur":

> You think it horrible that lust and rage
> Should dance attendance upon my old age;
> They were not such a plague when I was young;
> What else have I to spur me into song?

On that poem, Eliot commented:

> To what honest man, old enough, can these sentiments be entirely alien? They can be subdued and disciplined by religion, but who can say that they are dead? Only those to whom the maxim of La Rochefoucauld applies: "Quand les vices nous quittent, nous nous flattons de la créance que c'est nous qui les quittons." The tragedy of Yeats's epigram is all in the last line.[17]

The Yeats of "The Spur" is the poet who comes most powerfully into "Little Gidding." The perspective from which the ghost speaks is chiefly that of Yeats's last poems: "The Spur" was written in December 1936, a little more than two years before his death. It is especially appropriate that in "Little Gidding" the hope of the purgatorial experience and of passing through it to paradise is suggested in figurative terms common to Yeats and Dante:

> From wrong to wrong the exasperated spirit
>> Proceeds, unless restored by that refining fire
>> Where you must move in measure, like a dancer.

The refining fire is a translation, as we have seen, from Dante. It is also an allusion to the spiritual fire of Yeats's "Sailing to Byzantium" and "Byzantium." In the third stanza of "Sailing to Byzantium" Yeats summons the "sages standing in God's holy fire" to be "the singing-masters of my soul." The passage in "Little Gidding" is Eliot's version of this summoning, just as the words of the ghost are his judgment on the condition of being "caught in that sensual music." The moving in measure like a dancer is pure Yeats, not only the poet of "Among School Children"—

> Labour is blossoming or dancing where
> The body is not bruised to pleasure soul—

but the dramatist of the *Plays for Dancers.* Measure or dance is movement seen in the highest perspective of form.

The rest of "Little Gidding" is inhabited by four interrelated concerns: memory, the past, love, and language. Each is adduced in the light of the end of all merely temporal things, and each shows an aspect different from the one disclosed by its common provenance. Memory includes its voluntary and involuntary characters. Why, Eliot wondered in *The Use of Poetry and the Use of Criticism,* out of all the experiences that one has had, do a certain few assert themselves, keep coming back: like his own experience, as a boy on summer vacation in Gloucester, peering through sea water in a rock pool and finding for the first time a sea anemone? Voluntary memory is the act of summoning the otherwise gone figures from one's past, not in the hope of recovering them as they were but of finding one's apprehension of them becoming a new thing in the later light:

> See, now they vanish,
> The faces and places, with the self which, as it could, loved
>   them,
> To become renewed, transfigured, in another pattern.

Here the process of revision, which corresponds to a Jamesian scruple, is conveyed through the elaborately suspended syntax, as if no noun could reach its verb, no past participle settled upon, till every possible form of it had been considered.

But memory, in Eliot, is a morally complicated act. It was crucial to him not because he needed to retain sensitive continuity with gone occasions but because he felt impelled to release himself from their importunity. They could not make a claim upon him while he brooded upon their significance. Like certain mystics, he enriched his spirituality by detaching himself from every object that might claim his desire. There is a passage in Rilke's *The Notebooks of Malte Laurids Brigge* that might usefully be brought into Eliot's context: "And still it is not yet enough to have memories. One must be able to forget them when they are many and one must have the great patience to wait until they come again. For it is not yet the memories themselves. Not till they have turned to blood within us, to glance and gesture, nameless and no longer to be distinguished from ourselves—not till then can it happen that in a most rare hour the first word of a verse arises in their midst and goes forth from them."[18] In Eliot's case, the memories no longer to be distinguished from himself must not bring with them any intimation of desire; they must minister to his vision— love beyond desire—not to his appetitive zest. The possibility of achieving love beyond desire has been well understood in the history of ethics, and especially in those ethical principles, such as Balthasar's, that are in accord with aesthetic appreciation. It is a harder possibility when the object of love is a person. It is difficult, where human relations are concerned, to appeal to a perspective beyond desire: the appeal casts doubt on the reality of the feelings engaged. What Eliot speaks of as liberation is hard to distinguish from indifference; only the misgiving revealed in the poems keeps the distinction alive.

The past is the subject of much rumination in "Burnt Norton." The third section of "Little Gidding" seems to disavow nostalgia: let the dead bury their dead. Again the admonition is the same: consider the end, the idea, the ideal form of whatever claims your attention. In this passage Eliot distinguishes, among the dead, between the fortunate, those who have won, and the defeated, who in some sense have not—or not merely—lost. Walter Benjamin maintained, in his "Theses on the Philosophy of History," that history is always recited in favor of those who have won: there has never been a history of the defeated. But in the perspective of "Little Gidding,"

> Whatever we inherit from the fortunate
> We have taken from the defeated
> What they had to leave us—a symbol:
> A symbol perfected in death.

This symbol differs from Yeats's, which is always in nature and shared life even when he longs to find it, or to project himself, "out of nature." Eliot is unwilling to recognize a symbol as such until he has seen or imagined its force in the light of death; according to that vision, time is no longer mere *tempus,* one-thing-after-another, but *aevum,* time redeemed in the end and meanwhile lived in the light of that end.

And there is language. In "The Waste Land," Eliot was much concerned with the question of authority in language, with the sources, kinds, and degrees of authority that sustain our words or fail to sustain them. In "Little Gidding," released now from the familiar compound ghost, he speaks of language no longer in the apocalyptic or demonic terms of "The Waste Land," but by appeal to the idea of a decently composed sentence:

> And every phrase
> And sentence that is right (where every word is at home,
> Taking its place to support the others,
> The word neither diffident not ostentatious,
> An easy commerce of the old and the new,
> The common word exact without vulgarity,
> The formal word precise but not pedantic,
> The complete consort dancing together)
> Every phrase and every sentence is an end and a beginning,
> Every poem an epitaph.

Every poem is an epitaph in the sense that it commemorates feelings otherwise formless if not defunct. Wordsworth, another poet sensitive to memory and the decencies of our important occasions, wrote essays upon epitaphs that are among the finest considerations of the question: what should one say, given that an occasion calls for something to be said? "Little Gidding" continues:

> And any action
> Is a step to the block, to the fire, down the sea's throat
> Or to an illegible stone: and that is where we start.
> We die with the dying:

See, they depart, and we go with them.
We are born with the dead:
See, they return, and bring us with them.

III

"See, they return" is an allusion to a poem by Pound about the return
of the gods: the gods, figures of an otherwise lost time, are seen
returning, wavering, but they are still unmistakably gods. I take
Eliot's allusion to Pound's poem as indicating how we are to read this
one, "Little Gidding": it, too, is a poem about the return, the survival, of the gods. There is a well-established history of this motif, to
be consulted in Jean Seznec's *The Survival of the Pagan Gods*. Variations
on the theme are to be found in Heine's "The Gods in Exile" (1853),
Gautier's essay on Leonardo (1864), the chapter on Pico della Miran-
dola in Pater's *Studies in the History of the Renaissance* (1873), and his
"Apollo in Picardy" (1893). Heine describes, in a passage that Pater
quotes, how the gods of the older world, when Christianity tri-
umphed, hid themselves on earth under all sorts of disguises. That
Apollo should be imagined turning up in Picardy is only one such
instance of survival.

If we read "Little Gidding" as a poem about the survival of the
gods, it is hardly necessary to say that Eliot's gods are not Pound's,
Pater's, Gautier's, or Heine's. He finds his God according to the
theology of the Christian church and therefore can freely summon as
if they were lesser gods those men and women who were important
to him in the respects he cared about; figures from his personal history, his family, the history of literature—mainly in English, French,
and Dante's Italian. The allusion to Pound's poem is Eliot's way of
paying tribute to one of his masters and at the same time of separating
himself from Pound in the consideration that mattered more. Pound

took his gods where he found them, just as he took his myths oppor-
tunely if not opportunistically from Confucius, Ovid, Jefferson, and
anyone else he admired. Remember that I have remembered, Pound
said. It was far more important to Eliot that he believed and that he
subordinated to belief every other consideration. The communication of the dead is tongued with fire beyond the language of the living
because the dead are now complete, as we are not yet complete,
perfected in death. "Tongued with fire": an allusion, first and fore-
most, to the episode in the Acts of the Apostles when the apostles,
gathered in a room, suddenly heard what sounded like a great wind
from Heaven, and something appeared to them that seemed like
tongues of fire; the tongues separated and came to rest on the head of
each of them. The shape of the flame as in Isaiah 6 is associated with
prophecy, the gift of tongues. A further explication is given in the last
lines of "Little Gidding":

> And all shall be well and
> All manner of thing shall be well
> When the tongues of flame are in-folded
> Into the crowned knot of fire
> And the fire and the rose are one.

The immediate allusion is to the consolation offered to Lady Juliana in
a vision; then to the passage in *The Dark Night of the Soul* in which St.
John of the Cross says that love is like a fire, which always rises up
with the desire to be absorbed in the center of its sphere. A further
reference is to the passage in *Paradiso,* Canto 33, where Dante sees the
divine vision as scattered leaves of the universe, in-gathered now by
love in one mass: substance and accident and their relations ("sus-
tanza ed accidenti, e lor costume") as though fused together, "so that
what I speak of is one simple flame" ("che cio ch'io dico e un sem-
plice lume").

At the end of "Little Gidding," Eliot has reconciled, more completely than anywhere else in his poetry, myth and fact, mitigating the abstraction of the one, the rigidity of the other. That he saw his poetic aim in these terms, one can hardly doubt, especially in view of the admiration he expressed in his essay on Dante for "the power of the master who could thus at every moment realize the inapprehensible in visual images." Referring to the lines in *Paradiso* in which Neptune is imagined full of wonder at the passage of the Arno over his head, Eliot said that he did not know anywhere in poetry "a more authentic sign of greatness" than the power of association that could introduce the river and the god of the waves into a presentation of the divine vision.

IV

Eliot's problem in *Four Quartets* is a strategic one; how to evacuate practically all the areas in which his readers live. A proposal of this kind is tolerated only in wartime. Eliot wrote most of the poem during the second World War and perhaps he wanted to use the idiom of war in order to enforce a deeper discrimination of peacetime commitments. The critique is religious, dogmatic, and Christian. Eliot's hope is to clear a space, or if necessary to take over a bombed-out area, and there to build a new life of the spirit; to realize "the idea of a Christian society." He will approach meaning from several experimental directions, making fresh starts, because he can hardly hope— the conditions being unpropitious—that one will suffice. There is a sense in which he himself is the object of his persuasion. The redemption of time will be his theme, his case, but he will have to resist a Manichean force within himself which is notoriously subversive; it doesn't really believe that time can be redeemed, it fears that the human scale of action is puny beyond or beneath redemption. This is to give the Manichean force an extreme form, and it will not always be

so intransigent; but that it is a complication in Eliot's Christian poetry, I have no doubt. It is probably inevitable—or an occasional haz-
ard, at least—in all those "varieties of religious experience" which
are ascetic before they are anything else; taking their bearings from
the idiom of cleansing, surgery, and voiding. It is difficult to propose
the voiding of all human allegiances without implying that they are in
any event meretricious. The idiom of renunciation is all the greater if
what is renounced is indisputably fine. Therefore an "ideal" strategy
for a secular age would consist in persuading one's readers to void
their allegiances by showing up their daily preoccupations as mere
"fancies"; and then to translate this voiding into renunciation, a positive sacrifice which they are encouraged to make to a God now certified by the quality of the sacrifice itself. This is largely what Eliot
tries to do in the *Quartets*.

There is a passage in *The Trembling of the Veil* that throws light on
Eliot's object. Yeats has been discussing "Unity of Being" in his habitual idiom of Image, Mask, and Anti-Self. But he goes on to say that
there are people to whom this is irrelevant:

> I now know that there are men who cannot possess "Unity of
> Being," who must not seek it or express it—and who, so far from
> seeking an anti-self, a Mask that delineates a being in all things the
> opposite to their natural state, can but seek the suppression of the
> anti-self, till the natural state alone remains. These are those who
> must seek no image of desire, but await that which lies beyond
> their mind—unities not of the mind, but unities of Nature, unities
> of God—the man of science, the moralist, the humanitarian, the
> politician, Saint Simeon Stylites upon his pillar, Saint Anthony in
> his cavern, all whose preoccupation is to seem nothing . . . their
> imaginations grow more vivid in the expression of something
> which they have not created.[19]

The great example is George Herbert. Eliot would probably say, "all whose preoccupation is to *be* nothing," since seeming is not enough—he is not Wallace Stevens. The authority—if he needs one—comes from St. John of the Cross, "To be all things, be willing to be nothing." These men are the great exemplars, but they are only the most extreme forms of Eliot's ideal reader, his ideal person. In this sense the poetry does not matter: it merely "points" the reader—and perhaps the writer, too—toward one end.

The course of Eliot's persuasion in *Four Quartets* is to translate voiding into renunciation, negative into its corresponding positive. Some of the rhetoric whistles in the dark, warding off ghosts: there are moments in the *Quartets* when Eliot can't quite convince himself of human value, and even the pretty, inoffensive things are cleared away before they can be redeemed. Like the poor dancers of "East Coker":

> Keeping time,
> Keeping the rhythm in their dancing
> As in their living in the living seasons
> The time of the seasons and the constellations
> The time of milking and the time of harvest
> The time of the coupling of man and woman
> And that of beasts. Feet rising and falling.
> Eating and drinking. Dung and death.

It is a gruff dismissal, when all is said, and it points to the deepest quandary in Eliot's poetry; his feeling, in part, that all the declared values of human life are somehow illusory and, in part, that nevertheless God so loved the world that He gave up for its redemption His beloved Son. In *Four Quartets* when the first part of this feeling is predominant, the persuasion is all voiding; when the second part asserts itself, the persuasion is all renunciation. The poems are dogmatic, but there is often "the backward half-look / Over the shoulder, towards the primitive terror." For many readers this half-look redeems a poetry otherwise too imperiously set above the mire.

This is to say that the poem is animated, however precariously, by a profound sense of the process, the struggle, the writhing of ignorance and purpose. The motto is given in the second part of "The Dry Salvages":

And approach to the meaning restores the experience
In a different form. . . .

The meaning is given as the Incarnation, Love, figured in the dance. Readers take these terms as they find them and make of them what they can. But the poem does not depend on their goodwill, belief, or disbelief. It depends on their response to "the approach," the degree to which their own sense of the process is animated by Eliot's words. The approach is featured in several versions. There is the struggle to make valid sentences, the wrestling with last year's words. There is, to stand for everything, "the trying." "The rest is not our business." Eliot's greatest poetry is written in the tension between these polar terms, between the ineffable meaning and the temporal approach; between the Logos and the mere words, the dialect of the tribe. It is relevant also to note the Augustinian distinction between the meaning of a sentence and the syllables of which it is composed, which Kenneth Burke has linked to the distinction between spirit and matter.[20] If men and women are syllables, God is the meaning. So the higher term includes all the lower ones and transcends them; the tone of the transcendence can be urgent or reluctant. There is clearly a relation between the transcendence, the abstraction of Eliot's later poems, and his sense of the burden of objects, the despotism of finite things. The object, often canceled as an object, is entertained as form or shadow. But Eliot is not Mondrian or Kandinsky: he does not cancel the object in a fine flourish, his mind made up from the start. In the early poems the objects are seen from a distance and thus controlled: the distance is often the measure of the poet's distaste, the low vision, as of the "young man carbuncular" in "The Waste Land." The later mode is disciplinary and ascetic, and incidentally a way of gaining the highest and dearest property, the salvation of one's soul. But there is misgiving, either way. It is the poignancy of misgiving that keeps the poetry human. Here is another passage from "Little Gidding":

> If you came this way,
> Taking the route you would be likely to take
> From the place you would be likely to come from,
> If you came this way in may time, you would find the hedges
> White again, in May, with voluptuary sweetness.
> It would be the same at the end of the journey,
> If you came at night like a broken king,
> If you came by day not knowing what you came for,
> It would be the same, when you leave the rough road
> And turn behind the pig-sty to the dull façade
> And the tombstone.

This is not dramatic poetry, it does not find glory in the plenitude of the event, the thing, the object. In *Anna Karenina,* when the train is coming into the station at Petersburg, in the luggage-van, Tolstoy mentions, a dog is whining. This is not a symbol; it is an imagined fact, part of Tolstoy's vision of the event, the scene. Eliot's later poems do not go in this way: they are meditative poems, dealing with their objects at the remove of contemplation and generalization. In this kind of poetry we do not get the particular object, or even the feeling of that object: we get the feeling of all such objects, attracted into a single cadence. One thinks of George Herbert—

I know the wayes of Pleasure, the sweet strains,
The lullings and the relishes of it

—for whom the lullings and the relishes bring together, as flesh to
flesh, all those experiences which, in a decorous generalization, are
called pleasure; but not any particular instance of pleasure. In the
lines from "Little Gidding" the white hedges are provisional, moments in the approach to the meaning, and Eliot is prepared, at need,
to set them aside. But meanwhile the poetry acknowledges that kind
of whiteness, that kind of sweetness, the merging of a subject and an
object in those sensory terms; even if the cadence prepares us to
disengage ourselves from all such occasions, at need. The short name
for Eliot's later cadences is nostalgia. He writes of objects and experiences as if he had already left them behind—with whatever degree of
reluctance. In these lines the elaborate complicity with the "you" ("If
you came this way") is partly to register the delicacy of the occasion,
partly to make up for the poet's rejection of the objects, because he
has contracted to reject them, however reluctantly. The short way to
say this is too short: that Eliot's Christianity was not Franciscan, but
his poetry was enlivened by a Franciscan scruple. Perhaps this explains why the technical resources of the passage are lavished upon
the voluptuary sweetness; the single line, in the first part, which is
released from the elaborate grammatical chain. [21]

For me, the poetry is saved by the scruple. The way it is saved may
be indicated by a passage from *Varieties of Religious Experience,* where
William James discusses the character of sanctity, particularly its ascetic quality. He remarks that while it is normal and, apparently,
instinctive for us to seek "the easy and the pleasant," at the same time
it is also normal "in moderate degree" to seek the arduous: "Some
men and women, indeed, there are who can live on smiles and the
word 'yes' forever. But for others (indeed for most) this is too tepid

and relaxed a moral climate. Passive happiness is slack and insipid, and soon grows mawkish and intolerable. Some austerity and wintry negativity, some roughness, danger, stringency, and effort, some 'no! no!' must be mixed in, to produce the sense of an existence with character and texture and power."[22]

This is how *Four Quartets* lives, and how it communicates with those readers who do not share its Christian belief: by giving the sense of an existence with character and texture and power. I can't be persuaded by Geoffrey Hill that in the *Quartets* Eliot has ingratiated himself with his readers and neglected the responsibility he owes to his themes. Nor can Hill convince me that I must regard the achievement of "tone" as a sign of the writer's capitulation to his readers and audiences. Eliot's rhythm of yes-and-no, in something like William James's terms, determines the tone of his "approach" in the *Quartets*. He has always implied that the satisfactions of poetry are in this area of assent and dissent. The great poem helps to purify the dialect of the tribe by making tribal stupidity unendurable. A purified dialect then becomes the expression of joy as well as pain. Discussing "London" and "The Vanity of Human Wishes," Eliot remarked: "Those who demand of poetry a day-dream, or a metamorphosis of their own feeble desires and lusts, or what they believe to be 'intensity' of passion, will not find much in Johnson. He is like Pope and Dryden, Crabbe and Landor, a poet for those who want poetry and not something else, some stay for their own vanity."[23] *Four Quartets* is offered to the same readers for the same ascetic—but not only ascetic; sensuous, too—purpose. If the intimate procedures of Eliot's early verse invite attention to those of Tennyson and Swinburne as well as Baudelaire and Laforgue, the later poems should be read with Dante, Dryden, Pope, and Johnson in mind, as a poetry for those who want poetry and not something else.

Notes

Preface

1. T. S. Eliot, *Collected Poems, 1909–1962* (New York: Harcourt, Brace, 1963), pp. 79–80.
2. R. P. Blackmur, *A Primer of Ignorance,* edited by Joseph Frank (New York: Harcourt, Brace & World, 1967), p. 46.
3. Eliot, *Collected Poems, 1909–1962,* p. 82.
4. W. B. Yeats, *The Poems,* edited by Richard J. Finneran (New York: Macmillan, 1989), p. 7.

Chapter 1. Beginning

1. Ashley Brown and Frances Neel Cheney, editors, *The Poetry Reviews of Allen Tate, 1924–1944* (Baton Rouge: Louisiana State University Press, 1983), p. 47.
2. The original text is given in T. S. Eliot, *Inventions of the March Hare: Poems, 1909–1917,* edited by Christopher Ricks (London: Faber and Faber, 1996), pp. 39–47.
3. Hugh Kenner, *The Invisible Poet: T. S. Eliot* (New York: McDowell, Obolensky, 1959), pp. 40–41.
4. T. S. Eliot, *Collected Poems, 1909–1962* (London: Faber and Faber, 1963), p. 13.

5. Kristian Smidt, *Poetry and Belief in the Work of T. S. Eliot,* rev. ed., (London: Routledge and Kegan Paul, 1961), p. 85.

6. B. C. Southam, *A Guide to the Selected Poems of T. S. Eliot,* 6th ed., (New York: Harcourt, Brace, 1996), pp. 48–49.

7. Eliot, *Collected Poems, 1909–1962,* p. 13.

8. James T. Jones, editor, *Outsider at the Heart of Things: Essays by R. P. Blackmur* (Urbana: University of Illinois Press, 1988), p. 51.

9. J. Peter Dyson, "Words Heard: Prufrock Asks His Question," *Yeats Eliot Review* 5, no. 2 (1978): 34.

10. T. S. Eliot, *Selected Essays, 1917–1932* (London: Faber and Faber, 1932), p. 145.

11. Ibid., p. 146.

12. Ibid., p. 376.

13. The lecture is printed as "Tradition and the Practice of Poetry" in *Southern Review* 21, no. 4 (October 1985): 875–884.

14. Eliot, *Selected Essays, 1917–1932,* p. 21.

15. Jean de Boschère [*sic*], *Ulysse batit son lit,* edited by Michel Desbrueres (Paris: Granit: Collection de la clef, 1977), p. 11.

16. T. S. Eliot, "Reflections on Contemporary Poetry," *Egoist* 4, no. 9 (October 1917): 133.

17. De Bosschère, *Ulysse,* p. 13.

18. R. P. Blackmur, *Form and Value in Modern Poetry* (Garden City, N.Y.: Doubleday Anchor, 1957) pp. 251–252.

19. T. S. Eliot, *Complete Poems and Plays* (New York: Harcourt, Brace, 1952), p. 29.

20. William Arrowsmith, "Eros in Terre Haute: T. S. Eliot's "Lune de Miel," *New Criterion,* October 1982, p. 25.

21. Ibid., p. 34.

22. Ibid., p. 35.

23. R. P. Blackmur, *Anni Mirabiles, 1921–1925* (Washington, D.C.: Library of Congress, 1956), p. 29.

24. Wallace Stevens, *The Palm at the End of the Mind,* edited by Holly Stevens (reprint, New York: Vintage 1990), pp. 39–40.

Chapter 2. Voices

1. T. S. Eliot, *The Three Voices of Poetry* (Cambridge: Cambridge University Press, 1953), p. 4.

2. Ibid., p. 18.

3. T. S. Eliot, *The Use of Poetry and the Use of Criticism* (reprint, London: Faber and Faber, 1948), p. 68.

4. Ibid., p. 12.

5. Leonard Woolf, *Downhill All the Way: An Autobiography of the Years 1919 to 1939* (New York: Harcourt Brace Jovanovich, 1967), p. 109.

6. Ludwig Wittgenstein, *Zettel 55*, quoted in Guy Davenport, *The Geography of the Imagination* (San Francisco: North Point, 1981), p. 29.

7. T. S. Eliot, *On Poetry and Poets* (New York: Farrar, Straus and Cudahy, 1957), p. 306.

8. Francis Fergusson, *Sallies of the Mind,* edited by John McCormick and George Core (New Brunswick, N.J.: Transaction, 1997), p. 20.

9. R. P. Blackmur, *Outsider at the Heart of Things,* edited by James T. Jones (Urbana: University of Illinois Press, 1989), p. 62.

10. R. P. Blackmur, *A Primer of Ignorance,* edited by Joseph Frank (New York: Harcourt, Brace and World, 1967), p. 69.

11. T. S. Eliot, *Selected Essays, 1917–1932* (London: Faber and Faber, 1932), p. 313.

12. Ibid.

13. Eliot, *Use of Poetry,* pp. 118–119.

14. T. S. Eliot, *To Criticize the Critic and Other Writings* (New York: Farrar, Straus and Giroux, 1965), p. 31.

15. Eliot, *Use of Poetry,* p. 145.

16. Eliot, *Selected Essays, 1917–1932,* p. 228.

17. Ibid., p. 238.

18. Ibid., p. 229.

19. Quoted in Erich Auerbach, *Mimesis: The Representation of Reality in Western Literature,* translated by Willard R. Trask (reprint, Princeton: Princeton University Press, 1974), p. 5.

20. Eliot, *On Poetry and Poets,* pp. 161–162.

21. Ibid., pp. 161–163.

22. Ibid., p. 151.

23. Eliot, *To Criticize the Critic,* p. 32.

24. Ibid.

25. Eliot, *On Poetry and Poets,* p. 21.

26. T. S. Eliot, *The Sacred Wood: Essays on Poetry and Criticism* (New York: Knopf, 1930), p. 5.

27. Arthur Symons, *The Symbolist Movement in Literature,* 2nd ed. (London: Constable 1908), p. 4.

28. Ibid., p. 8.

29. Ezra Pound, *Gaudier Brzeska: A Memoir,* 2nd ed. (New York: New Directions, 1970), p. 89.

30. Symons, *Symbolist Movement,* p. 104.

31. T. S. Eliot, "Modern Tendencies in Poetry," *Shama'a* 1, no. 1 (April 1920): 12.

32. T. S. Eliot, "Reflections on Contemporary Poetry," *Egoist* 6, no. 3 (July 1919): 39–40. Cf. T. S. Eliot, *Inventions of the March Hare: Poems, 1909–1917,* edited by Christopher Ricks (London: Faber and Faber, 1996), p. 399.

33. Eliot, *Selected Essays, 1917–1932,* p. 276.

34. Jules Laforgue, *Derniers Vers,* edited by Michael Collie and J. M. L'Heureux (Toronto: University of Toronto Press, 1965), p. 45.

35. T. S. Eliot, *The Complete Poems and Plays* (New York: Harcourt, Brace, 1952), p. 14.

36. Eliot, *On Poetry and Poets,* p. 77.

37. William Carlos Williams, *Selected Essays* (New York: Random House, 1954), p. 106.

38. R. P. Blackmur, *Language as Gesture* (New York: Harcourt, Brace, 1952), p. 219.

39. Eliot, *Selected Essays, 1917–1932,* p. 181.

40. James Wood, *The Broken Estate: Essays on Literature and Belief* (London: Jonathan Cape, 1999), p. 141.

41. Eliot, *To Criticize the Critic,* p. 128.

42. René Girard, *Deceit, Desire, and the Novel,* translated by Yvonne Freccero (Baltimore: Johns Hopkins University Press, 1965), p. 4.

43. Geoffrey Hill, "Style and Faith," *Times Literary Supplement,* December 27, 1991, pp. 3–4.

Chapter 3. "La Figlia che Piange"

1. The most helpful elucidations of the Virgilian aspects of Eliot's poems are Gareth Reeves, *T. S. Eliot: A Virgilian Poet* (1989), Hugh Kenner, "The Urban Apocalypse," in A. Walton Litz, *Eliot in His Time* (1973), and Kenneth Reckford, "Recognizing Venus (II): Dido, Aeneas, and Mr. Eliot," *Arion,* Fall 1995–Winter 1996, pp. 43–80.

2. Irving Howe, *A Margin of Hope: An Intellectual Autobiography* (San Diego: Harcourt Brace Jovanovich, 1982), p. 336.

3. Immanuel Kant, *The Critique of Judgment,* translated by James Creed Meredith (Oxford: Clarendon, 1952), p. 289.

4. Ibid., p. 311.

5. Cf. J. M. Bernstein, *The Fate of Art: Aesthetic Alienation from Kant to Derrida and Adorno* (University Park: Pennsylvania State University Press, 1992), p. 18ff.

6. T. S. Eliot, *Letters,* vol. 1: *1898–1922,* edited by Valerie Eliot (San Diego: Harcourt Brace Jovanovich, 1988). Letter of September 8, 1921, to Richard Aldington, p. 468.

7. Guy Davenport, *The Geography of the Imagination* (San Francisco: North Point, 1981), p. 262.

8. Ibid., pp. 262–263.

9. T. S. Eliot, "Dryden the Dramatist," *Listener,* April 22, 1931, p. 681. My attention was drawn to this passage by Christopher Ricks, *T. S. Eliot and Prejudice* (Berkeley: University of California Press, 1988), p. 159.

10. Cf. Grover Smith, *T. S. Eliot's Poetry and Plays,* 2nd ed. (Chicago, 1974), pp. 27 and n21.

11. Virgil, *Aeneid,* the Loeb edition, translated by H. Rushton Fairclough (Cambridge, Mass.: Harvard University Press, 1978), Book 1, lines 327–328, p. 264 (translation modified).

12. Kenneth Reckford, "Recognizing Venus (I): Aeneas Meets His Mother," *Arion,* Fall 1995–Winter 1996, pp. 4–6.

13. Ibid., Book VI, lines 465–466 and 469–471, p. 539 (translation modified).

14. T. S. Eliot, *On Poetry and Poets* (New York: Farrar, Straus and Cudahy, 1957), pp. 63–64.

15. Ibid., p. 145.

16. *Aeneid,* p. 539.

17. T. S. Eliot, *Collected Poems, 1909–1962* (New York: Harcourt, Brace, 1963), p. 26.

18. Ronald Bush, *T. S. Eliot: A Study in Character and Style* (New York: Oxford University Press, 1983), p. 13.

19. T. S. Eliot, *Selected Essays* (London: Faber and Faber, 1963), p. 21.

20. Walter Pater, *The Renaissance: Studies in Art and Poetry: The 1893 Text,* edited by Donald L. Hill (Berkeley: University of California Press, 1980), p. xix.

21. Theodor W. Adorno, *Aesthetic Theory,* edited by Robert Hullot-Kentor (Minneapolis: University of Minnesota Press, 1997), p. 51.

22. Adorno, *Aesthetic Theory,* p. 196.

23. Ibid., p. 197.

24. J. M. Bernstein, *The Fate of Art: Aesthetic Alienation from Kant to Derrida and Adorno* (University Park: Pennsylvania State University Press, 1992), 235.

25. Ibid., p. 238.

26. Albrecht Wellmer, "Truth, Semblance, Reconciliation: Adorno's Aesthetic Redemption of Modernity," *Telos* 61 (1984–85): 107. Quoted in Bernstein, *Fate of Art,* p. 245.

Chapter 4. "Gerontion"

1. William H. Marshall, "The Text of T. S. Eliot's 'Gerontion,' " *Studies in Bibliography* 4 (1951–1952): pp. 213–217.

2. John Crowe Ransom, "Gerontion," in Allen Tate, editor, *T. S. Eliot: The Man and His Work* (New York: Delacorte, 1966), p. 149.

3. Henry Adams, *The Education of Henry Adams* (New York: Modern Library, 1996), p. 268.

4. *Explicator* 18, no. 5, item 30 (February 1960).

5. Adams, *Education of Henry Adams,* p. 316.

6. R. P. Blackmur, *Outsider at the Heart of Things,* edited by James T. Jones (Urbana: University of Illinois Press, 1989), p. 47.

7. Yvor Winters, *In Defense of Reason* (Denver: Alan Swallow, 1947), p. 86.

8. Ibid., pp. 496–497.

9. Ransom, "Gerontion," p. 152.

10. Alfred Kazin, *An American Procession* (New York: Knopf, 1984), p. 19.

11. Ibid.

12. T. S. Eliot, *The Sacred Wood: Essays on Poetry and Criticism* (New York: Knopf, 1930), pp. 31–32.

13. T. S. E[liot], "A Sceptical Patrician," *Athenaeum,* no. 4647 (May 23, 1919): 362.

14. Ibid., p. 362.

15. T. S. Eliot, *Selected Essays, 1917–1932* (London: Faber and Faber, 1932), p. 273.

16. T. S. Eliot, *On Poetry and Poets* (New York: Farrar, Straus, 1957), p. 303.

17. Ransom, "On Gerontion," p. 151.

18. Sherna Vinograd, "The Accidental: A Clue to Structure in Eliot's Poetry," *Accent* 9, no. 4 (Summer 1949).

19. T. S. Eliot, "Reflections on Contemporary Poetry," *Egoist* 6, no. 3 (July 1919): 39–40.

20. Eliot, *Elected Essays, 1917–1932,* pp. 130–131.

21. Johannes Fabricius, *The Unconscious and Mr. Eliot: A Study in Expressionism* (Copenhagen: Nyt Nordisk Forlag Arnold Busck, 1967), p. 55.

22. T. S. E[liot], "A Foreign Mind," *Athenaeum,* no. 4653 (July 4, 1919): 552–553.

23. T. S. Eliot, *After Strange Gods: A Primer of Modern Heresy* (London: Faber and Faber, 1934), p. 45.

24. Ibid., p. 46.

25. Ibid.

26. E. M. Cioran, *The Temptation to Exist,* translated by Richard Howard (Chicago: Quadrangle, 1968), pp. 126, 127, 133.

27. T. S. Eliot, *The Use of Poetry and the Use of Criticism* (London: Faber and Faber, 1933), pp. 147–148.

28. Ibid.

Chapter 5. "Burbank with a Baedeker: Bleistein with a Cigar"

1. W. B. Yeats, editor, *Oxford Book of Modern Verse, 1892–1935* (New York: Oxford University Press, 1937), pp. xxi–xxiii.

2. *The Letters of T. S. Eliot,* vol. 1: *1898–1922,* edited by Valerie Eliot (New York: Harcourt Brace Jovanovich, 1988), p. 363. Letter of February 15, 1920, to Henry Eliot.

3. *Poetry* 58 (1946): 335. Quoted in Christopher Ricks, "Gautier and Eliot's Openings," *Times Literary Supplement,* June 11, 1993.

4. Quoted in B. C. Southam, *A Guide to the Selected Poems of T. S. Eliot,* 6th ed. (New York: Harcourt Brace, 1994), p. 79.

5. Robert Crawford, *The Savage and the City in the Work of T. S. Eliot* (Oxford: Clarendon, 1987), p. 116.

6. Guy Davenport, *Cities on Hills: A Study of I–XXX of Ezra Pound's Cantos* (Ann Arbor: UMI Research Press, 1983), pp. 228–229.

7. Karl Miller, *Rebecca's Vest: A Memoir* (London: Hamish Hamilton, 1993), p. 81.

8. William Empson, *Using Biography* (Cambridge, Mass.: Harvard University Press, 1984), pp. 195–197.

9. T. S. Eliot, *Selected Essays, 1917–1932* (London: Faber and Faber, 1932), p. 415.

10. Christopher Ricks, *T. S. Eliot and Prejudice* (Berkeley: University of California Press, 1988), pp. 33–38.

11. Ibid., p. 34.

12. Ibid., p. 70.

13. Anthony Julius, *T. S. Eliot, Anti-Semitism, and Literary Form* (Cambridge: Cambridge University Press, 1995), p. 2.

14. Giorgio Melchori, "Henry James: Burbank or Bleistein," in Sergio Perosa, editor, *Henry James e Venezia* (Florence: Leo S. Olschki Editore, 1987), p. 118.

15. Tony Tanner, *Venice Desired* (Cambridge, Mass.: Harvard University Press, 1992), p. 329.

16. R. P. Blackmur, *Outsider at the Heart of Things,* edited by James T. Jones (Urbana: University of Illinois Press, 1989), p. 51.

17. Hans-Georg Gadamer, *Truth and Method* (reprint, London: Sheed and Ward, 1985), p. 240.

18. Ibid., p. 246.

19. Ibid., p. 249.

20. Southam, *Guide to the Selected Poems,* pp. 79–92.

21. James Joyce, *A Portrait of the Artist as a Young Man,* edited by Hans Walter Gabler with Walter Hettche (New York: Garland, 1993), p. 81.

22. Southam, *Guide to the Selected Poems,* pp. 86.

Chapter 6. "The Waste Land"

1. Nathaniel Hawthorne, *The House of the Seven Gables* (Columbus: Ohio State University Press, 1955), vol. 2, p. 855.

2. T. S. Eliot, "In Memory," *The Little Review* 5, no. 4 (August 1918): 44.

3. T. S. Eliot, *To Criticize the Critic* (London: Faber and Faber, 1965), p. 54.

4. Harold Rosenberg, *The Tradition of the New* (reprint, London: Paladin, 1970), pp. 86, 89.

5. Roland Barthes, *Writing Degree Zero,* translated by Annette Lavers and Colin Smith (London: Cape, 1967), pp. 54–55.

6. R. P. Blackmur, *Form and Value in Modern Poetry* (New York: Anchor, 1957), p. 143.

7. R. P. Blackmur, *Anni Mirabiles, 1921–1925* (Washington, D.C.: Library of Congress, 1956), p. 31.

8. T. S. Eliot, *The Waste Land: A Facsimile and Transcript of the Original Drafts,* p. 31. edited by Valerie Eliot (London: Faber and Faber, 1971).

9. Plato, *The Republic,* Book IX, 592-A-B, quoted from the Loeb edition in

the Facsimile *The Waste Land*, p. 128. Frank Kermode has pointed out that the phrase is remembered in Eliot's reference to Kipling's vision of empire: "The vision is almost that of an idea of empire laid up in Heaven" (Eliot, *On Poetry and Poets* [New York: Farrar, Straus and Cudahy, 1957], p. 245). Plato's phrase is also quoted, in Greek, in *Criterion* 14, no. 56 (April 1935): 435, immediately after Eliot's assertion that "the City of God is at best only realisable on earth under an imperfect likeness." Cf. Frank Kermode, *The Classic* (London: Faber and Faber, 1975), p. 38.

10. T. S. Eliot, *Collected Poems, 1909–1962* (New York: Harcourt, Brace 1963), pp. 70–71.

11. Blackmur, *Form and Value in Modern Poetry*, p. 247.

12. T. S. Eliot, *Knowledge and Experience in the Philosophy of F. H. Bradley* (London: Faber and Faber), pp. 19, 30, 31, 27.

13. F. H. Bradley, *Essays on Truth and Reality* (Oxford, 1914), p. 194.

14. Eliot, *Knowledge and Experience*, pp. 22, 25.

15. Ibid., pp. 147–148.

16. F. H. Bradley, *Appearance and Reality* (London, 1902), p. 346.

17. Ibid., p. 258.

18. Eliot, *On Poets and Poetry*, p. 38.

19. E. M. Cioran, *The Temptation to Exist*, translated by Richard Howard (Chicago: Quadrangle, 1968), p. 152.

20. Seamus Heaney, *Preoccupations: Selected Prose, 1968–1978* (New York: Farrar, Straus and Giroux, 1980), p. 211.

21. *Heraclitus*, translated by Philip Wheelwright (New York: Atheneum, 1964), p. 19 (fragment 2).

22. Quoted in William Empson, *Using Biography* (Cambridge, Mass.: Harvard University Press, 1984), p. 193.

23. T. S. Eliot, *Letters*, edited by Valerie Eliot, vol. 1: *1898–1922*, (New York: Harcourt Brace Jovanovich, 1988), p. 197.

24. Paul Valéry, "Avant-Propos à la connaissance de la déesse": "Ils ont réouvert aussi sur les accidents de l'être les yeux que nous avions fermés pour nous faire plus semblables à sa substance." *Oeuvres*, edited by Jean Hytier (Paris: Gallimard, 1957), vol. 1, p. 1276.

25. Hugh Kenner, "The Urban Apocalypse," in W. K. Wimsatt, editor, *Literary Criticism: Idea and Act* (Berkeley: University of California Press, 1974), p. 630.

26. Georg Simmel, *Philosophische Kultur* (1923), quoted in Jean Starobinski, *The Invention of Liberty, 1700–1789,* translated by Bernard C. Swift (Geneva: Skira, 1964), p. 180.

Chapter 7. The Music of "Ash-Wednesday"

1. Donald Davie, *The Poet in the Imaginary Museum: Essays of Two Decades,* edited by Barry Alpert (New York: Persea, 1977), p. 33.

2. Ibid., p. 111.

3. Ibid., p. 112.

4. Donald Davie, *Articulate Energy: An Inquiry into the Syntax of English Poetry* (London: Routledge and Kegan Paul, 1955), p. 148.

5. Ibid., p. 73.

6. Susanne K. Langer, *Philosophy in a New Key: A Study in the Symbolism of Reason, Rite, and Art* (Cambridge, Mass.: Harvard University Press, 1942), pp. 238, 240.

7. Davie, *Articulate Energy,* p. 87.

8. T. S. Eliot, *Selected Essays,* 3rd ed. (London: Faber and Faber, 1963), p. 145.

9. Ibid., pp. 189–190.

10. Ibid., p. 190.

11. T. S. Eliot, *Collected Poems, 1909–1962* (New York: Harcourt Brace, 1963), p. 29.

12. Davie, *Articulate Energy,* pp. 88–89.

13. Ibid., p. 76.

14. Eliot, *Collected Poems, 1909–1962,* p. 85.

15. I. A. Richards, *Science and Poetry,* 2nd ed. (London: Kegan Paul, Trench, Trubner, 1935), pp. 70–71, fn. 1.

16. T. S. Eliot, "Preface," in St.-Jean Perse, *Anabasis,* translated into English by T. S. Eliot: *Anabase* (New York: Harcourt, Brace, 1938), p. 8.

17. Perse, *Anabase,* p. 62. In Eliot's translation: "Select a wide hat with the

brim seduced. The eye withdraws by a century into the provinces of the soul. Through the gate of living chalk we see the things of the plain: living things . . . " (p. 63).

18. I. A. Richards, *Coleridge on Imagination* (London: Kegan Paul, Trench, Trubner, 1934), pp. 216–217.

19. S. T. Coleridge, *Selected Poetry and Prose,* edited by Donald A. Stauffer (New York: Random House, Modern Library Edition, 1951), p. 85.

20. F. R. Leavis, *New Bearings in English Poetry* (reprint, London: Penguin in association with Chatto and Windus, 1963), p. 99.

21. Ibid., p. 100.

22. Ibid., p. 98.

23. T. S. Eliot, *For Lancelot Andrewes: Essays on Style and Order* (Garden City, N.Y.: Doubleday, Doran, 1929), pp. 21–22.

24. T. S. Eliot, *On Poetry and Poets* (New York: Farrar, Straus and Cudahy, 1957), p. 32.

25. T. S. Eliot, "Thinking in Verse: A Survey of Early Seventeenth-Century Poetry," *Listener* 3, no. 61 (March 12, 1930): 442.

26. Leonard Woolf, *Downhill All the Way: An Autobiography of the Years 1919 to 1939* (New York: Harcourt Brace Jovanovich, 1967), pp. 109–111.

27. Northrop Frye, *T. S. Eliot* (Edinburgh: Oliver and Boyd, 1963), p. 74.

28. Eliot, *Collected Poems, 1909–1962,* pp. 90–91.

29. Paul Valéry, "La Pythie," quoted in Elizabeth Sewell, *Paul Valéry: The Mind in the Mirror* (New Haven: Yale University Press, 1952), p. 33.

30. Sewell, *Paul Valéry,* p. 56.

31. Ibid., p. 33.

32. Ibid., p. 87.

33. R. P. Blackmur, *Language as Gesture* (New York: Harcourt, Brace, 1952), p. 196.

34. Hugh Kenner, *The Invisible Poet: T. S. Eliot* (New York: McDowell, Obolensky, 1959), p. 265.

35. Eliot, *Collected Poems, 1909–1962,* p. 168.

36. T. S. Eliot: "Note sur Mallarmé et Poe," translated by Ramon Fernandez: *La Nouvelle Revue Française* 14, no. 158 (November 1926): 524–526.

37. Frank Kermode, *Romantic Image* (New York: Chilmark, 1961), p. 163.

38. Ibid., p. 62.

39. W. B. Yeats, *Autobiographies* (London: Macmillan, 1961), p. 321.

Chapter 8. *"Marina"*

1. Hugh Kenner, *Historical Fictions* (San Francisco: North Point, 1990), p. 216.

2. Quoted in James Olney, editor, *T. S. Eliot* (London: Oxford University Press, 1988), p. 211.

3. Quoted in Richard Abel, "The Influence of St. Jean Perse on T. S. Eliot," *Contemporary Literature* 14, no. 2 (Spring 1973): 235.

4. From an unpublished lecture quoted in Elizabeth Drew, *T. S. Eliot: The Design of His Poetry* (New York: Scribner, 1949), p. 127.

5. T. S. Eliot, Introduction to G. Wilson Knight, *The Wheel of Fire,* enlarged ed., (London: Methuen, 1949), p. xviii.

6. Ibid., p. xv.

7. T. S. Eliot, *The Varieties of Metaphysical Poetry,* edited by Ronald Schuchard (New York: Harcourt, Brace, 1993), pp. 151–152. Schuchard has corrected Eliot's misquotations of Chapman's play.

8. Henry James, *The Art of the Novel: Critical Prefaces,* with an introduction by Richard P. Blackmur (New York: Scribner, 1962), p. 33.

9. Ibid., pp. 31–32.

10. T. S. Eliot, *Selected Essays* (London: Faber and Faber, 1963), pp. 194–195.

11. Wallace Stevens, *Letters of Wallace Stevens,* edited by Holly Stevens (New York: Knopf, 1966), p. 434.

12. Wilhelm Worringer, *Abstraction and Empathy,* translated by Michael Bullock (London: Routledge and Kegan Paul, 1953), pp. 15, 24.

13. Wallace Stevens, *The Palm at the End of the Mind,* edited by Holly Stevens (New York: Vintage, 1972), p. 212.

14. F. R. Leavis, *Education and the University: A Sketch for an "English School,"* 2nd ed. (London: Chatto and Windus, 1948), pp. 88–89.

15. *Seneca: His Tenne Tragedies,* edited by Thomas Newton with an introduction by T. S. Eliot (London: Constable, 1927), p. 46.

16. T. S. Eliot, *Collected Poems, 1909–1962* (New York: Harcourt, Brace, 1963), p. 105.

17. Eliot, *Complete Poems and Plays* (New York: Harcourt, Brace, 1952), p. 71.

18. Leavis, *Education and the University*, p. 90.

19. A draft of "Marina" gives the bird of Pride as a peacock rather than a hummingbird. Robert Crawford has noted in his *The Savage and the City in the Work of T. S. Eliot* (Oxford: Clarendon, 1987), pp. 21–22, that one of the sources of the poem is this passage from Mayne Reed's *The Boy Hunters: Adventures in Search of a White Buffalo* (1853): "Listen to his whirring wings, like the hum of a great bee. It is from that he takes his name of 'humming-bird.' See his throat, how it glitters—just like a ruby."

20. Leavis, *Education and the University*, p. 91.

21. Christopher Ricks, *T. S. Eliot and Prejudice* (London: Faber and Faber, 1988), p. 234.

22. Graham Martin, *Eliot in Perspective*, p. 114. Quoted in Ricks, *T. S. Eliot and Prejudice*, p. 213.

23. A. D. Moody, *Thomas Stearns Eliot: Poet* (Cambridge: Cambridge University Press, 1979), p. 186.

24. Eliot, *Complete Poems and Plays*, p. 142.

25. William Empson, *Argufying: Essays on Literature and Culture*, edited by John Haffenden (Iowa City: University of Iowa Press, 1987), p. 356.

26. James, *Art of the Novel*, p. 5.

27. Stevens, *Palm at the End of the Mind*, p. 367.

28. Julia Kristeva, *Desire in Language: A Semiotic Approach to Literature and Art*, edited by Leon S. Roudiez (Oxford: Basil Blackwell, 1980), p. 55.

29. Augustine, *Confessions*, translated by R. S. Pine-Coffin (Harmondsworth: Penguin, 1961), p. 269.

30. Empson, *Argufying*, p. 359.

Chapter 9. Stevens and Eliot

1. G. W. F. Hegel, *The Phenomenology of Mind*, translated by J. B. Baillie (New York: Harper, 1967), pp. 588–589.

2. Michel Foucault, "What Is Enlightenment?" in *The Foucault Reader,* edited by Paul Rabinow (Harmondsworth: Penguin, 1984), p. 44.

3. T. S. Eliot, "A Contemporary Thomist," *New Statesman,* December 10, 1917, p. 312.

4. Stanley Cavell, *In Quest of the Ordinary* (Chicago: University of Chicago Press, 1988), p. 52.

5. M. H. Abrams, *Natural Supernaturalism: Tradition and Revolution in Romantic Literature* (New York: Norton, 1971), p. 12.

6. Josiah Royce, *The Problem of Christianity,* 2 vols. (1913; Hamden, Conn.: Archon, 1967), 1: xv.

7. Ibid., 1: 17–18.

8. Ibid., 2: 428–429.

9. Wallace Stevens, *Collected Poems* (New York: Vintage, 1990), p. 336.

10. Wallace Stevens, *Letters of Wallace Stevens,* edited by Holly Stevens (New York: Knopf, 1966), p. 250.

11. Ibid., pp. 67–68.

12. Wallace Stevens, "Two or Three Ideas," in *Opus Posthumous,* edited by Samuel French Morse (New York: Knopf, 1957), pp. 205–206.

13. Ibid., p. 206.

14. Royce, *Problem of Christianity,* 2: 331–332.

15. Stevens, *Collected Poems,* pp. 383–384.

16. Charles S. Peirce, *Values in a Universe of Chance,* edited by Philip P. Wiener (New York: Doubleday, 1958), p. 158.

17. Wallace Stevens, *The Necessary Angel* (New York: Knopf, 1951), p. 96.

18. Stevens, *Letters,* p. 434.

19. Quoted in Jeffrey M. Perl, *Skepticism and Modern Enmity: Before and After Eliot* (Baltimore: Johns Hopkins University Press, 1989), p. 66.

20. Ibid., p. 71.

21. Ibid., p. 68.

22. Ibid., p. 413.

23. Ibid., p. 27.

24. Ibid., p. 374.

25. Ibid., p. 398.

26. T. S. Eliot, *Collected Poems, 1909–1962* (London: Faber and Faber, 1963), p. 199.

27. Jürgen Habermas, *The Philosophical Discourse of Modernity,* translated by Frederick Lawrence (Cambridge, Mass.: MIT Press, 1987), p. 296.

28. Ibid., p. 298.

29. Emmanuel Levinas, *Totality and Infinity,* translated by Alphonso Lingis (Pittsburgh: Duquesne University Press, 1969), p. 58.

30. Emmanuel Levinas, *Collected Philosophical Papers,* translated by Alphonso Lingis (Dordrecht, Neth.: Martinis Nijhoff, 1987), p. 183.

31. Wallace Stevens, *Collected Poetry and Prose* (New York: Library of America, 1997), p. 940.

32. Wallace Stevens, *Letters,* edited by Holly Stevens (Berkeley: University of California Press, 1996), pp. 378, 677, 813.

33. Stevens, *Collected Poetry and Prose,* pp. 274–275.

34. Ibid., pp. 229–230.

Chapter 10. *The Idea of a Christian Society*

1. T. S. Eliot, "Last Words," *Criterion* 18, no. 71 (January 1939): 274.

2. T. S. Eliot, *Christianity and Culture: The Idea of a Christian Society and Notes Towards the Definition of Culture* (San Diego: Harcourt Brace Jovanovich, 1988), pp. 50–51.

3. T. S. Eliot, *The Use of Poetry and the Use of Criticism* (London: Faber and Faber, 1933), p. 130.

4. Ibid., p. 137.

5. Ibid.

6. Ibid., p. 137n.

7. T. S. Eliot, *Collected Poems, 1909–1962* (New York: Harcourt, Brace and World, 1963), pp. 215–216.

8. Eliot, *Christianity and Culture,* p. 10.

9. Ibid., p. 20.

10. Ibid., p. 14.

11. Ibid., p. 116.

12. Ibid., p. 25.

13. T. S. Eliot, *After Strange Gods: A Primer of Modern Heresy* (London: Faber and Faber, 1934), p. 20.

14. J. M. Cameron, *The Night Battle* (London: Catholic Book Club, 1962), p. 25.

15. I am grateful to Ronald Schuchard for drawing my attention to this correspondence in the Harry Ransom Humanities Research Center, University of Texas at Austin.

16. Eliot, *Collected Poems*, p. 205.

17. Eliot, *Christianity and Culture*, p. 15.

18. Ibid.

19. S. T. Coleridge, *On the Constitution of Church and State*, edited by John Colmer (Princeton: University Press, 1976), p. 12.

20. Ibid., p. 13.

21. Ibid.

22. Plato, *Dialogues*, translated by B. Jowett (Oxford: Clarendon, 1953), p. 467.

23. T. S. Eliot, *On Poetry and Poets* (New York: Farrar, Straus and Cudahy, 1957), p. 286.

24. Gilles Deleuze, *Kant's Critical Philosophy*, translated by Hugh Tomlinson and Barbara Habberjam (London: Athlone, 1984), p. 19.

25. R. P. Blackmur, *The Expense of Greatness* (New York: Arrow Editions, 1940), p. 241.

26. Ibid., pp. 241–242.

27. Deleuze, *Kant's Critical Philosophy*, p. 19.

28. Harold Bloom, *Shakespeare: The Invention of the Human* (London: Fourth Estate, 1999), p. 174.

29. Cameron, *Night Battle*, p. 30.

30. Ibid., p. 32.

Chapter 11. Reading Four Quartets

1. Translation by Lionel D. Barnett, *Bhagavad-Gita* (London: Dent, 1905), p. 123. Cf. Canto II, verses 38, 47.

2. The most relevant passages of *Paradiso* are Canto 31, lines 10–24, and Canto 33, lines 85–145.

3. "Eliot's Moral Dialectic," *Hudson Review* 2 (1949). See also Hugh Ken-

ner, *The Invisible Poet* (New York: McDowell, Obolensky, 1959). Donald Davie's essay, first published in *The Twentieth Century,* April 1956, is conveniently reprinted in Hugh Kenner, editor, *Twentieth Century Views on T. S. Eliot* (New York: Prentice-Hall, 1962).

Chapter 12. "Burnt Norton"

1. T. S. Eliot, "Note sur Mallarmé et Poe," translated by Ramon Fernandez, *La Nouvelle Revue Français* 14, no. 158 (November 1, 1926), pp. 524–526. (English text not published.)
2. F. R. Leavis, *The Living Principle: "English" as a Discipline of Thought* (London: Chatto and Windus, 1975), p. 179.
3. William Empson, *Some Versions of Pastoral* (reprint, New York: New Directions, 1974), pp. 260–261.
4. D. W. Harding, *Experience into Words* (reprint, Harmondsworth: Penguin Books, 1974), pp. 107–108.

Chapter 13. The Communication of the Dead

1. Letter of August 3, 1929, quoted in B. A. Harries, "The Rare Contact: A Correspondence Between T. S. Eliot and P. E. More," *Theology* 75, no. 621 (March 1972): 136.
2. Quoted in Harries, "Rare Contact," p. 141.
3. Ibid., p. 137n.
4. Ibid., p. 141.
5. T. S. Eliot, *On Poetry and Poets* (London: Faber and Faber, 1957), p. 209.
6. T. S. Eliot, "Literature, Science, and Dogma," *Dial* 82 (March 1927): 241.
7. Quoted in Harries, "Rare Contact," p. 142.
8. T. S. Eliot, "A Note on Poetry and Belief," *Enemy* 1 (January 1927): 15.
9. T. S. Eliot, *After Strange Gods* (New York: Harcourt, Brace, 1934), pp. 45–46.
10. T. S. Eliot, *Selected Essays, 1917–1932* (London: Faber and Faber, 1932), pp. 256–257.

11. Ibid., p. 255.

12. Quoted in Harries, "Rare Contact," p. 143.

13. Helen Gardner, *The Composition of Four Quartets* (London: Faber and Faber, 1978), p. 157.

14. Eliot, *Selected Essays,* pp. 256–257.

15. Ibid., p. 275.

16. Gardner, *Composition of Four Quartets,* p. 157.

17. Eliot, *Selected Essays,* pp. 257–258.

18. Rainer Maria Rilke, *The Notebooks of Malte Laurids Brigge,* translated by M. D. Herter Norton (New York: Capricorn, 1958), pp. 26–27.

19. W. B. Yeats, *Autobiographies* (London: Macmillan, 1955), pp. 247–248.

20. Kenneth Burke, *A Rhetoric of Religion* (Boston: Beacon, 1961), p. 68.

21. A few points to note in a technical analysis. (*a*) The coincidence of clause and meter. (*b*) The semantic stresses, normally four to a line, also serve the purposes of metrical stresses, keeping the lines going, in this case, at the speed of refined conversation. (*c*) More important: in these unrhymed lines, grammar takes the place of rhyme. The italicized phrases, below, are grammatical cousins, running in the sequence ABBA; two sets: This has the effect, one among many, of pointing up the odd-lines-out precisely because they are thus released from the grammatical "rhymes." (Donald Davie shows a similar procedure at work in "Ash-Wednesday," the opening lines. See his *Articulate Energy* [London: Routledge and Kegan Paul, 1955], pp. 90ff.)

22. William James, *Varieties of Religious Experience* (reprint, London: Collins, 1960), p. 295.

23. T. S. Eliot, *Selected Prose* (London: Penguin, 1953), pp. 168–169.

Index